• T R O P H I E S •

Intervention
TEACHER'S GUIDE
Grade 3

Harcourt

Orlando   Boston   Dallas   Chicago   San Dieg

Visit *The Learning Site!*
www.harcourtschool.com

D1088345

Printed in the United States of America

ISBN 0-15-325345-2

4 5 6 7 8 9 10 048 10 09 08 07 06 05 04 03

Table of Contents

What are Intervention Strategies?

Intervention strategies are designed to facilitate learning for those students who may experience some difficulty no matter how well we have planned our curriculum. These strategies offer support and guidance to the student who is struggling. The strategies themselves are no mystery. They are based on the same time-honored techniques that effective teachers have used for years—teaching students on their instructional reading level; modeling previewing and predicting; and giving direct instruction in strategic-reading, vocabulary, phonics, fluency, and writing.

Intervention works best in conjunction with a strong core program. For an intervention program to be effective, instruction should focus on specific needs of students, as determined by systematic monitoring of progress.

Components of the Intervention Program

The goal of the *Trophies* Intervention Program is to provide the scaffolding, extra support, and extra reading practice that below-level readers need to succeed in the mainstream reading program. The program includes the following components:

- *Skill Cards* to preteach and reteach the Focus Skill for each lesson
- *Intervention Practice Book* with the following practice pages for each lesson:

  Fluency Page with word lists and phrase-cued sentences that parallel the reading level of the *Intervention Reader* selection

  Phonics Practice Page that reinforces prerequisite phonics/decoding skills and can be used as a teacher-directed or independent activity

  Comprehension Practice Page that gives students an opportunity to respond to the *Intervention Reader* selection and show that they have understood it

  Focus Skill Review Page that provides an additional opportunity to practice and apply the focus skill for that lesson

- *Intervention Reader* to provide reading material at students' instructional reading level
- *Vocabulary Game Boards* and related materials to provide additional practice and application of vocabulary skills
- *Intervention Assessment Book* opportunities to monitor progress and ensure success

Using the *Intervention Teacher's Guide* with *Trophies*

The *Intervention Teacher's Guide* gives support for below-level readers in key instructional strands of *Trophies*, plus prerequisite phonics skills and oral-reading fluency. Each *Intervention Teacher's Guide* lesson includes the following resources:

- The **Phonics/Decoding Lesson** reviews prerequisite phonics and word analysis skills. Each skill is systematically applied in the corresponding *Intervention Reader* selection.

- **Preteach/Reteach Vocabulary** activities to teach key vocabulary that appears in both the *Intervention Reader* selection and the corresponding *Trophies Pupil Edition* selection.

- **Fluency Builders** reinforce important vocabulary while providing reading practice to promote oral reading fluency. You may also wish to use the *Oral Reading Fluency Assessment* periodically to measure student progress.

- **Preteach/Reteach Focus Skill** activities reinforce the objective of *Trophies* Focus Skills, ensuring that below-level readers get the in-depth instruction they need to reach grade skill-level standards.

- **Preview and Summarize** provide support for comprehension of each main selection in *Trophies Pupil Editions*.

- **Directed Reading Lesson** for the *Intervention Reader* selection that reinforces basic comprehension skills, using questions and teacher modeling.

- **Writing Support** for writing lessons in *Trophies* provides interactive writing experiences for the key aspects of the corresponding writing forms and skills.

- **Weekly Review** provides additional support as students review phonics, vocabulary, and focus skills and prepare for testing.

- **Self-Selected Reading** suggests titles that students can read independently with success and also offers specific suggestions for encouraging student expression and participation through conferencing.

The *Intervention Teacher's Guide* lessons clearly identify the most appropriate times during the *Trophies* lesson plan to provide supplemental instruction. Look for the BEFORE or AFTER tag that appears next to each of the key instructional strands, along with page numbers from the core program. For example:

BEFORE
Reading
pages 306–320

This tag alerts you that *before* students read the literature selection that appears in *Trophies* on pages 306–320, intervention strategies may be useful. Appropriate preteaching activities are provided. Reteaching activities are indicated by the AFTER tag.

Depending on your individual classroom and school schedules, you can tailor the "before" and "after" instruction to suit your needs. The following pages show two options for pacing the instruction in this guide.

Suggested Lesson Planners

Option 1:

DAY 1	DAY 2
BEFORE Building Background and Vocabulary	**BEFORE** Reading the *Trophies* Selection
Review Phonics ■ Identify the sound ■ Associate letters to sound ■ Word blending ■ Apply the skill **Introduce Vocabulary** ■ Preteach lesson vocabulary	**Focus Skill** ■ Preteach the skill ■ Use Skill Card Side A **Prepare to Read the *Trophies* selection** ■ Preview the selection ■ Set purpose
AFTER Building Background and Vocabulary	**AFTER** Reading the *Trophies* Selection
Apply Vocabulary Strategies ■ Use decoding strategies ■ Reteach lesson vocabulary **Fluency Builder** ■ Use *Intervention Practice Book*	**Reread and Summarize** **Fluency Builder** ■ Use *Intervention Practice Book*

Option 2:

DAY 1	DAY 2
AFTER Weekly Assessments	**AFTER** Building Background and Vocabulary
Self-Selected Reading ■ Choosing books ■ Conduct student-teacher conferences **Fluency Performance** ■ Use passage from *Intervention Reader* selection	**Apply Vocabulary Strategies** ■ Use decoding strategies ■ Reteach lesson vocabulary **Fluency Builder** ■ Use *Intervention Practice Book*
BEFORE Building Background and Vocabulary	**BEFORE** Reading the *Trophies* Selection
Review Phonics ■ Identify the sound ■ Associate letters to sound ■ Word blending ■ Apply the skill **Introduce Vocabulary** ■ Preteach lesson vocabulary	**Focus Skill** ■ Preteach the skill ■ Use Skill Card Side A **Prepare to Read the *Trophies* selection** ■ Preview the selection ■ Set purpose

DAY 3

BEFORE Making Connections

Directed Reading of Intervention Reader selection
- Read the selection
- Summarize the selection
- Answer *Think About It* Questions

AFTER Skill Review

Focus Skill
- Reteach the skill
- Use Skill Card Side B

Fluency Builder
- Use *Intervention Practice Book*

DAY 4

BEFORE Writing Lesson

Writing Support
- Build on prior knowledge
- Construct the text
- Revisit the text
- On Your Own

AFTER Spelling Lesson

Connect Spelling and Phonics
- Reteach phonics
- Build and read longer words

Fluency Builder
- Use passage from *Intervention Reader* selection

DAY 5

BEFORE Weekly Assessments

Review Vocabulary
- Vocabulary activity

Review Focus Skill
- Use *Intervention Practice Book*

Review Test Prep
- Use the core *Pupil Edition*

AFTER Weekly Assessments

Self-Selected Reading
- Choosing books
- Conduct student-teacher conferences

Fluency Performance
- Use passage from *Intervention Reader* selection

DAY 3

AFTER Reading the *Trophies* Selection

Reread and Summarize

Fluency Builder
- Use *Intervention Practice Book*

BEFORE Making Connections

Directed Reading of Intervention Reader selection
- Read the selection
- Summarize the selection
- Answer *Think About It* Questions

DAY 4

AFTER Skill Review

Focus Skill
- Reteach the skill
- Use Skill Card Side B

Fluency Builder
- Use *Intervention Practice Book*

BEFORE Writing Lesson

Writing Support
- Build on prior knowledge
- Construct the text
- Revisit the text
- On Your Own

DAY 5

AFTER Spelling Lesson

Connect Spelling and Phonics
- Reteach phonics
- Build and read longer words

Fluency Builder
- Use passage from *Intervention Reader* selection

BEFORE Weekly Assessments

Review Vocabulary
- Vocabulary activity

Review Focus Skill
- Use *Intervention Practice Book*

Review Test Prep
- Use the core *Pupil Edition*

Fluency

*"**S**o that students will understand why rereading is done, we have involved them in a discussion of how athletes develop skill at their sports. This discussion brings out the fact that athletes spend considerable time practicing basic skills until they develop speed and smoothness at their activity. Repeated readings uses this same type of practice."*

S. Jay Samuels
The Reading Teacher, February 1997
(originally published January 1979)

In the years since S. Jay Samuels pioneered the technique of repeated reading to improve fluency, continuing research has confirmed and expanded upon his observations. Ideally, oral reading mirrors the pacing, smoothness, and rhythms of normal speech. Fluency in reading can be defined as a combination of these key elements.

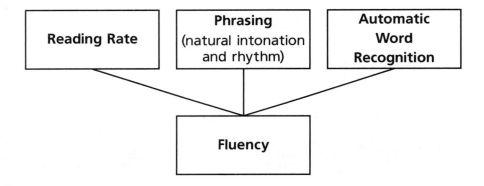

How Do Students Become More Fluent Readers?

Research and the experiences of classroom teachers make it clear that certain practices can and do lead to significant improvements in reading fluency. Techniques that have been shown to be successful include

- **Teacher modeling**

- **Repeated reading of short passages**

- **Daily monitoring of progress**

A program that incorporates these three elements will help struggling readers gain fluency and improve their comprehension.

Using Fluency Builders in the *Intervention Teacher's Guide*

The plan for each lesson in the *Intervention Teacher's Guide* includes daily fluency practice that incorporates the elements of teacher modeling, repeated reading, and self-monitoring.

The fluency portion of the lesson is designed to be completed in five or ten minutes, although you may adjust the time according to students' needs and as your schedule allows.

About the *Intervention Practice Book* Fluency Page

The *Intervention Practice Book* Fluency page is designed to correlate with the phonics elements taught in the *Intervention Teacher's Guide*, as well as with key vocabulary from the *Trophies* and *Intervention Reader* selections. A total of twenty words that fall into these three categories are listed at the top of the Fluency Page for each lesson.

On the bottom half of the page, you will find a set of numbered sentences that incorporate the words from the lists. Slashes are used to divide each sentence into phrases. To help students improve natural phrasing, model reading each phrase smoothly, as a unit, and encourage students to follow the same procedure in their repeated-reading practice.

This chart gives an overview of the fluency portion of the Intervention Program.

Day	Materials	Explanation
1	*Intervention Practice Book* Fluency Page	Teacher models reading aloud word lists. Students then practice reading aloud the word lists with partners.
2	*Intervention Practice Book* Fluency Page	Teacher models reading aloud the phrased fluency sentences. Students then practice repeated rereadings of the sentences with partners.
3	*Intervention Practice Book* Fluency Page	Students read the fluency sentences on tape, assess their own progress, and then reread the sentences on tape to improve pacing and tone.
4	*Intervention Reader* selection	Students read aloud a selected short passage from the *Intervention Reader* selection three times, monitoring their progress after each reading.
5	*Intervention Reader* selection	Students read the same passage aloud to the teacher. Both teacher and student assess the student's progress.

Phonemic Awareness

Rhyming Activities

Rhyme-a-Day

Start each day by teaching students a short rhyme. Periodically throughout the day, repeat the rhyme with them. Say the rhyme together, have them say it alone, pause and leave out words for them to insert, or ask volunteers to say each line. Students will develop a repertoire of favorite rhymes that can serve as a storehouse for creating their own rhymes.

Rhyme Sort

Place on a tabletop pictures of items that rhyme. Have students sort the pictures into groups, according to names that rhyme. You may also want to try an "open sort" by having students create categories of their own to sort the picture cards.

Rhyme Pairs

To assess students' ability to recognize pairs of words that rhyme, say a list of twenty or more pairs of words. Half of the word pairs should rhyme. Students tell which word pairs rhyme and which do not. Have students indicate *yes* with a card marked *Y* or another symbol.

If working with **one child** (or small group), have students use one of the Game Boards. From each correct response, the player can move a marker ahead one space. Provide word pairs until the player has completed the game.

What Word Rhymes?

Use theme-related words from across the curriculum to focus on words that rhyme. For example, if you are studying animals, ask: *What rhymes with snake? bear? fox? deer? ant? frog? goat? hen? fish? whale?* If a special holiday is approaching, ask: *What rhymes with flag, year, or heart?* Use these word groups for sound-matching, sound-blending, or sound-segmenting activities.

Sound-Matching Activities

Odd Word Out

Form a group of four students. Say a different word for each group member to repeat. The student with the word that does not begin (or end) like the other words must step out of the group. For example, say *basket, bundle, cost, bargain.* The student whose word is *cost* steps from the group. The odd-word-out player then chooses three students to form a new group and the procedure continues.

Head or Toes, Finger or Nose?

Teach students the following rhyme. Be sure to say the sound, not the letter, at the beginning of each line. Recite the rhyme together several times while touching the body parts.

> /h/ is for *head.*
>
> /t/ is for *toes.*
>
> /f/ is for *finger.*
>
> /n/ is for *nose.*

Explain that you will say a list of words. Students are to touch the head when you say a word that begins with /h/, the toes for the words that begin with /t/, a finger for words that begin with /f/, and the nose for words that begin with /n/. Say words such as *fan, ten, horn, hat, feet, nut, ham, nest, toy, fish, note, tub, nail, time, fox,* and *house.*

Souvenir Sound-Off

Have students imagine that a friend has traveled to a special place and has brought them a gift. Recite the following verse, and ask a volunteer to complete it. The names of the traveler, the place, and the gift must begin with the same letter and sound.

- My friend [person]
  My friend Hannah
- who went to [place]
  who went to Hawaii
- brought me back a [gift].
  brought me back a hula skirt.

After repeating this activity a few times, ask **partners** to recite the missing words. As an alternative, you can focus on words with initial blends and digraphs. Students can focus on social studies and phonics skills by using a world map or globe to find names of places.

Match My Word

Have students match beginning or ending sounds in words. Seat students in pairs, sitting back-to-back. One student in each pair will say a word. His or her partner will repeat the word and say another word that begins with the same sound. Repeat the activity, reversing the roles of partners and focusing on ending sounds.

Sound Isolation Activities

What's Your Name N-N-N-Name?

Invite students to say their names by repeating the initial phoneme in the name, such as *M-M-M-M-Michael* or by drawing out and exaggerating the initial sound, such as *Sssss-erena.* Have students say the names of others, such as friends or family members.

Singling Out the Sounds

Form groups of three students. Students can decide who will name the beginning, the middle, and the ending sounds in one-syllable picture names. Given a set of pictures, the group identifies a picture name, and then each group member isolates and says the sound he or she is responsible for. Group members can check one another.

Chain Reaction

Have students form a circle. The student who begins will say a word such as *bus.* The next child must isolate the ending sound in the word, /s/, and say a word that begins with that sound, such as *sun.* If the word is correct, the two students link arms, and the procedure continues with the next child isolating the final sound in *sun* and giving a word that begins with /n/. You will want all students to be able to link arms and complete the chain, so provide help when needed.

Sound-Addition, Deletion, or Substitution Activities

Add-a-Sound

Explain that the beginning sound is missing in each of the words you will say. Students must add the missing sound and say the new word. Some examples follow.

Add:

/b/ to *at* (bat)	/f/ to *ox* (fox)	/k/ to *art* (cart)
/f/ to *ace* (face)	/p/ to *age* (page)	/h/ to *air* (hair)
/w/ to *all* (wall)	/j/ to *am* (jam)	/r/ to *an* (ran)
/b/ to *and* (band)	/d/ to *ark* (dark)	/f/ to *arm* (farm)
/d/ to *ash* (dash)	/s/ to *it* (sit)	/s/ to *oak* (soak)
/h/ to *eel* (heel)	/b/ to *end* (bend)	/m/ to *ice* (mice)
/n/ to *ear* (near)	/f/ to *east* (feast)	/b/ to *each* (beach)
/f/-/l/ to *at* (flat)	/sk/ to *ate* (skate)	/t/-/r/ to *eat* (treat)
/g/-/r/ to *ill* (grill)	/sh/ to *out* (shout)	/p/-/l/ to *ant* (plant)

Remove-a-Sound

Reinforce rhyme while focusing on the deletion of initial sounds in words to form new words. Ask students to say:

- *hat* without the /h/ (at)
- *fin* without the /f/ (in)
- *tall* without the /t/ (all)
- *box* without the /b/ (ox)
- *will* without /w/ (ill)
- *peach* without the /p/ (each)
- *nice* without the /n/ (ice)
- *meat* without the /m/ (eat)
- *band* without the /b/ (and)

Continue with other words in the same manner.

Mixed-Up Tongue Twisters

Think of a simple tongue twister such as *ten tired toads*. Say the tongue twister for students, but replace the initial letter in each word with another letter, such a *p*, to create nonsense words: *pen pired poads*. Explain to students that you need their help to make sense of the tongue twister by having them replace /p/ with /t/ and say the new tongue twister. Use the same procedure for other tongue twisters.

- copper coffee cups
- nine new nails
- two ton tomatoes
- long lean legs

Then ask partners to do this activity together.

The Name Game

Occasionally when a new sound is introduced, students might enjoy substituting the first sound of their names for the name of a classmate. Students will have to stop and think when they call one another by name, including the teacher. For example, Paul would call Ms. Vega, Ms. Pega; Carmen becomes Parmen; Jason becomes Pason; and Kiyo becomes Piyo. Just make certain beforehand that all names will be agreeable.

Take Away

New words can be formed by deleting an initial phoneme from a word. Have students say the new word that is formed.

flake without the /f/
(lake)

bring without the /b/
(ring)

swing without the /s/
(wing)

swell without the /s/
(well)

shrink without the /sh/
(rink)

shred without the /sh/
(red)

spread without the /s/-/p/
(read)

gloom without the /g/
(loom)

fright without the /f/
(right)

snout without the /s/-/n/
(out)

score without the /s/
(core)

slip without the /s/
(lip)

bride without the /b/
(ride)

block without the /b/
(lock)

spoke without the /s/
(poke)

snail without the /s/
(nail)

Sound-Blending Activities

I'm Thinking of a Word

Play a guessing game with students. Tell students that you will give them clues to a word. Have them listen closely to blend the sounds to say the word.

- I'm thinking of something that has words—
/b/-/o͞o/-/k/. (book)

- I'm thinking of something that comes in bunches—
/g/-/r/-/ā/-/p/-/s/. (grapes)

- I'm thinking of something that shines in the night sky—
/s/-/t/-/är/-/z/. (stars)

- I'm thinking of something that moves very slowly—
/s/-/n/-/ā/-/l/. (snail)

What's in the Box?

Place various objects in a box or bag. Play a game with students by saying **In this box is a /k/-/r/-/ā/-/o/-/n/. What do you think is in the box?** (crayon) Continue with the other objects in the box, segmenting the phonemes for students to blend and say the word.

Sound-Segmenting Activities

Sound Game

Have **partners** play a word-guessing game, using a variety of pictures that represent different beginning sounds. One student says the name on the card, separating the beginning sound, as in **p-late**. The partner blends the sounds and guesses the word. After students are proficient with beginning sounds, you could have them segment all the sounds in a word when they give their clues, as in **d-o-g**.

Count the Sounds

Tell students that you are going to say a word. Have them listen and count the number of sounds they hear in that word. For example, say the word *task*. Have children repeat the word and tell how many sounds they hear. Students should reply *four*.

tone (3)	four (3)
great (4)	peak (3)
pinch (4)	sunny (4)
stick (4)	clouds (5)
flake (4)	feel (3)
rain (3)	paint (4)

Vocabulary Games

Vocabulary Game Boards

To give students additional vocabulary practice, use the Vocabulary Game Boards and copying masters provided in the Intervention Kit. Two different games can be played on each game board. Directions for each game are printed on the back of the board on which the game is played. There are a total of five game boards, which students can use to play ten different games. For best results, use the games to review vocabulary at the end of each theme, so that there are more words to play with.

Copying Masters

The copying masters that accompany the game boards provide some other materials that students will need to play the games. These include:

- spinners
- game pieces
- game cards

Illustrated directions on the copying masters show students how to create the game materials. They may need scissors, crayons or colored markers, and glue. Pencils and paper clips are used to construct spinners. When game markers are called for, provide students with buttons, counters, or some other small item.

Additional Materials

When the directions for a game call for **word cards**, use the vocabulary word cards from *Trophies*. In addition, some games require the use of a vocabulary list, definition cards that students can create, a dictionary, and commonly available items such as a paper bag.

Use the following charts to plan for and organize the vocabulary games.

Game Board I: Hopscotch			
Games	**Skills Practiced**	**Players**	**Additional Materials**
Wordscotch	definitions	2	Wordscotch Copying Master *Trophies* word cards dictionary game markers
Syllable Hop-Along	number of syllables	2	Syllable Hop-Along Copying Master *Trophies* word cards dictionary game markers

Game Board 2: Tic-Tac-Toe

Games	Skills Practiced	Players	Additional Materials
Tic-Tac-Know	creating sentences	2	word cards with meaning on back (to be made by students) game markers
Riddle Me	definitions and number of syllables	4	word cards with meaning on back (to be made by students) paper bag vocabulary list game markers

Game Board 3: Do You Remember?

Games	Skills Practiced	Players	Additional Materials
Match a Pair	definitions	2	word cards with meaning on back (to be made by students) *Trophies* word cards
Syllable Match	number of syllables	2	*Trophies* word cards dictionary

Game Board 4: Safari

Games	Skills Practiced	Players	Additional Materials
Safari Spin	number of syllables	2	Safari Spin Copying Master *Trophies* word cards dictionary
Safari Wordwatch	definitions	2–4	Safari Wordwatch Copying Masters vocabulary list dictionary

Game Board 5: Word Castle

Games	Skills Practiced	Players	Additional Materials
Castle Construction	definitions	2	Castle Construction Copying Master *Trophies* word cards dictionary
Knight's Syllablle Spin	number of syllables	2	Knight's Syllable Spin Copying Masters *Trophies* word cards dictionary

Vocabulary Activities

The six activities on the following pages provide additional opportunities for vocabulary practice and application. Two activities are offered for individual students, two for pairs of students, and two for small groups of three or four students. All require a minimum of preparation and call for materials that are readily available in the classroom.

Word Book

INDIVIDUAL ACTIVITY

MATERIALS
- paper
- markers
- stapler
- simple binding materials

As students progress through a theme, encourage them to identify new vocabulary that they find interesting or that they think will be useful to them. Have students create a page for each of the special words they choose. Encourage them to check the spelling of the word and to include the definition and other information they might find helpful, such as how the word is divided into syllables, how it is pronounced, whether it has a prefix or a suffix, synonyms and antonyms, and how the word may be related to other words they know. Students can also draw pictures and include captions and labels.

Upon completion of the theme, have students make a cover for the book. Staple the pages together or help students use simple materials to bind them. Encourage them to share their word books with classmates and to use them as a resource for their writing.

Draw a Smile

PARTNER ACTIVITY

MATERIALS
- list of vocabulary words from a complete theme
- two sheets of paper and markers or chalk and chalkboard
- dictionary

Pairs of students can play this game on paper or on the board. Players should be designated Player 1 and Player 2. Player 1 begins by choosing a vocabulary word from the list for Player 2 to define. If Player 2 defines the word correctly, he or she gets to draw one part of a smiling face. If Player 2 cannot define the word correctly, he or she cannot draw on that turn. Players take turns choosing words for each other to define and adding parts to their drawings each time they define a word correctly. Encourage students to use a dictionary to check definitions as necessary.

A completed drawing has five parts, to be drawn in this order: (1) head, (2) one eye, (3) the other eye, (4) nose, (5) smile. The first player to draw a complete smiling face wins the game.

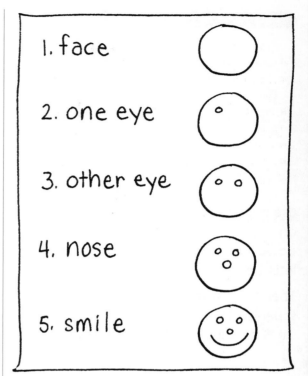

1. face

2. one eye

3. other eye

4. nose

5. smile

Make a Word Garden

MATERIALS
- bulletin board
- colored construction paper
- markers
- scissors
- masking tape
- pencil
- paper

Students can create a word garden by drawing and cutting out large flowers from construction paper. Encourage them to use their imaginations to create flowers in a variety of shapes and colors. Have students use markers to write a vocabulary word on each flower and then arrange the flowers to make a garden on the bulletin board.

Then have students create a key on a separate sheet of paper by making a small drawing of each of the large

flowers and writing the definition of the word that appears on the matching large flower. Students should display the key on the bulletin board with their garden.

What's the Score?

MATERIALS
- list of vocabulary words from a theme or several lessons within a theme
- pencil and paper
- dictionary

Make a list of six to eight vocabulary words that may have given students some difficulty. Have students copy the words from the list and write a definition for each word from memory. Then have them use a dictionary to check their definitions. Tell them to keep score by writing down the number of words they defined correctly.

Then have students copy the words from the list in reverse order, beginning at the bottom. Have them again write a definition for each word from memory, check the definitions in a dictionary, and count the words they defined correctly. Tell students to compare this score to their first score to see how much they improved.

Finger Puppets

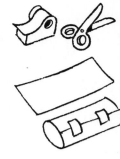

Give students a simple pattern that they can trace to make finger puppets. Have students use construction paper and markers to create puppets that represent favorite characters from a particular theme.

Have students work together to make up simple dramatizations using the finger puppets. Challenge students to use as many words as possible from the vocabulary list. They can keep track of the words they use by checking them off the list.

Guess My Word

Display the list of vocabulary words where both players can see it. Students take turns choosing a word from the list for each other to guess.

The student who is guessing may ask questions about the meaning of the word, how it is spelled, the number of syllables, or any other information they think may help them, as long as the questions can be answered with *yes* or *no*. Encourage students to jot down information that they find out about the word that can help narrow down the list. You may want to give examples of questions that players might ask and explain how they can use the information they obtain.

QUESTION: Does the word begin with a consonant?

INFORMATION: If the answer is *yes*, you can look at the words that begin with consonants and ask more questions to figure out which of those is the correct word. If the answer is *no*, you can rule out the words that begin with consonants and focus on those that begin with vowels.

QUESTION: Does the word have an -*ed* ending?

INFORMATION: If the answer is *no*, you can rule out all words with -*ed* endings. If the answer is yes, focus on the words with -*ed* endings. Ask more questions to figure out which of those words is the correct one.

Use with

"Officer Buckle and Gloria"

Review Phonics: Short Vowel /a/a

Identify the sound. Tell students to listen for the /a/ sound as you say *hat*. Then have them repeat three times: *The cat Sam has is fat*. Ask students to identify the four words with the /a/ sound. (*cat, Sam, has, fat*)

Associate letter to sound. Write on the board: *The cat Sam has is fat*. Circle *cat, Sam, has*, and *fat*. Ask how these words are alike. (*All have the short* a *vowel sound*.) Underline *a* in each word. Tell students that in *cat, Sam, has*, and *fat*, the *a* stands for the /a/ sound. Point out the CVC pattern in each word, and tell students that the vowel in a word with this pattern usually stands for the short vowel sound.

Word blending. Model how to blend the word *cap*. Slide your hand under *ca* as you elongate the sounds /kkaa/. Add the /p/, and have students say *cap* along with you. Follow a similar procedure with *man* and *sad*.

Apply the skill. *Consonant Substitution* Tell students that once they can read words such as *cap, man*, and *sad*, they can read many other words that end in the same way. Replace initial consonants as shown to form new words with the /a/ sound. Ask a volunteer to read each aloud.

INTERVENTION
PRACTICE
BOOK

page 4

cap	(tap)	(lap)	(nap)
man	(ran)	(fan)	(pan)
sad	(mad)	(bad)	(had)

Introduce Vocabulary

PRETEACH **lesson vocabulary.** Tell students that they are going to learn seven new words that they will see again when they read a selection called "Officer Buckle and Gloria." Teach each Vocabulary Word using the process shown at the right.

Use these suggestions or similar ideas to give the meaning or context.

> Write the word.
> Say the word.
> Track the word and have students repeat it.
> Give the meaning or context.

department Give familiar examples, such as the police department or the fire department.

audience Remind students that when they go to see a movie, a play, or a concert, they are members of the audience.

obeys Give examples of school safety rules that should be obeyed.

commands Role-play giving commands, such as "sit" or "stay," to a dog.

expression	Demonstrate speaking with expression by reading part of a familiar story.
accident	Relate to a car accident or spilling a glass of water.
noticed	Have a student pretend to notice something new in the classroom. Point out the *-ed* ending showing past action.

For vocabulary activities, see Vocabulary Games on pages 2–7.

For vocabulary activities, see Vocabulary Games on pages 2–7.

Vocabulary Words

department a separate part of a large organization, such as a government or business

audience a group of people who gather to see or hear a performance, such as a play

obeys carries out wishes, orders, or instructions

commands directions or orders

expression a way of speaking that shows feeling

accident something bad that happens without being planned

noticed became aware of; saw for the first time

AFTER
Building Background and Vocabulary

Apply Vocabulary Strategies

Use reference sources. Write the word *audience* on the board. Tell students that this is a word you do not recognize. Explain that sometimes readers can figure out new words by looking for word parts they know or by breaking a word into syllables. Sometimes, though, the best strategy is to look up the meaning in a dictionary. Model using the strategy.

> **MODEL** In a dictionary the words are listed in alphabetical order, so I'll turn to the *a* section. To find *audience*, I look at the guide words in dark type at the top of each page. I'll find *audience* after words that begin with *at* but before words that begin with *av*. When I locate the word, I find its pronunciation, the part of speech it is, its meaning or meanings, and example sentences that show it used correctly.

Guide students in using the dictionary to look up the word *obey(s)*.

RETEACH lesson vocabulary. Provide patterns for a circle and an arrow. Have students make a simple spinner by cutting a circle and arrow from cardboard and joining them with a brad. Tell students to write the Vocabulary Words on the spinner. Students take turns with the spinner, saying the word the arrow lands on, and using it in a sentence.

FLUENCY BUILDER Use *Intervention Practice Book* page 3. Read each word in the first column aloud and have students repeat it. Then have students work in pairs to read the words in the first column aloud to each other. Repeat the procedure with the remaining columns. After partners have practiced reading aloud the words in each column, have them listen to each other as they practice the entire list.

INTERVENTION PRACTICE BOOK

page 3

BEFORE

Reading "Officer Buckle and Gloria"
pages 16–35

USE SKILL CARD 1A

Focus Skill Decode Long Words

PRETEACH the skill. Tell students that all readers at times come upon long words they do not know. Encourage students to share briefly some of their own experiences with unfamiliar words. Then have them look at **side A of Skill Card 1: Decode Long Words.** Read and discuss the diagram that shows the steps for reading long words. Then have students follow the steps to decode the three words.

Prepare to Read: "Officer Buckle and Gloria"

CHANGING PATTERNS
pp. 16–35

Preview. Tell students that they are going to read a selection called "Officer Buckle and Gloria." Explain that this selection is a fantasy story, which tells about events that could not really happen. Point out that students probably know many fantasy stories, such as stories about animals that talk and act like people and creatures that visit Earth from outer space. Tell them that parts of a fantasy story may be realistic, but other parts are more like a daydream. After discussing the genre, preview the selection.

- **Pages 16–17:** On these pages, I see the title of the story and the name of the author and illustrator. I think the man who looks like a police officer must be Officer Buckle. I wonder who Gloria is. Maybe she is the dog doing a flip, or one of the children. From the illustration, I think this will be a funny story.
- **Pages 18–19:** The picture on these pages looks funny, too. I will read page 18 to see what I can find out about the story. (*Read page 18 aloud.*) Now I understand what the picture shows.
- **Pages 20–21:** On page 20, Officer Buckle is giving a speech to some children. The setting looks like a school auditorium. The children look really bored! On page 21, children are falling down and getting hurt, and a woman is standing on a swivel chair. Down in the corner, I see Officer Buckle and the dog.
- **Pages 22–23:** Here is Officer Buckle giving another speech. This time the dog is with him. The dog is doing tricks, and the children seem very interested, not bored.

Set purpose. Model setting a purpose for reading "Officer Buckle and Gloria."

MODEL **From my preview, I know that this is a funny story about a police officer who gives talks to students. At first they are bored, but they pay attention when he brings his dog. I know that readers often read stories for the purpose of enjoyment. I'll enjoy reading to find out more about Officer Buckle's dog and why the children seem to like the dog so much.**

Reread and Summarize

Have students reread and summarize "Officer Buckle and Gloria"
in sections, as described in the chart below.

Pages 18–20
**Let's reread pages 18–20 to recall what happens when Officer Buckle
goes to Napville School.**

Summary: Officer Buckle knows a lot of safety tips. He shares the tips
with students, but no one ever listens.

Pages 21–27
Now let's reread pages 21–27 to find out how Gloria changes things.

Summary: Officer Buckle brings Gloria with him when he talks to the
students. He thinks she is sitting quietly, but she is really acting out the
tips. The children like the speech. Officer Buckle and Gloria are invited
to speak at many other schools.

Pages 28–30
**As we reread pages 28–30, let's see how Officer Buckle finds out
why his speeches are so popular.**

Summary: A TV news team tapes Officer Buckle's speech. When he
sees it on the news, he realizes that everyone is watching Gloria.

Pages 31–35
Let's reread pages 31–35 to recall how the story ends.

Summary: Gloria goes to the school by herself, but everyone falls
asleep. Then Napville School has a big accident. Officer Buckle realizes
that he and Gloria should stick together.

FLUENCY BUILDER Use *Intervention Practice Book* page 3. Call
attention to the sentences on the bottom half of the page. The slashes
break the sentences into phrases to allow you to work
on natural phrasing. Tell students that their goal is to
read each phrase or unit smoothly. Model appropriate
pace, expression, and phrasing as you read each
sentence, and have students read it after you. Then
have students practice by reading the sentences aloud
three times to a partner.

**INTERVENTION
PRACTICE
BOOK**
page 3

Directed Reading: "Dan and Fran," pp. 6–12

BRIGHT SURPRISES
pp. 6–12

Page 6

Read the title aloud. Explain that Dan Craft works in a post office and that he has an important problem to solve. Have students read page 6 to find out about Dan's problem. (*He has many letters to send out, but he doesn't know who will help him.*) **SYNTHESIZE**

Page 7

After students read page 7, ask: **Why can't anyone help Dan?** (*Nan and Hank are too busy, and Brad had an accident.*) **CAUSE AND EFFECT**

What do you think Dan will do? (*Accept reasonable responses.*) **MAKE PREDICTIONS**

Pages 8–9

Have students read pages 8–9 to find out how Dan solves his problem. Ask: **Why is everyone glad to see Fran?** (*because she brings them their letters*) **DRAW CONCLUSIONS**

Ask: **What does Dan mean when he says, "We are in a jam!"?** Model using context to confirm meaning.

> **MODEL** I know that *jam* has more than one meaning. I can put jam on my toast, but I can tell that this is not the right meaning in this sentence. From the other words and sentences around it, I can figure out that Dan uses *jam* to mean "problem."
> ⭐(Focus Strategy) **USE CONTEXT TO CONFIRM MEANING**

Page 10

Read page 10 aloud to students. Ask: **Does Fran do a good job? How do you know?** (*Yes. She takes letters to the police department and to Ann Grant's class.*) **SUMMARIZE**

Page 11

Before students read, ask what Fran is. (*a kangaroo*) Then have them read page 11 to find out what the students do when Fran comes back. Ask: **How did you figure out the word *clapped* on page 11?** (*Possible response: looked for familiar word parts; used -ed ending and sounds for letters*)
⭐(Focus Skill) **DECODE LONG WORDS**

Why doesn't Fran give a speech? (*because kangaroos can't talk*) **DRAW CONCLUSIONS**

Were you surprised to find out that Fran was a kangaroo? Why or why not? (*Responses will vary.*) **EXPRESS PERSONAL OPINIONS**

Summarize the selection. Have students think about what happens first, next, and last in the story. Help them summarize the story in three or four sentences. Then have students complete *Intervention Practice Book* page 5.

INTERVENTION PRACTICE BOOK

page 5

Answers to *Think About It* Questions

1. Fran delivers the letters. **SUMMARY**

2. Fran cannot make a speech because she is a kangaroo. **INTERPRETATION**

3. Discuss with students the 5 *W*s of a news story: *Who, What, Where, When,* and *Why.* Remind students to choose one of these and give only the important information in their sentences. **WRITE FOR A TV NEWS REPORT**

AFTER

Skill Review
pages 40–41

USE SKILL CARD 1B

(Focus Skill) Decode Long Words

RETEACH **the skill.** Have students look at **side B of Skill Card 1: Decode Long Words.** Read aloud and discuss the skill reminder with them. Then read aloud the suggestion in the box. Explain that students can try this idea for breaking some long words into parts. Point out the first long word (*catlike*), but do not read it aloud. Have students identify each word part, sounding out the first syllable if necessary. Then have them blend the parts to say the word. Follow a similar procedure with the second word (*flapjack*), having students sound out both syllables. Work with students to break the additional words into parts and then pronounce them.

FLUENCY BUILDER Use *Intervention Practice Book* page 3. Explain that students will practice the sentences on the bottom half of the page by reading them aloud on tape. Assign new partners. Have students take turns reading the sentences aloud to each other and then reading them on tape. After they listen to the tape, have them tell how they think they have improved their reading of the sentences. Then have them read the sentences aloud on tape a second time, with improved pacing and tone.

INTERVENTION PRACTICE BOOK

page 3

Expressive Writing: Sensory Detail Sentences

Build on prior knowledge. Tell students that an author may use special words and phrases to help readers see, hear, smell, taste, or feel what he or she is writing about. Ask students why an author might say that a bell made a sweet tinkly sound or that a blanket felt soft and cuddly. Explain that colorful words and phrases like *soft, cuddly* and *sweet tinkly sound* are called sensory details.

Tell students that they are going to write descriptive sentences that use sensory details to tell about a walk in the forest. Display a graphic organizer like the one shown here. Work with students to list words and phrases that give sensory details.

Construct the text. "Share the pen" with students in a collaborative group writing effort. As students dictate words and phrases, write them in the organizer, guiding the process by asking questions and offering suggestions as needed. Encourage students to think of more than one detail for Sight and Sound.

Guide students in using the completed organizer to write three or four descriptive sentences.

- You might begin with a simple sentence frame, such as "On my walk in the woods, I saw _____." After a noun is supplied, students can expand the sentence with colorful adjectives.

- Additional sentences might focus on other specific senses.

Revisit the text. With students, reread the sentences you wrote together. Ask: **Can we add anything to these sentences to make it easier for the reader to picture the scene?**

- Have students assess the sentences to see if any vivid adverbs or adjectives can be added.

- Students can also look at the sentences to see whether any can be combined.

On Your Own

Think of sensory details to describe the weather either today or on another day when you felt the weather was interesting, and write the details in a web. Then use details from your web to write three descriptive sentences.

Connect Spelling and Phonics

RETEACH **short vowel /a/a.** Tell students that you will say some words in which the letter *a* stands for the /a/ sound. Have volunteers write each word on the board. Work together to proofread their work.

I. nap	2. bat	3. jam*	4. bags*
5. can*	6. glad*	7. stamp*	8. flap

* Word appears in "Dan and Fran."

Dictate the following sentence and have students write it: *A man can plan to camp on the sand.*

Build and Read Longer Words

Remind students that they have learned that the letter *a* can stand for the /a/ sound. Now they will use what they have learned to help them read some longer words.

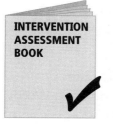

INTERVENTION ASSESSMENT BOOK

Write the word *camping* on the board. Remind students that they can read longer words by dividing a word into syllables and looking for familiar spelling patterns. Underline the familiar ending *-ing*. Cover *-ing* and point out the CVC pattern in the first syllable. Have students use letter-sound associations to pronounce the first syllable. Then uncover the rest of the word and have students blend the syllables to read the word *camping*. Use appropriate strategies to help students decode the words *standing, banner, damper, grassy, handbag, grandstand*. Encourage students to build other long words in which the letter *a* has the /a/ sound. Suggest that they use a dictionary to look up words they are not sure about.

FLUENCY BUILDER Have students choose a passage from "Dan and Fran" to read aloud to a partner. You may have students choose passages that they found particularly interesting, or have them choose one of the following options:

- Read pages 6 and 7. (Total: 69 words)
- Read page 10 and the first three paragraphs on page 11. (Total: 61 words)

SCALE	
I	Not good
2	Pretty good
3	Good
4	Great!

Students read the selected passage aloud to their partners three times. Have students rate each of their own readings on a scale of I to 4.

Encourage readers to note their improvement from one reading to the next by completing sentence frames such as *I know my reading improved because* _____. The partner who listens to the reading should also be encouraged to offer positive comments on the reader's improvement.

Review Vocabulary

To revisit Vocabulary Words with students prior to the weekly assessment, display a word line like the one shown here.

not silly at all ——————————————————— very silly

Have students listen to the following questions and take turns indicating on the word line how silly each event would be. Have them explain their reasons. If needed, ask follow-up questions to check students' understanding of the Vocabulary Words.

How silly would it be if . . .

1. the clothing **department** of a store begins to sell pots and pans?
2. an **audience** decides to perform a play?
3. a driver **obeys** the traffic laws?
4. a trainer gives **commands** to a dog?
5. someone reads a comic strip aloud with no **expression**?
6. a cook has an **accident** with a tall stack of pancakes?

You may want to display the Vocabulary Words and definitions on page 9 and have students copy them to use when they study for the vocabulary test.

 ## Review Decode Long Words

To review the focus skill before the weekly assessment, distribute *Intervention Practice Book* page 6. Point out the title, Decode Long Words, and read the directions aloud. Guide students to decode the words, using the strategies they have learned in this lesson, or have them work independently. Then have students share and explain the pictures they drew.

INTERVENTION
PRACTICE
BOOK

page 6

Review Test Prep

Ask students to turn to page 41 of the *Pupil Edition*. Call attention to the tips for answering the test questions. Tell students that paying attention to these tips can help them answer not only the test questions on this page but also other test questions like these.

CHANGING
PATTERNS
p. 41

Read the directions to students, and have a volunteer read the paragraph aloud. Then have students follow along as you read aloud the first test question and answer choices and the tip that goes with that question. Have students identify the correct choice and explain how they figured out the pronunciation of the word. Remind them to look back at the paragraph to be sure the word they pronounced makes sense in the sentence. Follow a similar procedure with the second question. Encourage students to tell how they might apply the tips on this page in other test situations as well.

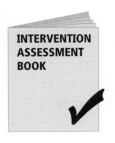

INTERVENTION
ASSESSMENT
BOOK

Self-Selected Reading

Have students select their own books to read independently. They might choose books from the classroom library shelf, or you may wish to offer a group of appropriate books from which students can choose. Titles might include the following:

- *The Best Stunt of All.* (See page 41K of the *Teacher's Edition* for a lesson plan.)

- *Hugo at the Park* by Anne Rockwell. Simon and Schuster, 1990.

- *Can I Help?* by Marilyn Janovitz. North-South Books, 1998.

You might also like to choose additional books that are the same genre or by the same author as the selection.

After students have chosen their books, give each student a copy of My Reading Log, which can be found on page R42 in the back of the *Teacher's Edition*. Have students fill in the information at the top of the form. Then have them use the log to keep track of their reading and to record their responses to the literature.

Conduct student-teacher conferences. Arrange time for each student to meet with you individually about his or her self-selected reading. Have students bring their Reading Logs to share with you at the conference. Students might also like to choose a favorite passage to read aloud to you. Ask questions designed to stimulate discussion of the book. For example, you might ask what the student liked best about the story or how the author used sensory words to express feelings.

FLUENCY PERFORMANCE Have students read aloud to you the passage from "Dan and Fran" that they selected and practiced earlier with their partners. Keep track of the number of words the student reads correctly. Ask the student to rate his or her own performance on the 1–4 scale. If students are not happy with their oral reading, give them an opportunity to continue practicing and then to reread the passage to you.

See *Oral Reading Fluency Assessment* for monitoring progress.

LESSON 2

BEFORE

Building
Background
and Vocabulary

Use with

"Pepita Talks Twice"

Phonics Review: Short Vowel /i/*i*

Identify the sound. Tell students to listen for the /i/ sound as you say the word *lid.* Then have them repeat the following sentence three times: *Did the big hat fit on Kim?* Ask students to identify the four words that have the /i/ sound. (*Did, big, fit, Kim*)

Associate letter to sound. Write on the board *Did the big hat fit on Kim?* Circle *Did, big, fit, Kim.* Ask how these words are alike. (*All have the short i vowel sound.*) Underline *i* in each word. Tell students that in *Did, big, fit,* and *Kim,* the *i* stands for the /i/ sound. Point out the CVC pattern in each word, and remind students that the vowel in a word with this pattern usually stands for the short vowel sound.

Word blending. Model how to blend the word *fit.* Slide your hand under the letters *fi* as you elongate the sounds /ffii/. Then point to the letter *t* as you say /t/, and have students say *fit* along with you. Slide your hand under the whole word and say the word naturally—*fit.* Follow a similar procedure with the words *big, pig, sit,* and *swim.*

INTERVENTION
PRACTICE
BOOK

page 8

Apply the skill. *Vowel Substitution* Write the following words on the board, and have students read each aloud. Make the changes necessary to form the word in parentheses. Have a volunteer read aloud each new word.

had (hid)	**sat** (sit)	**lap** (lip)	**clap** (clip)
tan (tin)	**pan** (pin)	**crab** (crib)	**hat** (hit)

Introduce Vocabulary

PRETEACH **lesson vocabulary.** Tell students that they are going to learn seven new words that they will see again when they read a selection called "Pepita Talks Twice." Teach each Vocabulary Word using the process shown at the right.

Use these suggestions or similar ideas to give the meaning or context.

grumble	Demonstrate picking up a tall stack of books with a grumble.
exploded	Relate to fireworks or volcanic action.
languages	Mention different languages students might speak, such as Spanish, Italian, or Japanese.

Write the word.

Say the word.

Track the word and have students repeat it.

Give the meaning or context.

mumbled	Point out the *-ed* ending that shows an action in the past. Mumble an instruction to a student. Note that *mumble* rhymes with *grumble*.
streak	Demonstrate by moving quickly from one place to another.
stubborn	Relate to the idea and image of a mule that won't budge.
darted	Relate to a game in which children run quickly from one tree to another, hiding behind each. Point out the *-ed* ending.

For vocabulary activities, see Vocabulary Games on pages 2–7.

Vocabulary Words

grumble a muttered complaint

exploded burst apart

languages systems of sounds and symbols used to communicate ideas

mumbled said in a low, unclear way

streak a quick flash of movement

stubborn headstrong or unyielding

darted moved swiftly

AFTER

Building Background and Vocabulary

Apply Vocabulary Strategies

Use syllabication. Write *grumble* on the board. Remind students that they can sometimes figure out how to pronounce a new word by dividing it into syllables. Model using the strategy.

> **MODEL** I know that when a word ends in a consonant and *-le*, I divide it into syllables before the consonant: *grum/ble*. Now I see the CVC pattern in the first syllable, and since I know that the *u* has the short vowel sound, I pronounce it /grum/. I have seen the *-le* ending in Officer Buckle's name in the last story we read, so I know how to say that syllable. I can blend the sounds to pronounce the whole word.

Guide students in using a similar procedure to decode the words *mumbled* and *stubborn*.

RETEACH **lesson vocabulary.** Provide a set of word cards for each student or pair of students. Read aloud or write on the board the meaning of one of the Vocabulary Words and the first letter in that word. Students match the correct word card to the definition. Continue until students have matched all the words.

FLUENCY BUILDER Using *Intervention Practice Book* page 7, read each word in the first column aloud and have students repeat it. Then have students work in pairs to read the words in the first column aloud to each other. Follow the same procedure with each of the remaining columns. After partners have practiced reading aloud the words in each column, have them listen to each other as they practice the entire list.

INTERVENTION PRACTICE BOOK

page 7

⭐ (Focus Skill) **Narrative Elements**

PRETEACH the skill. Ask whether students enjoy reading, hearing, and seeing different kinds of stories. Have them look at **side A of Skill Card 2: Narrative Elements.** Read aloud the definition of *characters,* and ask students to identify different kinds of characters they see in the illustration. Point out that characters may be realistic or make-believe. Then read aloud the definition of *setting,* and ask students to identify the places they see and to point out clues about whether the pictures show modern or long-ago times. Read aloud the definition of *plot,* and have students describe the pictured events. Then have volunteers name stories and answer the bulleted questions. Encourage students to name both fantasy and realistic fiction stories, which may include some they have seen as movies or videos.

Prepare to Read: "Pepita Talks Twice"

Preview. Tell students that they are going to read a story called "Pepita Talks Twice." Tell them that this selection is realistic fiction. Explain that a realistic fiction story tells about characters who are like people in real life. The characters do and say things that real people might do, and they have the same kinds of problems, thoughts, and feelings as real people. The setting of a realistic fiction story could be a real place, and the story events are things that could happen in real life. After discussing the genre, preview the selection.

CHANGING PATTERNS

pages 44–62

- **Pages 44–45:** On these pages I see the title of the story and the names of the author and illustrator. The illustration shows a girl and her dog. The setting looks like a real neighborhood, and the story probably takes place in our own time.

- **Pages 46–47:** On page 46 I see a girl running. She is wearing a backpack. I will read the first sentence of the story to see what I can find out. (*Read the first sentence aloud.*) I guess that the girl in the picture is Pepita. On page 47 she has stopped to talk to some neighbors. She still looks like she is in a hurry, though.

- **Pages 48–49:** On page 49 a boy is giving a dog a hug. Pepita looks very angry! I wonder what happened to make her feel that way.

Set purpose. Model setting a purpose for reading "Pepita Talks Twice."

MODEL From my preview, I know that this story is about a girl named Pepita, who speaks Spanish and English. One purpose for reading realistic fiction is to enjoy a story. I think I will enjoy reading about Pepita. I want to find out why she is angry and what she does about it.

Reread and Summarize

Have students reread and summarize "Pepita Talks Twice" in sections, as described below.

Pages 46–49

Let's reread pages 46–49 to recall what makes Pepita angry.

Summary: Pepita wants to get home to teach her dog Lobo a new trick. She has to stop and help people because she can speak both Spanish and English. She is angry when her brother gets home first and teaches Lobo the trick.

Pages 50–54

Now let's reread pages 50–54 to find out what Pepita decides.

Summary: Pepita decides she is not going to speak Spanish any more. People tell her it is a good thing to speak two languages, but Pepita thinks it is not good to have to speak twice.

Pages 55–59

As we reread pages 55–59, let's see how Pepita's idea is working.

Summary: Pepita finds that not speaking Spanish causes some problems she had not thought about, but she still will not change her mind.

Pages 60–62

Let's reread pages 60–62 to recall why Pepita decides to speak Spanish again.

Summary: Lobo runs into the street because he doesn't understand when Pepita calls him in English. She calls him in Spanish just in time to save him from being hit by a car. Then she is glad that she can speak two languages.

FLUENCY BUILDER Use *Intervention Practice Book* page 7. Call attention to the sentences on the bottom half of the page. The slashes break the sentences into phrases to allow you to work on natural phrasing. Tell students that their goal is to read each phrase or unit smoothly. Model appropriate pace, expression, and phrasing as you read each sentence, and have students read it after you. Then have students practice by reading the sentences aloud three times to a partner.

INTERVENTION PRACTICE BOOK

page 7

Directed Reading: "Miss Mack's Tricks," pp. 14–21

Pages 14–15

Have students read the title of the story aloud. Ask them to read pages 14–15 to find out who Miss Mack is. (*a big, pink pig*) Ask: **Where does this story take place?** (*in Kim's yard*) **What problem does Kim have?** (*She wants to teach Miss Mack tricks, but Miss Mack does not listen.*) 🟊 **NARRATIVE ELEMENTS**

Pages 16–17

Read page 16 aloud to students. Ask: **Do you think Jill will be able to get Miss Mack to listen?** Model using the strategy of making and confirming predictions.

> **MODEL** I predict that Jill will find a way to get Miss Mack to listen. I'll look for clues in the illustrations that might help explain how Jill gets Miss Mack to sit and stand. I see that Jill uses hand signals to show Miss Mack what she wants her to do. I also read on page 17 that Miss Mack sits and stands when Jill tells her to. So I'm right; she did find a way to get Miss Mack to listen. 🟊 **MAKE AND CONFIRM PREDICTIONS**

Pages 18–19

Ask students to read pages 18–19 to find out what happens next. Ask: **What story event takes place when Ink the cat meets Miss Mack?** (*Ink runs away.*) 🟊 **NARRATIVE ELEMENTS**

Page 20

Have students read page 20 to find out what happens to Ink. (*Miss Mack grabs her and saves her.*) Ask: **Why does the author tell you that Kim used her hands?** (*Miss Mack does not pay attention until the children learn to use hand signals. When Kim uses her hands, Miss Mack understands what Kim wants her to do.*) **DRAW CONCLUSIONS**

**INTERVENTION
PRACTICE
BOOK**

page 9

Summarize the selection. Have small groups of students summarize the story by acting it out. Students can play the roles of Kim, Nick, Jill, Tim, and Jim and use stuffed animals or puppets for Miss Mack and Ink.

Answers to *Think About It* Questions

1. Miss Mack does not listen to Kim. **SUMMARY**
2. Possible responses: She may have trained her own cat or dog and knows that pets respond to motions or gestures. She may know that people use sign language to communicate. **INTERPRETATION**
3. Ask questions like the following to help students brainstorm ideas for their story: *Where do Miss Mack and Ink live? What other animals might live in their neighborhood? What might Ink teach or show Miss Mack?* **WRITE A STORY IDEA**

(Focus Skill) Narrative Elements

RETEACH the skill. Have students look at **side B of Skill Card 2: Narrative Elements.** Read aloud and discuss the skill reminder with them. Then read the direction line. Have students take turns reading the captions and telling what they see in the pictures. Call on volunteers to read aloud and answer the questions. Encourage students to explain how they identified the characters, setting, and plot events.

 FLUENCY BUILDER Use *Intervention Practice Book* page 7. Explain that students will practice the sentences on the bottom half of the page by reading them aloud on tape. Assign new partners. Have students take turns reading the sentences aloud to each other and then reading them on tape. After they listen to the tape, have them tell how they think they have improved their reading of the sentences. Then have them read the sentences aloud on tape a second time, with improved pacing and tone.

INTERVENTION PRACTICE BOOK

page 7

Expressive Writing: Expressive Sentences

Build on prior knowledge. Tell students that people write in a journal, which can be a blank notebook or just sheets of paper, to record events and to express their feelings about the events. Ask them to imagine how Kim in "Miss Mack's Tricks" might have felt when she tried to teach Miss Mack tricks but Miss Mack did not listen. Tell students you will work together to write a journal entry Kim might have made.

	Miss Mack did not listen to me.
Event	
Feelings	
Details	

Display a graphic organizer like the one shown here.

Construct the text. "Share the pen" with students in a collaborative group writing effort. As students dictate words and phrases, write them in the organizer, guiding the process by asking questions and offering suggestions as needed.

- Have a student read aloud the event shown in the chart. Ask students how they think Kim might feel about this event. Have them dictate words or phrases for you to write in the Feelings section of the chart.

- Have students supply details that show Kim's feelings in an interesting, colorful way. For example, if they have suggested that Kim was angry, details might include *so angry that I stamped my foot.*

- Guide students to develop the material into a journal entry of two or three sentences that tell about the event and how the writer, Kim, felt about it. Write the entry on the board or on chart paper as students dictate.

Revisit the text. Go back and read the journal entry together. Ask: **Did we express Kim's thoughts and feelings clearly?**

- Ask: **Did we use colorful words to describe the event? Can we add other colorful words?**

- Have students check to be sure they have written complete sentences with correct capitalization and punctuation.

On Your Own

Think of an experience you have had with a pet, either your own or someone else's. Maybe you made friends with a neighbor's dog or saw a cat climb a tree. Write one or two sentences describing the event. Include your feelings and details that show how you felt. Then use what you wrote to tell a partner about the event.

Connect Spelling and Phonics

RETEACH short vowel /i/ i. Tell students that you will say some words in which the letter *i* stands for the /i/ sound. Have volunteers write each word on the board. Work together to proofread their work.

I. sit*	2. big*	3. pink*	4. tricks*
5. swim	6. twins*	7. did*	8. flip

Word appears in "Miss Mack's Tricks."

Dictate the following sentence and have students write it: *Can a pig pick a wig from a bin?*

Build and Read Longer Words

Remind students that they have learned that the letter *i* can stand for the /i/ sound. Now they will use what they have learned to help them read some longer words.

Write the word *within* on the board. Remind students that they can read longer words by looking for smaller words in a longer word or by looking for familiar spelling patterns. Cover *in* and point out the familiar word *with*. Then cover *with* and point out the familiar word *in*. Have students read the word *within*. Use appropriate strategies to help students decode the words *misspell, skipper, winner, ridden, finger, given*. Encourage students to build other long words like these in which an *i* stands for the short vowel *i* sound. Suggest that they use a dictionary to look up words they are not sure about.

INTERVENTION
ASSESSMENT
BOOK

FLUENCY BUILDER Have students choose a passage from "Miss Mack's Tricks" to read aloud to a partner. You may have students choose passages that they found particularly interesting, or have them choose one of the following options:

- Read page 14 and the first two paragraphs on page 15. (Total: 68 words)

- Read page 16 and the first two paragraphs on page 17. (Total: 70 words)

Students read the selected passage aloud to their partners three times. Have students rate each of their own readings on a scale of 1 to 4.

Encourage readers to note their improvement from one reading to the next by completing sentence frames such as *I know my reading improved because* _____ . The partner who listens to the reading should also be encouraged to offer positive comments on the reader's improvement.

SCALE
1 Not good
2 Pretty good
3 Good
4 Great!

Vocabulary Review

To revisit the Vocabulary Words prior to the weekly assessment, have students listen as you read aloud each of the following sentence beginnings. Call on a volunteer to complete each sentence so that it makes sense. Alternatively, you might write the sentence beginnings on the board with the Vocabulary Words underlined. Have volunteers read aloud and complete the sentences.

1. When the fireworks **exploded**, _____.
2. John **mumbled** the answer because _____.
3. If you run like a **streak**, you _____.
4. People learn other **languages** so _____.
5. The cat **darted** across the street because _____.
6. Jeremy **grumbled** when _____.
7. Sarah was so **stubborn** that she _____.

You may want to display the Vocabulary Words and definitions on page 19 and have students copy them to use when they study for the vocabulary test.

(Focus Skill) Review Narrative Elements

To review narrative elements before the weekly assessment, distribute *Intervention Practice Book* page 10. Point out the title, Narrative Elements, and read aloud the directions. Explain that students should recall the names of the characters and write them in the Characters box in the story map. Help students identify the time and place of the story and then complete the Setting box. Next, elicit simple sentences to describe important events that take place at the beginning, middle, and end of the story. You may want to write students' sentences on the board for everyone to copy in the Plot box to complete the story map.

INTERVENTION
PRACTICE
BOOK

page 10

Review Test Prep

Ask students to turn to page 67 of the *Pupil Edition*. Call attention to the tips for answering the test questions. Tell students that paying attention to these tips can help them answer not only the test questions on this page but also other test questions like these.

CHANGING
PATTERNS
page
67

Have a volunteer read the story aloud. Read the directions aloud. Then have students follow along as you read aloud the first test question and the tip that goes with it. Have students identify the correct choice and explain how they knew which was the main character. Read aloud the second question and tip, and have students give an oral response. Encourage students to tell how they might apply the tips on this page in other test situations as well.

INTERVENTION
ASSESSMENT
BOOK

✔

Self-Selected Reading

Have students select their own books to read independently. They might choose books from the classroom library shelf, or you may wish to offer a group of appropriate books from which students can choose. Titles might include the following:

- *Le Anne Joins the Show.* (See page 67M of the *Teacher's Edition* for a lesson plan.)

- *D.W. the Picky Eater* by Marc Brown. Little, Brown, 1997.

- *The Doorbell Rang* by Pat Hutchins. Morrow/Avon, 1989.

You might also like to suggest other books that are by the same author as the selection or are the same genre. After students have chosen their books, give each student a copy of My Reading Log, which can be found on page R42 in the back of the *Teacher's Edition*. Have students fill in the information at the top of the form. Then have them use the log to keep track of their reading and to record their responses to the literature.

Conduct student-teacher conferences. Arrange time for each student to confer with you individually about his or her self-selected reading. Have students bring their Reading Logs to share with you at the conference. Students might also like to choose a favorite passage to read aloud to you. Ask questions about the book to stimulate discussion. For example, you might ask which story character a student liked best, or ask what the problem is in the story and how it is solved.

FLUENCY PERFORMANCE Have students read aloud to you the passage from "Miss Mack's Tricks" that they selected and practiced earlier with their partners. Keep track of the number of words the student reads correctly. Ask the student to rate his or her own performance on the 1–4 scale. If students are not happy with their oral reading, give them an opportunity to continue practicing and then to read the passage to you again.

Use with

"Nate the Great, San Francisco Detective"

Review Phonics: Short Vowel /o/o

Identify the sound. Tell students to listen for the short *o* vowel sound as you say the words *hop* and *rock*. Then have students repeat the following sentence twice: *Rob will not stop.* Ask them to identify the three words that have the /o/ sound. (*Rob, not, stop*)

Associate letter to sound. Write on the board *Rob will not stop.* Circle *Rob, not,* and *stop.* Ask how these words are alike. (*All have the short o vowel sound.*) Underline *o* in each word. Tell students that in *Rob, not,* and *stop,* the *o* stands for the /o/ sound. Point out the CVC pattern in each word, and remind students that the vowel in a word with this pattern usually stands for the short vowel sound.

Word blending. Model how to blend and read the word *stop.* Slide your hand under the letters *sto* as you elongate the sounds /ssttoo/. Then point to the letter *p* as you say the /p/ sound. Slide your hand under the whole word and say the word naturally—*stop.* Follow a similar procedure with the words *trot, mop, job,* and *sob.*

INTERVENTION PRACTICE BOOK

page 12

Apply the skill. *Vowel Substitution* Write these words on the board, and have students read each aloud. Make the changes needed to form the words in parentheses. Have a volunteer read aloud each new word.

hip (hop)	**map** (mop)	**slit** (slot)	**flap** (flop)
hat (hot)	**tip** (top)	**lick** (lock)	**drip** (drop)

Introduce Vocabulary

PRETEACH lesson vocabulary. Tell students that they are going to learn seven new words that they will see again when they read a story called "Nate the Great." Teach each Vocabulary Word using the following process.

Use these suggestions or similar ideas to give the meaning or context.

> Write the word.
> Say the word.
> Track the word and have students repeat it.
> Give the meaning or context.

detective	Relate to the word *detect,* meaning "to discover."
case	Point out that this is a multiple-meaning word. Discuss the idea of a detective solving a case.
specific	Relate to the familiar word *special.*
assistant	Relate to the word *assist,* meaning "to help."

definitely	Point out the suffix. Explain that *definite* means "certain" or "sure." Substitute *definitely* for *certainly* in an example sentence.
returned	Point out the *-ed* ending. Have a volunteer pretend to leave the classroom and return.
positive	Point out the CVC pattern and short *o* vowel sound in the first syllable. Discuss similar meanings of *positive* and *definite*.

For vocabulary activities, see Vocabulary Games on pp. 2–7.

Vocabulary Words

detective a person who solves mysteries

specific exact

positive completely sure

case a mystery or problem a detective is working to solve

returned brought back

definitely surely

assistant a person who helps someone do a job

AFTER

Building Background and Vocabulary

Apply Vocabulary Strategies

Use familiar word parts. Write *returned* on the board. Tell students that they can sometimes figure out the pronunciation of a word by looking for word parts they know. Model using the strategy.

> **MODEL** When I look at this word, I see the familiar prefix *re-*, which I know from words like *repeat* and *repair.* I also see the ending *-ed,* which is often added to a word to show action that has happened in the past. Between these two word parts is the familiar word *turn.* I'll blend all three parts to pronounce the whole word.

Guide students in using a similar procedure to decode the words *detective* and *positive.*

RETEACH **lesson vocabulary.** Provide patterns for a circle and an arrow. Have students make a simple spinner by cutting a circle and arrow from cardboard and joining them with a brad. Tell students to divide the spinner into sections and write a Vocabulary Word in each one. Students take turns spinning the spinner, saying the word the spinner lands on, and using the word in a sentence.

FLUENCY BUILDER Use *Intervention Practice Book* page 11. Read each word in the first column aloud and have students repeat it. Then have students work in pairs to read the words in the first column aloud to each other. Follow the same procedure with each of the remaining columns. After partners have practiced reading aloud the words in each column, have them listen to each other as they practice the entire list.

INTERVENTION PRACTICE BOOK

page 11

★ Focus Skill ## Decode Long Words

PRETEACH **the skill.** Tell students that long words may look difficult at first, but there are often ways to figure them out. Have students look at **side A of Skill Card 3: Decode Long Words.** Ask a volunteer to read the first sentence aloud. Then have students take turns reading the steps in the diagram and explaining each step in their own words. Work with students to decode the underlined words, using the steps listed.

Prepare to Read: "Nate the Great"

Preview. Tell students that they are going to read a selection called "Nate the Great, San Francisco Detective." Explain that this is a type of fiction story called a mystery in which the main character is often a detective who has to solve or figure out a crime or other event. Explain that readers may also use story clues to try to figure out the solution. Then preview the selection.

CHANGING PATTERNS
pages 70–94

- **Pages 70–71:** On page 71, I see the title and the names of the authors and illustrator. The boy with the dog may be Nate. I know that San Francisco is a city in California. That must be the city in the picture.

- **Page 72:** At the top of page 72, I see "Chapter 1" and the chapter title. This tells me that the story is divided into chapters. On page 72 I see a lot of people with signs. A man has a sign that says "Nate the Great." The same boy and dog from the title page are in this picture, too. The boy seems to be looking around. I think he must have just arrived at a place like an airport and is looking for the person who is supposed to meet him.

- **Pages 73–77:** On these pages the boy and the dog are riding in a long car called a limousine, or limo, and the boy is talking on the telephone. I wonder where they are going and what the telephone calls are about. Maybe they have something to do with solving a crime or mystery.

- **Pages 76–80:** The message on the answering machine mentions a California case and the end of the entire world. This sounds interesting, so I look at the next few pages and see a new character on page 79, the same character reading a joke book on page 80, and a funny picture of Nate with three stacks of pancakes floating around his head. I think these are all important to this story.

Set purpose. Model setting a purpose for reading "Nate the Great."

MODEL From my preview, I think that Nate the Great is a young detective who has come to San Francisco to try to solve a case. It seems to have something to do with a joke book and pancakes. I know that one purpose for reading fiction is for enjoyment. I'll enjoy reading to find out how Nate the Great solves the case.

Reread and Summarize

Have students reread and summarize "Nate the Great" in sections, as described in the chart below.

Pages 72–78

Let's reread the first three chapters on pages 72–78 to recall why Nate the Great goes to San Francisco and what happens when he arrives there.

Summary: Nate the Great goes to San Francisco to see his cousin Olivia. He agrees to help Olivia's friend Duncan find a lost joke book.

Pages 79–83

Now let's reread Chapters 4 and 5 on pages 79–83 to find out where Duncan lost his joke book.

Summary: Duncan tells Nate the Great how he lost the joke book at Perry's Pancake House. Nate the Great goes to the pancake house, but the joke book is not there.

Pages 84–89

As we reread Chapters 6, 7, and 8 on pages 84–89, let's see where else Nate the Great looks for the missing joke book.

Summary: Nate the Great thinks the joke book might be in the bag of frozen pancakes in Duncan's freezer, but it isn't. Then Nate and Duncan go to the bookstore where Duncan bought the book to see if anyone returned it.

Pages 90-94

Let's reread Chapters 9 and 10 on pages 90–94 to recall how Nate the Great solves the case.

Summary: Nate the Great figures out that the joke book was returned to the cookbook section because it is called "Joke Stew." The case is solved.

FLUENCY BUILDER Use *Intervention Practice Book* page 11. Call attention to the sentences on the bottom half of the page. The slashes break the sentences into phrases to allow you to work on natural phrasing. Tell students that their goal is to read each phrase or unit smoothly. Model appropriate pace, expression, and phrasing as you read aloud each sentence, and have students read it after you. Then have students practice by reading the sentences aloud three times to a partner.

INTERVENTION PRACTICE BOOK

page 11

Directed Reading: "The Case of the Missing Letter" pp. 22–28

**BRIGHT
SURPRISES**
pp. 22–28

Pages 22–23

Read aloud the title. Call attention to the illustration, and ask a volunteer to read the sign. Then read pages 22–23 aloud while students listen to find out why the girl in the picture needs help from Detective Tom. Ask: **What is Min's problem?** *(Possible response: She mailed two letters to her mom, but her mom got only one of them.)* **DRAW CONCLUSIONS**

Ask: **How can you figure out the long word *letterbox*?** *(Possible response: by breaking it into smaller words)* (Focus Skill) **DECODE LONG WORDS**

Pages 24–25

Have students read page 24 to find out what might have happened to Min's letter. Ask: **What does Tom think might have happened to the letter?** *(Possible response: He thinks the letter might have fallen out of the letterbox because the box is very full.)* **CAUSE/EFFECT**

Ask a volunteer to read page 25 aloud while students listen to find out what Tom learns. Ask: **What does Tom find out from Mr. Bond?** *(Possible response: Some letters did drop out of the box.)* **IMPORTANT DETAILS**

Pages 26–27

Read aloud the first three paragraphs on page 26. **Ask: Will the stamp help Tom solve the case?** Model the strategy of reading ahead.

> **MODEL** I read that Tom thinks the case is solved. I know the stamp is a clue, but I do not understand how it helps Tom solve the case. I will read ahead to see if I can find out what Tom is thinking. (Read aloud the rest of page 26 and the first paragraph on page 27.) Now I see how the stamp helped Tom solve the case. The missing letter was not delivered to Min's mother because the stamp came off when the letter fell out of the letterbox.
> (Focus Strategy) **READ AHEAD**

Ask: **Do you think the letter will be in Min's box? Why or why not?** *(Responses may vary.)* Then have students read the rest of page 27 to see if their predictions are correct. **MAKE AND CONFIRM PREDICTIONS**

**INTERVENTION
PRACTICE
BOOK**

page 13

Summarize the selection. Ask students to think about the problem in the story and how Tom solves it. Then have them complete *Intervention Practice Book* page 13.

Answers to *Think About It* Questions

1. The stamp came off one of the letters when the letters fell out of the box because it was full. That letter did not get delivered to Min's mother because it had no stamp. **SUMMARY**

2. Possible response: Yes. He finds clues and solves the mystery. **INTERPRETATION**

3. Review the format of a friendly letter before students begin writing. **WRITE A LETTER**

AFTER

Skill Review
pages 98–99

USE SKILL CARD 3B

(Focus Skill) Decode Long Words

RETEACH **the skill.** Have students look **at side B of Skill Card 3: Decode Long Words**. Have a volunteer read the skill reminder aloud. Then read the directions with students. Ask a volunteer to read aloud the first word, identify the matching picture, and tell how he or she figured out the word. Repeat the same procedure with each of the words.

Have students copy the five words on their papers. Tell them to show how each word is divided into parts or syllables by writing the parts in different colors.

FLUENCY BUILDER Use *Intervention Practice Book* page 11. Explain that students will practice the sentences on the bottom half of the page by reading them aloud on tape. Assign new partners. Have students take turns reading the sentences aloud to each other and then reading them on tape. After they listen to the tape, have them tell how they think they have improved their reading of the sentences. Then have them read the sentences aloud on tape a second time, with improved pacing and tone.

INTERVENTION PRACTICE BOOK

page 11

Expository Writing: Personal Narrative

Build on prior knowledge. Choose a recent class or school event, such as a special project or parent visiting day, to model focusing on main ideas. Explain that a personal narrative is a piece of writing that tells about something that really happened and also tells the writer's own thoughts and feelings. A personal narrative has a beginning, a middle, and an ending. Tell students that to prepare for writing, they should think of the most important ideas, or main ideas, that they want to tell about.

As students talk about the event, jot down their ideas in a graphic organizer like this one.

Our Puppet Show		
Beginning	**Middle**	**Ending**
We decided to have a puppet show.	We made puppets. We wrote a script. It was fun.	Ms. Ortiz's class came to see our puppet show. They liked the show.

Construct the text. "Share the pen" with students in a collaborative writing effort. As students dictate words or phrases, write them in the graphic organizer, guiding the process by asking questions and offering suggestions as needed.

- Help students develop sentences that tell the beginning, middle, and ending.

- Remind students that a personal narrative tells the writer's thoughts and feelings. If necessary, ask questions such as **How did you feel about that? What did you think when that happened?**

Revisit the text. With students, read the sentences in the completed graphic organizer.

- Ask: **Should any of our sentences be exclamatory sentences?** Make changes as appropriate.

- After any needed revisions are made, help students develop an oral narrative using the sentences you wrote.

> **On Your Own**
>
> Write sentences that tell the main ideas about a birthday or holiday you enjoyed with your family. Tell your narrative to a partner, using your sentences as a guide.

Connect Spelling and Phonics

RETEACH **short vowel /o/o.** Tell students that you will say some words in which the letter *o* stands for the short *o* vowel sound. Have volunteers write each word on the board. Work together to proofread their work.

1. Tom*	2. not*	3. box*	4. mom*
5. got*	6. pond	7. drop*	8. job*

Word appears in "The Case of the Missing Letter."

Dictate the following sentence and have students write it: *Can a frog hop on top of a fox?*

Build and Read Longer Words

Remind students that they have learned how to decode words with the short *o* vowel sound spelled *o.*

Write the word *bobsled* on the board. Tell students that when they see a long word, they can look to see if it is made up of two smaller words. Cover the word *sled,* and have students read the shorter word *bob.* Then cover the word *bob,* and have students read the shorter word *sled.* Finally, slide your hand under the entire word as students read it aloud. Follow a similar procedure with the words *doghouse* and *potluck.* Encourage students to build other long words in which the letter *o* stands for the short *o* vowel sound. Suggest that they use a dictionary to look up words they are not sure about.

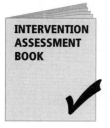

INTERVENTION
ASSESSMENT
BOOK

FLUENCY BUILDER Have students choose a passage from "The Case of the Missing Letter" to read aloud to a partner. You may have students choose passages that they found particularly interesting, or have them choose one of the following options:

- Read the last paragraph on page 22 and all of page 23. (From *How can you* to *information.* Total: 73 words)

- Read page 26. (Total: 62 words)

Students read the selected passage aloud to their partners three times. Have students rate each of their own readings on a scale of 1 to 4.

Encourage readers to note their improvement from one reading to the next by completing sentence frames such as *I know my reading improved because* _____ . The partner who listens to the reading should also be encouraged to offer positive comments on the reader's improvement.

SCALE
1 Not good
2 Pretty good
3 Good
4 Great!

Review Vocabulary

To revisit Vocabulary Words prior to the weekly assessment, have students listen as you read aloud each of the following sentence beginnings. Call on a volunteer to complete each sentence so that it makes sense. Alternatively, you might write the sentence beginnings on the board with the Vocabulary Words underlined. Have volunteers read aloud and complete the sentences.

1. You might call a **detective** if _____ .
2. Be sure to give **specific** information when you _____ .
3. Juan was **positive** it was raining because _____ .
4. It would be hard to solve a **case** if _____ .
5. Alice **returned** the jacket because _____ .
6. A teacher **definitely** needs to _____ .
7. Someone might need an **assistant** to _____ .

You may want to display the Vocabulary Words and definitions on page 29 and have students copy them to use when they study for the vocabulary test.

 ## Review Decode Long Words

To review the focus skill before the weekly assessment, distribute *Intervention Practice Book* page 14. Call attention to the title, Decode Long Words. Read the directions at the top of the page with students. Point out the list of four words at the left. Remind students that they may be able to read long words like these by looking for smaller parts. Guide them in breaking the first word into two smaller words and writing the parts in the boxes. (*back + pack*) Tell them to use the word parts to help them read the long word. Have a student read the long word aloud. Follow the same procedure with each of the other words. (*paint + ing*, *sudden + ly*, *un + able*) Then have volunteers read the sentences at the bottom of the page.

INTERVENTION
PRACTICE
BOOK

page 14

Review Test Prep

Ask students to turn to page 99 of the *Pupil Edition*. Call attention to the tips for answering the test questions. Tell students that paying attention to these tips can help them answer not only the test questions on this page but also other test questions like these.

CHANGING
PATTERNS
page 99

Have students follow along as you read aloud each test question and the tip that goes with it. Ask volunteers to identify the consonant-vowel-consonant pattern and the vowel sound in each syllable of *pumpkin*, and the letter pattern that is the same in *scramble* and *table*. Encourage students to tell how they might apply the tips on this page in other test situations.

INTERVENTION
ASSESSMENT
BOOK

Self-Selected Reading

Have students select their own books to read independently. They might choose books from the classroom library shelf, or you may wish to offer a group of appropriate books from which they can choose. Titles might include the following:

- *A Visit to San Francisco.* (See page 99M of the *Teacher's Edition* for a lesson plan.)

- *Detective Dinosaur Lost and Found* by James Skofield. HarperCollins, 1999.

- *In the Attic* by Hiawyn Oram. Henry Holt, 1988.

You may also wish to choose additional books that are the same genre, are by the same author, or that have the same kind of text structure as the selection.

After students have chosen their books, give each one a copy of My Reading Log, which can be found on page R42 in the back of the *Teacher's Edition*. Have students fill in the information at the top of the form. Then have them use the log to keep track of their reading and to record their responses to the literature.

Conduct student-teacher conferences. Arrange time for each student to confer with you individually about his or her self-selected reading. Have students bring their Reading Logs to share with you at the conference. Students might also like to choose a favorite passage to read aloud to you. Ask questions about the book to stimulate discussion. For example, you might ask where the story took place, who the main character was, and what happened at the beginning, middle, and end of the story.

FLUENCY PERFORMANCE Have students read aloud to you the passage from "The Case of the Missing Letter" that they selected and practiced earlier with their partners. Keep track of the number of words each student reads correctly. Ask the student to rate his or her own performance on the 1–4 scale. If students are not happy with their oral reading, give them an opportunity to continue practicing and then to read the passage to you again.

See *Oral Reading Fluency Assessment* for monitoring progress.

LESSON 4

BEFORE

Building
Background
and Vocabulary

**INTERVENTION
PRACTICE
BOOK**

page 16

Use with

"Allie's Basketball Dream"

Review Phonics: Short Vowel /e/e

Identify the sound. Tell students to listen for the /e/ sound as you say the words *let* and *hen*. Then have students repeat this sentence three times: *Ken lends Jen ten red sleds.* Ask them to identify the words that have the /e/ sound they hear in *let*. (*Ken, lends, Jen, ten, red, sleds*)

Associate letter to sound. Write on the board *Ken lends Jen ten red sleds.* Underline the *e* in each word. Tell students that the letter *e* in each of these words stands for the short *e* vowel sound. Point out the CVC pattern, and remind students that a vowel that comes between two or more consonants usually stands for a short vowel sound.

Word blending. Model how to blend and read the word *red*. Slide your hand under the letters *re* as you elongate the sounds /rree/. Then point to the letter *d* and say /d/. Slide your hand under the whole word, and say the word naturally—*red*. Repeat the procedure using the words *bed*, *fed*, *send*, *spend*, *hen*, and *men*.

Apply the skill. *Vowel Substitution* Write the following words on the board, and have students read them aloud. Make the changes necessary to form the words in parentheses. Have students read each new word.

sit (set)	**pig** (peg)	**tin** (ten)	**sand** (send)
pan (pen)	**bad** (bed)	**rod** (red)	**stop** (step)

Introduce Vocabulary

PRETEACH **lesson vocabulary.** Tell students that they are going to learn six new words that they will see again when they read a selection called "Allie's Basketball Dream." Teach each Vocabulary Word using the following process.

Use these suggestions or similar ideas to give the meaning or context.

> Write the word.
> Say the word.
> Track the word and have students repeat it.
> Give the meaning or context.

professional	Relate to professional athletes that students have seen on TV. Explain that this word is sometimes shortened to *pro*.
familiar	Point out the similarity to the word *family* and the fact that the people in your family are usually the ones you know best, or are most familiar with.
captain	Give examples, such as the captain of a ship or a team.

pretended	Point out the *-ed* ending that shows past tense. Have students pretend to shoot a basketball or wash their hands.
aimed	Point out the *-ed* ending. Crumple a paper and aim it at a target on the board.
monitor	Give an example of someone students know, such as a lunch-room or hallway monitor or a crossing guard.

For vocabulary activities, see Vocabulary Games on pages 2–7.

Vocabulary Words

professional doing something as a job

familiar known well or recognized

captain the leader of a group

pretended made believe

aimed pointed one thing at another

monitor a person who watches over something

AFTER

Building Background and Vocabulary

Apply Vocabulary Strategies

Use synonyms/antonyms. Write the following sentences on the board:

John <u>pretended</u> he was on a ship. He made believe the ship was sinking.

Tell students that they can sometimes figure out a word by looking for a synonym or antonym in the sentence or another sentence nearby. Model using the strategy.

> **MODEL** I'm not sure what the word *pretended* means. The first sentence says that John pretended he was on a ship. I'll look at the second sentence to see if it has any clues. This one also mentions a ship and says he made believe. I think that *pretended* means the same thing as *made believe*. These are synonyms.

Guide students in looking for an antonym to figure out the underlined word in this sentence: **This word is <u>familiar</u>, but the other word is strange to me.** (antonym: *strange*)

RETEACH lesson vocabulary. Write the letters of the Vocabulary Words on small squares of construction paper. If possible, use a different color for each word. Place the letters for each word in a separate envelope, and write a clue sentence on the front. Students figure out the correct word from the clue and put the letters together to form that word. You may wish to write the words on the board to help students with spelling.

FLUENCY BUILDER Use *Intervention Practice Book* page 15. Read each word in the first column aloud and have students repeat it. Then have students work in pairs to read the words in the first column aloud to each other. Follow the same procedure with each of the remaining columns. After partners have practiced reading aloud the words in each column separately, have them listen to each other as they practice the entire list.

INTERVENTION PRACTICE BOOK

page 15

(Focus Skill) ★ **Narrative Elements**

PRETEACH **the skill.** Tell students that a story has three main parts, or elements—setting, characters, and plot. Ask volunteers to explain briefly each element. Then have students look at **side A of Skill Card 4: Narrative Elements.** After reading the sentences at the top, have students read the words in the boxes and discuss the diagram.

Then call attention to the pictures at the bottom. Ask volunteers to read aloud what the character says and to describe what he does. Have students explain what they can tell about this character from what he says and does. (*Possible response: He is lonesome.*)

Prepare to Read: "Allie's Basketball Dream"

Preview. Tell students that they are going to read a story called "Allie's Basketball Dream." Explain that this selection is realistic fiction, which means that the characters and events in the story are like people and events in real life. The characters may have traits, feelings, and problems like those of real people that students know. Then do a preview of the selection.

CHANGING
PATTERNS
pages
102–119

- **Pages 102–103:** I see the title and the names of the author and illustrator. A girl is soaring through the air toward a basketball hoop. She must be Allie. Maybe her dream is to become a great basketball player. Clues in the illustration tell me that the setting is a city in the present time.

- **Page 104 :** I see a man carrying a box with a bow like a gift. I'll read the paragraph to see if I can find out who he is. Now I know that he's Allie's father, and the gift is a basketball for her.

- **Page 105:** Allie is with her father. She has her basketball. In the background is a basketball court. I think Allie and her father are on their way there so Allie can play with her new basketball.

- **Pages 106–107:** I see some older, bigger boys playing basketball. Allie is holding her ball. I wonder if she is going to play basketball with them.

- **Pages 108–111:** On page 108 the big boys watch Allie miss a shot. On page 109, Allie is throwing the basketball through a hula hoop. On pages 110 and 111 Allie is still playing with her basketball, but she's not taking any shots. I wonder if she is getting discouraged.

Set purpose. Model setting a purpose for reading "Allie's Basketball Dream."

> **MODEL** From my preview I know that this story is about a girl named Allie who dreams of playing basketball. In realistic fiction the main character often has a problem that people in real life might have. I think maybe Allie will have to solve a problem to make her basketball dream come true. One purpose for reading fiction is for enjoyment. I'll read to enjoy finding out whether Allie learns to shoot her basketball the way she dreams of doing.

Reread and Summarize

Have students reread and summarize "Allie's Basketball Dream" in sections, as described in the chart below.

Pages 104–107

Let's reread pages 104–107 to recall how Allie begins learning to play basketball.

Summary: Allie's father gives her a basketball and takes her to the playground to practice shooting baskets.

Pages 108–111

Now let's reread pages 108–111 to find out what Allie does with her new basketball.

Summary: Some older boys laugh when Allie shoots and misses. She tries to get some friends to play basketball with her, but they are doing other things.

Pages 112–115

As we reread pages 112–115, let's see whether Allie's feelings about playing basketball have changed.

Summary: Allie begins to feel discouraged. Her friend Buddy offers to trade his volleyball for her basketball. Allie thinks it over and remembers how much she loved basketball the first time her father took her to a game.

Pages 116–119

Let's reread pages 116–119 to recall what Allie decides to do.

Summary: Allie decides to keep her basketball. Her friends join in playing with her. Everyone applauds when she makes a basket, including her father.

FLUENCY BUILDER Be sure students have copies of *Intervention Practice Book* page 15. Point out the sentences on the bottom half of the page. The slashes break the sentences into phrases to allow students to work on natural phrasing. Tell students that their goal is to read each phrase or unit smoothly. Model appropriate pace, expression, and phrasing as you read each sentence, and have students read it after you. Then have students practice by reading the sentences aloud three times to a partner.

INTERVENTION PRACTICE BOOK

page 15

Directed Reading: "Just a Little Practice" pp. 30–37

Page 30

Read aloud the title on page 30. Ask students what kinds of things they have needed "just a little practice" to learn. Then have them read page 30 to find out who needs practice and at what. Model the thinking:

BRIGHT SURPRISES pp. 30–37

> **MODEL** I read that Pat takes a shot and makes a basket. Then Ted tells his basketball, "Now you go in." That makes me think that Ted will need practice shooting baskets. **MAKE PREDICTIONS**

Pages 31–32

Have students read pages 31–32 to confirm the prediction and to figure out what kind of person Pat is. Ask: **Do you think Pat is a friendly person? Why or why not?** (*Possible response: yes; because she doesn't laugh when Ted misses; she introduces herself and says, "Let's test that basketball!"*) (Focus Skill) **NARRATIVE ELEMENTS**

Pages 33–34

Have students read pages 33-34 to find out what happens next. Model using the strategy of summarizing.

> **MODEL** I can summarize the events on these two pages by retelling them briefly in my own words. Pat makes a shot. Ted takes a shot with Pat's ball, but he misses again. Pat says she will be his teacher, but Ted keeps missing. (Focus Strategy) **SUMMARIZE**

Page 35

Have students read page 35 to find out whether Ted makes a basket. Ask: **How do you think Ted feels now?** (*happy, excited, proud*) **CHARACTERS' EMOTIONS**

How do you think Pat feels, and how can you tell? (*She must feel happy because she applauds and says, "You did it!"*) (Focus Skill) **NARRATIVE ELEMENTS**

Page 36

INTERVENTION PRACTICE BOOK

page 17

Have students read page 36 to find out about Jack Wick. Ask: **What trade does Jack Wick suggest?** (*Pat was Ted's teacher. Now Jack Wick will trade places with Pat and teach her to dribble.*) **MAIN IDEA**

Summarize the selection. Ask students to think about what happened in the story. Help them summarize the story in three or four sentences. Then have them complete *Intervention Practice Book* page 17.

Page 37

Answers to *Think About It* Questions

1. He practices and practices, and Pat helps him. **SUMMARY**

2. Possible response: He can see that Pat is doing a good job and that Ted is learning. He wants Ted to feel proud. **INTERPRETATION**

3. Ask questions like the following to help students brainstorm ideas for the next scene: *What happens when Pat tries to dribble? Does Ted help Pat, too? What does Jack Wick say when Pat starts to dribble?* **WRITE A STORY**

(Focus Skill) **Narrative Elements**

RETEACH **the skill.** Have students look at **side B of Skill Card 4: Narrative Elements**. Read the skill reminder and directions with them. Give students time to read the story silently, and then have a volunteer read it aloud. As you draw a diagram on the board, have students draw their own diagrams on their papers. Through discussion, guide them to complete the diagram on the board interactively and copy the information in their individual diagrams. *Possible responses are shown.*

What the Character Says

Where's your lunch, Sam?
Why aren't you eating?
You can help me eat it.

What the Character Does

She gives Sam part of her sandwich, even though she is hungry.

What the Character Is Like

Jenna is a caring and generous friend.

 FLUENCY BUILDER Be sure students have copies of *Intervention Practice Book* page 15. Explain that students will practice the sentences on the bottom half of the page by reading them aloud on tape. Assign new partners. Have students take turns reading the sentences aloud to each other and then reading them on tape. After they listen to the tape, have them tell how they think they have improved their reading of the sentences. Then have them read the sentences aloud on tape a second time, with improved pacing and tone.

INTERVENTION PRACTICE BOOK

page 15

Expressive Writing: Story

Build on prior knowledge. Tell students that they are going to prepare to write a story about a person who solves a problem with the help of a new friend. Remind them that the elements of a story are the setting, characters, and plot.

Brainstorm with students' ideas for the story elements. Record the ideas in a story outline. Ask questions such as the following to help students focus on the narrative elements.

- When and where does the story take place?

- Who is the main character? What other character or characters will be in the story?

- What is the main character's problem?

- What events take place in the middle of the story?

- How is the problem solved? How does the story end?

Construct the text. "Share the pen" with students in a collaborative group writing effort. As students dictate words and phrases, write them on the board or chart paper, guiding the process by asking questions and offering suggestions as needed. Work with students to create a story.

- Point out that students will need to decide on a setting, the main character, and at least one other character.

- Help students compose one or more sentences that present the main character's problem.

- As you work together on outlining the middle of the story, remind students to tell events in the correct order and to include sensory details that will help readers create mental images.

- Guide students in coming up with a strong ending that explains how the main character's problem is solved.

Revisit the text. As you review the outline with students, ask them to check whether all the story elements have been included. Ask: **Have we listed characters, a setting, a problem for the main character, events that lead to the solution, and an ending in which the problem is solved?**

- Have students read the completed outline aloud.

On Your Own

Choose something that takes practice, like learning to swim, make cookies, or play the piano. Write an outline of a story about a girl or boy who needs to practice something. Remember that the main character should have a problem that gets solved at the end of the story.

Connect Spelling and Phonics

RETEACH **short vowel /e/e.** Tell students that you will say some words in which the letter e stands for the short e vowel sound. Have volunteers write each word on the board. Work together to proofread their work.

I. get*	2. bed	3. ten	4. let*
5. step	6. test*	7. best*	8. went*

*Word appears in "Just a Little Practice."

Dictate this sentence, and have students write it: *Ben fed a red hen in the pen*.

Build and Read Longer Words

Remind students that they have learned that the letter e can stand for the /e/ sound. Now they will use what they have learned to help them read some longer words.

**INTERVENTION
ASSESSMENT
BOOK**

Write the word *tested* on the board. Remind students that they can read longer words by looking for word parts that they know or by dividing the word into syllables. Underline *ed*, and have a volunteer identify this familiar ending. Then have students use what they know about letters and sounds to read the word *test*. Have them blend word parts to read the word *tested*. Similarly, use appropriate strategies to help students decode the words *bedroom, getting, better, presses, kettle,* and *settle*. Encourage students to build other long words in which the letter e stands for the short e vowel sound. Suggest that they use a dictionary to look up words they are not sure about.

FLUENCY BUILDER Have students choose a passage from "Just a Little Practice" to read aloud to a partner. You may have students choose passages that they found particularly interesting, or have them choose one of the following options:

- Read page 30 and the first paragraph on page 31. (Total: 70 words)

- Read page 34 and the first paragraph on page 35. (Total: 75 words)

Students read the selected passage aloud to their partners three times. Have students rate each of their own readings on a scale of I to 4.

Encourage readers to note their improvement from one reading to the next by completing sentence frames such *as I know my reading improved because* _____ . The partner who listens to the reading should also be encouraged to offer positive comments on the reader's improvement.

Review Vocabulary

To revisit Vocabulary Words with students prior to the weekly assessment, have students demonstrate understanding by answering questions such as the following.

1. Who is your favorite **professional** athlete, and why?
2. Where are you likely to see people who are **familiar** to you?
3. Do you enjoy being the **captain** of a team? Why or why not?
4. What is something you **pretended** when you were little?
5. When have you **aimed** at something? What happened?
6. In what part of our school do you think we most need a **monitor** to see that students obey school rules?

You may want to display the Vocabulary Words and definitions on page 39 and have students copy them to use when they study for the vocabulary test.

Review Narrative Elements

To review the focus skill before the weekly assessment, distribute *Intervention Practice Book* page 18. Point out the title, Narrative Elements, and have a student read aloud the directions. Review briefly what students have learned about how to figure out what a character is like. Then have them read the story and write their answers to the questions. Have students share and discuss their answers.

INTERVENTION
PRACTICE
BOOK

page 18

Review Test Prep

Ask students to turn to page 129 of the *Pupil Edition*. Call attention to the tips for answering the test questions. Tell students that paying attention to these tips can help them answer not only the test questions on this page but also other test questions like these.

CHANGING
PATTERNS
page 129

Have a volunteer read the story aloud. Then have students follow along as you read aloud the first test question and the tip that goes with it. Have students point out parts of the story that help them know what Mike is like. Then have a student read aloud the second test item and the tip that goes with it. Ask students to tell how they would answer this test question and give examples from the story that they could use in their answers. Encourage students to tell how they might apply the tips on this page in other test situations as well.

INTERVENTION
ASSESSMENT
BOOK

Self-Selected Reading

Have students select their own books to read independently. They might choose books from the classroom library shelf, or you may wish to offer a group of appropriate books from which students can choose. Titles might include the following:

- *Tiny Terrific Debbie Black.* (See page 129K of the *Teacher's Edition* for a lesson plan.)

- *Amelia's Fantastic Flight* by Rose Bursik. Henry Holt, 1994.

- *Flower Garden* by Eve Bunting. Harcourt, 2000.

After students have chosen their books, give each one a copy of My Reading Log, which can be found on page R42 in the back of the *Teacher's Edition*. Have students fill in the information at the top of the form. Then have them use the log to keep track of their reading and to record their responses to the literature.

Conduct student-teacher conferences. Arrange time for each student to confer with you individually about his or her self-selected reading. Have students bring their Reading Logs to share with you at the conference. Students might also like to choose a favorite passage to read aloud to you. Ask questions about the book designed to stimulate discussion. For example, you might ask who the characters were, what they said and did, and what they were like.

FLUENCY PERFORMANCE Have students read aloud to you the passage from "Just a Little Practice" that they selected and practiced earlier with their partners. Keep track of the number of words the student reads correctly. Ask the student to rate his or her own performance on the 1–4 scale. If students are not happy with their oral reading, give them an opportunity to continue practicing and then to reread the passage to you.

See *Oral Reading Fluency Assessment* for monitoring progress.

Use with

"The Olympic Games: Where Heroes Are Made"

Review Phonics: Short Vowel /u/u

Identify the sound. Tell students to listen for the /u/ sound as you say the word *cut.* Then have them repeat three times: *Gus can run and have fun in the sun.* Ask students to identify the four words with the /u/ sound.

Associate letter to sound. Write on the board: *Gus can run and have fun in the sun.* Circle *Gus, run, fun,* and *sun.* Ask how they are alike. (*All have the short* u *vowel sound.*) Underline *u* in each word. Tell students that in *Gus, run, fun,* and *sun,* the *u* stands for the /u/ sound. Point out the CVC pattern in each word, and remind students that the vowel in a word with this pattern usually stands for the short vowel sound.

Word blending. Model how to blend the word *run.* Slide your hand under the letters as you slowly elongate the sounds /rruunn/. Slide your hand under the whole word and say the word naturally—*run.* Follow a similar procedure with the words *tub, scrub, snug, bug, strut,* and *drum.*

INTERVENTION PRACTICE BOOK

page 20

Apply the skill. *Vowel Substitution* Write the following words on the board, and have students read each aloud. Change as needed to form the word in parentheses. Have a volunteer read aloud each new word.

rob (rub)	**mad** (mud)	**lamp** (lump)	**spin** (spun)
hit (hut)	**cap** (cup)	**mitt** (mutt)	**stick** (stuck)

Introduce Vocabulary

PRETEACH lesson vocabulary. Tell students that they are going to learn eight new words that they will see again when they read a selection called "The Olympic Games: Where Heroes Are Made." Teach each Vocabulary Word using the following process.

Use these suggestions or similar ideas to give the meaning or context.

> Write the word.
> Say the word.
> Track the word and have students repeat it.
> Give the meaning or context.

ancient	Relate to ancient art, such as cave paintings.
host	Explain to students that if they gave a book party for another class, they would be the hosts.
stadium	Relate to a stadium where fans watch a baseball game from the stands.
compete	Give examples of familiar events in which people compete, such as sporting events.

earned	Explain ways to earn something such as money, someone's respect, or an award.
record	Give examples of records that have been set, such as the one for the fastest mile.
ceremonies	Give examples of familiar ceremonies, such as weddings.
medals	Use a prop, and role-play pinning a medal on a student.

For vocabulary activities, see Vocabulary Games on pages 2–7.

AFTER
Building Background and Vocabulary

Apply Vocabulary Strategies

Use syllabication. Write the word *medals* on the board. Remind students that they can sometimes figure out the pronunciation of a new word by dividing it into syllables. Model using the strategy.

> **MODEL** I can divide *medals* into syllables as *med/als*. Now I see the *CVC* pattern in the first syllable, so I know the *e* has a short *e* vowel sound. The first syllable is /med/. I recognize the letter pattern *al* from words like *pedal* and *principal*. I also see the *-s* ending. I can blend all these sounds to say the whole word.

Guide students in using a similar method to decode *compete* and *record*.

RETEACH lesson vocabulary. Have students print the Vocabulary Words neatly on cards. Tell them to cut the words apart to make letter cards and then mix the letters in a box. Using the word cards on page T27 as a reference, have students pick out the letters to reconstruct each word. Have them tell the meaning of each word after they have completed it.

Vocabulary Words

ancient very old

host one who provides the place for an event

stadium an arena or building with rows of seats built around the field

compete to take part with others in a contest of skill

earned gained as a result of effort

record the best performance in a competition

ceremonies formal acts performed in honor of an occasion

medals small, flat pieces of metal given as awards

FLUENCY BUILDER Using *Intervention Practice Book* page 19, read each word in the first column aloud and have students repeat it. Then have students work in pairs to read the words in the first column aloud to each other. Follow the same procedure with each of the remaining columns. After partners have practiced reading aloud the words in each column separately, have them listen to each other as they practice the entire list.

INTERVENTION PRACTICE BOOK

page 19

(Focus Skill) Elements of Nonfiction

PRETEACH **the skill.** Ask students to name some fiction stories that they have read. Explain that fiction stories are made up, but nonfiction tells facts. Have students look at **side A of Skill Card 5: Elements of Nonfiction**. Read aloud and discuss the introductory sentences, and have students look at the pictures. Give help as needed to identify the images. Point out that these are examples of topics that a nonfiction book might tell about. Call attention to the book page. Explain that this is a page from a nonfiction book about ducks. Have a volunteer read aloud the text and caption. Then read and discuss each of the bulleted items.

Prepare to Read: "The Olympic Games"

Preview. Tell students that they are going to read a selection called "The Olympic Games: Where Heroes Are Made." Explain that it is expository nonfiction, which means that it explains information and ideas about a topic. Remind students that nonfiction tells about real people and events. Expository nonfiction may be divided into sections with headings and subheadings. It may also include photos with captions. After discussing the genre, preview the selection.

CHANGING PATTERNS

pages 132–147

- **Pages 132–133:** On these pages I see the title and the author's name. I see fireworks and a set of five colored rings. I know they are the symbol of the Olympic Games.

- **Pages 134–137:** The picture caption at the bottom of page 134 tells about chariot races in an ancient stadium. The caption for the picture on page 135 says this picture is from 1928, but the pictures on pages 136–137 are modern. I think that this section might tell about the history of the Olympic Games.

- **Pages 138–139:** At the top of page 138 is the heading "Track and Field." The picture shows runners on a track. There is a smaller heading at the top of page 139, "Sprinting for Gold," and the name Evelyn Ashford. I can tell from the caption that the woman in the photo is Evelyn Ashford, an American athlete, so I know that this page is about her.

Set purpose. Model setting a purpose for reading "The Olympic Games: Where Heroes Are Made."

MODEL From my preview, I know that this selection is an expository nonfiction article about the Olympic Games. One purpose for reading nonfiction is to learn about the topic of the selection. I will read to find out about the athletes in the pictures and why the Olympic Games are so important.

Reread and Summarize

Have students reread and summarize "The Olympic Games: Where Heroes Are Made" in sections, as described below.

Pages 134–137

Let's reread pages 134–137 to recall how the Olympic Games began and how they have changed.

Summary: The first Olympic Games were held in ancient Greece. The modern Olympic Games began in 1896. The Games begin with a parade of athletes from all over the world and the lighting of the Olympic torch.

Pages 138–140

Now let's reread pages 138–140 to learn about track and field events.

Summary: Track events are races between runners. Evelyn Ashford and Michael Johnson are great American runners who won many Olympic gold medals.

Pages 141–145

Now we can reread pages 141–145 to find out about other Olympic events and athletes.

Summary: Mark Spitz and Lenny Krayzelburg are two great American athletes who won gold medals in swimming events. Many Olympic events are team sports, like softball. Lisa Fernandez is a great pitcher who helped the United States softball team win a gold medal.

Page 146

Let's reread page 146 to recall how the Olympic Games end.

Summary: At the closing ceremonies, the Olympic flag is given to the mayor of the host city for the next games, and the Olympic flame is put out.

FLUENCY BUILDER Use *Intervention Practice Book* page 19. Call attention to the sentences on the bottom half of the page. The slashes break the sentences into phrases to allow you to work on natural phrasing. Tell students that their goal is to read each phrase or unit smoothly. Model appropriate pace, expression, and phrasing as you read each sentence, and have students read it after you. Then have students practice by reading the sentences aloud three times to a partner.

INTERVENTION PRACTICE BOOK

page 19

Directed Reading: "You Are in the Olympics," pp. 38–45

Pages 38–39

Have students read the title aloud. Ask them to read pages 38–39 to find out what the selection is about. Ask: **What is the topic of this selection?** (*what it is like to be in the Olympics*) (Focus Skill) **ELEMENTS OF NONFICTION**

**BRIGHT
SURPRISES**
pp. 38–45

Page 40

Read page 40 aloud, slowing your reading rate when you come to longer, more complicated sentences or longer words, such as *competitions* and *information*. Model the strategy of adjusting reading rate.

> **MODEL** When I start to read this page, I can read it fairly quickly, but then I come to some unfamiliar words, such as *competitions*. I realize that I need to slow down when I come to longer words or complicated sentences. By adjusting my reading rate, I'm better able to understand the information in this section. (Focus Strategy) **ADJUST READING RATE**

Pages 41–42

Ask students to read pages 41–42 to find out what else the girl does to get ready for the race. Ask: **Why is it important for the girl to be rested and to eat a good breakfast?** (*so she will be strong and do well in the race*) **DRAW CONCLUSIONS**

Do you think the girl will win a medal? Why or why not? (*Responses may vary.*) **MAKE PREDICTIONS**

Pages 43–44

Have students read pages 43–44 to find out whether their predictions are correct. Ask: **Did the ending surprise you? Why or why not?** (*Responses will vary.*) **CONFIRM PREDICTIONS**

**INTERVENTION
PRACTICE
BOOK**

page 21

Why do you think the author ends many of the sentences on these pages with exclamation marks? (*to show excitement; because this is the most exciting part of the story*) **AUTHOR'S CRAFT**

Summarize the selection. Have pairs of students summarize the selection by role-playing an interview between the girl and a TV news reporter. They can then complete *Intervention Practice Book* page 21.

Page 45

Answers to *Think About It* Questions

1. Your run is not perfect, but you win the race. **SUMMARY**
2. They are pleased to be at the Olympics. **INTERPRETATION**
3. Tell students to think about the difficult parts of competing in the Olympics that they learned about in the story and to compare them to the enjoyable parts of competing. Then have them give reasons why they would or would not like to compete. **WRITE AN OPINION**

Elements of Nonfiction

RETEACH **the skill.** Have students look at **side B of Skill Card 5: Elements of Nonfiction.** Read aloud and discuss the skill reminder with them. Have students follow along as you read aloud the text for the first book. Ask students what they might expect to find in the book *Trees.* (*facts about trees, photos with captions, sections with headings*) Follow a similar procedure to review the information for each of the other books. Ask volunteers to show the examples they found and to explain how they identified the type.

 FLUENCY BUILDER Use *Intervention Practice Book* page 19. Explain that today students will practice the sentences on the bottom half of the page by reading them aloud on tape. Assign new partners. Have students take turns reading the sentences aloud to each other and then reading them on tape. After they listen to the tape, have them tell how they think they have improved their reading of the sentences. Then have them read the sentences aloud on tape a second time, with improved pacing and tone.

INTERVENTION
PRACTICE
BOOK

page 19

Expressive Writing: Personal Narrative

Build on Prior Knowledge. Tell students that you are going to talk about some ideas for doing well on a writing test that asks them to write a personal narrative. Remind them that they wrote a personal narrative for the first lesson of this theme, and help them recall what they learned.

Tell students that when they take a writing test, a prompt tells them what to write about. Write this prompt on the board: *Think of something you have done that made you feel good about yourself. Now write a story for your classmates about what you did. Describe the event in detail, and tell how it made you feel good about yourself.*

Explain that the first thing students should do when taking a writing test is to read and analyze the prompt. Explain that they need to identify the **writing form**, the **topic**, the **audience**, and any **special instructions**. Point out that details and feelings are important elements in their description.

Tell students to imagine that the girl in "You Are in the Olympics" is writing a personal narrative about something that made her feel good about herself—winning a gold medal. Display a graphic organizer like the one shown here.

Topic: Winning a Gold Medal at the Olympics	
Details About Event	Writer's Feelings

Construct the Text. "Share the pen" with students in a collaborative group writing effort. As students dictate words and phrases, write them in the graphic organizer, guiding the process by asking questions and offering suggestions as needed.

- Remind students to express feelings from the girl's point of view and to use the words *I*, *me*, and *my*.

- Prompt students to provide details by asking questions such as "What did you hear when you crossed the finish line?" Encourage them to use vivid words.

Revisit the text. Go back and reread the prompt together. Ask: **Can we use the topic and details in our chart to follow the instructions in this prompt?**

- Have students use the topic and details in the chart to develop a personal narrative.

> **On Your Own**
>
> Think of an experience you have had when you were on a team. Make your own graphic organizer that lists details and your feelings about what happened. Use your organizer to write two or three sentences. Describe what you did and how you felt.

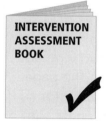

Connect Spelling and Phonics

RETEACH **short vowel /u/u.** Tell students that you will say some words in which the letter *u* stands for the /u/ sound. Have volunteers write each word on the board. Have students work together to proofread their work.

1. run*	2. just	3. fun*	4. sun*
5. must*	6. bus*	7. hut*	8. jump

***Word appears in "You Are in the Olympics."**

Dictate the following sentence, and have students write it: *The pup can jump up to the tub.*

Build and Read Longer Words

Remind students that they have learned that the letter *u* can stand for the /u/ sound. Now they will use what they have learned to help them read some longer words.

Write the word *unplug* on the board. Remind students that they can read longer words by looking for familiar word parts. Underline the familiar word part *un-*, which means "not." Then cover *un-* and blend the sounds to read the word *plug*. Point out the short *u* sound in *un-* and *plug*. Have students read the word *unplug*. Use appropriate strategies to help students decode the words *unpack*, *unlimited*, *sudden*, *runner*, *summer*, and *buttermilk*. Encourage students to build other long words in which the letter *u* stands for the short *u* vowel sound. Suggest that they use a dictionary to look up words they are not sure about.

INTERVENTION ASSESSMENT BOOK

FLUENCY BUILDER Have students choose a passage from "You Are in the Olympics" to read aloud to a partner. You may have students choose passages that they found particularly interesting, or have them choose one of the following options:

- Read the first paragraph on page 38 and the first three sentences on page 39. (From *An ancient . . .* through . . . *the stadium.* Total: 75 words)

- Read page 40. (Total: 71 words)

Students read the selected passage aloud to their partners three times. Have students rate each of their own readings on a scale of 1 to 4. Encourage readers to note their improvement from one reading to the next by completing sentence frames such as *I know my reading improved because* _____. The partner who listens to the reading should also be encouraged to offer positive comments on the reader's improvement.

Review Vocabulary

To revisit Vocabulary Words with students prior to the weekly assessment, display or read aloud the following sentences. Have students tell whether each statement is true or false and explain why.

1. Something that is **ancient** was made a short time ago.
2. When you **compete**, there is no winner.
3. A **host** is someone who goes to a party.
4. Winners in the Olympics receive **medals**.
5. **Ceremonies** are held for important occasions.
6. If you **earned** something, you probably worked hard for it.
7. A **stadium** can hold many people.

You may want to display the Vocabulary Words and definitions on page 49 and have students copy them to use when they study for the vocabulary test.

Review Narrative Elements

INTERVENTION PRACTICE BOOK

page 22

To review the focus skill before the weekly assessment, distribute *Intervention Practice Book* page 22. Point out the title, Elements of Nonfiction, and read aloud the directions. Call attention to the words and phrases in the box, and have students read each of them aloud with you. Then have students look at the books and articles pictured on the page. Explain that they should choose from the box the best description for each of these nonfiction works and write the word or words under the picture. After students have completed the page, have them share and explain their work. Ask what kind of information students would expect to learn from each of these books and articles.

Review Test Prep

CHANGING PATTERNS

page 153

Ask students to turn to page 153 of the *Pupil Edition*. Call attention to the tips for answering the test questions. Tell students that paying attention to these tips can help them answer not only the test questions on this page but also other test questions like these.

Have a student read aloud the paragraph. Then have students follow along as you read aloud the first question, the answer choices, and the tip for that question. Have students identify the correct choice and explain how they figured it out. Follow a similar procedure for question 2.

INTERVENTION ASSESSMENT BOOK

Self-Selected Reading

Have students select their own books to read independently. They might choose books from the classroom library shelf, or you may wish to offer a group of appropriate books from which students can choose. Titles might include the following:

- *Tara Lipinski: Olympic Champion* (See page 153M of the *Teacher's Edition* for a lesson plan.)

- *The Best Vacation Ever* by Stuart J. Murphy. HarperCollins, 1997.

- *First Flight* by David McPhail. Little Brown, 1991.

After students have chosen their books, give each one a copy of My Reading Log, which can be found on page R42 in the back of the *Teacher's Edition*. Have students fill in the information at the top of the form. Then have them use the log to keep track of their reading and to record their responses to the literature.

Conduct student-teacher conferences. Arrange time for each student to confer with you individually about his or her self-selected reading. Have students bring their Reading Logs to share with you at the conference. Students might also like to choose a favorite passage to read aloud to you. Ask questions designed to stimulate discussion of the book. For example, you might ask what information the student learned from a nonfiction text, how the author structured the text or how illustrations or diagrams helped the student understand the topic.

FLUENCY PERFORMANCE Have students read aloud to you the passage from "You Are in the Olympics" that they selected and practiced earlier with their partners. Keep track of the number of words the student reads correctly. Ask the student to rate his or her own performance on the 1–4 scale. If students are not happy with their oral reading, give them an opportunity to continue practicing and then to reread the passage to you again.

Use with

"Turtle Bay"

Review Phonics: Digraphs /th/*th*, /hw/*wh*

Identify the sound. Tell students to listen for the /th/ sound as you say *thorn* and *tooth*. Then have them repeat the following sentence three times: *I think I see a moth on my path.* Ask students to identify the words that have the /th/ sound. (*think, moth, path*) Follow a similar procedure for the /hw/ sound, using this sentence: *What do you do when you get a whiff of a smell?*

Associate letters to sounds. Write on the board and read aloud *I think I see a moth on my path.* Circle the words *think*, *moth*, and *path*. Ask how these words are alike. (the letters *th*; the /th/ sound) Underline *th* in each word and tell students that when the letters *th* come together in a word, they usually stand for the /th/ sound. Follow a similar procedure with the letters *wh* and the /hw/ sound, using the sentence *What do you do when you get a whiff of a smell?*

Word blending. Model how to blend and read the word *path*. Slide your hand under the letters as you elongate the sounds /ppaatthh/. Slide your hand under the whole word, and say it naturally—*path*. Repeat the procedure using the words *thank*, *thing*, *thick*. Follow a similar procedure with the words *whiff*, *when*, *where*.

Apply the skill. *Consonant Substitution* Write the following words on the board, and have students read them aloud. Make the changes necessary to form the words in parentheses. Have students read each new word.

tin (thin)	**hen** (when)	**bat** (bath)	**wit** (with)
tick (thick)	**hip** (whip)	**pat** (path)	**mat** (math)

Introduce Vocabulary

PRETEACH **lesson vocabulary.** Tell students that they are going to learn six new words that they will see again when they read a selection called "Turtle Bay." Teach each Vocabulary Word using the process shown in the box.

Use these suggestions or similar ideas to give the meaning or context.

message	Give examples, such as taking a phone message.	Write the word.
litter	Give examples of types of litter, such as candy wrappers.	Say the word.
trained	Relate to training a dog to sit. Point out the *-ed* ending.	Track the word and have students repeat it.

Write the word.
Say the word.
Track the word and have students repeat it.
Give the meaning or context.

patiently	Point out the suffix -*ly*, meaning "in a way." Demonstrate the contrast between patient and impatient behavior.
wise	Give examples of familiar story characters who are wise.
eager	Show how someone acts when he or she is eager.

For vocabulary activities, see Vocabulary Games on pages 2–7.

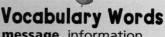

Vocabulary Words

message information that is passed on to someone

litter trash left on the ground

trained taught a person or animal how to do something

patiently in a way that shows a person is able to wait without complaining

wise able to understand important things

eager full of energy and desire to do something

AFTER

Building Background and Vocabulary

Apply Vocabulary Strategies

Use familiar word parts. Write the word *litter* on the board. Remind students that they can sometimes figure out how to pronounce a word by looking for word parts they recognize. Model using the strategy.

> **MODEL** The beginning of this word reminds me of the beginning of another word I know—*little*. When I cover up *litt*, I see *er*, an ending I know from the words *father* and *mother*. I can blend these word parts to read the whole word.

Guide students in using a similar procedure to decode the word *trained*.

RETEACH **lesson vocabulary.** Have students take turns acting out or pantomiming scenes that illustrate the meanings of the Vocabulary Words. The other students guess the words and hold up the correct word cards. You may want to have students act out the following clues:

- Take a **message** over the phone.
- Toss **litter** on the ground.
- Show how you **trained** your dog to sit.
- Wait **patiently** for something.
- Show how a **wise** person looks thinking important thoughts.
- Pretend you are **eager** to answer a question in class.

FLUENCY BUILDER Use *Intervention Practice Book* page 23. Read each word in the first column aloud and have students repeat it. Then have students work in pairs to read the words in the first column aloud to each other. Follow the same procedure with each of the remaining columns. After partners have practiced reading aloud the words in each column, have them listen to each other as they practice the entire list.

INTERVENTION PRACTICE BOOK

page 23

★
Focus
Skill

Author's Purpose

PRETEACH the skill. Explain that the authors of the books and selections that students read have a reason, or purpose, for writing. Then have students look at **side A of Skill Card 6: Author's Purpose**. Read aloud the sentence at the top of the card. Have students look at and discuss the picture and book cover below the sentence. Point out that the child in the picture is enjoying a funny story but that authors also write other types of stories to interest and entertain readers, such as mysteries or realistic fiction. Ask students to name some stories they have read that were written to entertain readers. Follow a similar procedure to guide students in discussing writing to inform and writing to persuade.

Prepare to Read: "Turtle Bay"

Preview. Tell students that they are going to read a selection called "Turtle Bay," which is realistic fiction. The characters are made up, but they act the way people do in real life. The setting could be a real place, and the events could really happen. After discussing the genre, preview the selection.

CHANGING
PATTERNS
pages
158–175

- **Pages 158–159:** I see the title and the names of the author and illustrator. Two children and a large turtle are on a beach. I also see a man with a broom. I wonder what he is doing.

- **Pages 160–163:** In the picture on page 160, a boy and a man are in the water. I will read the first sentence of the story to see what I can find out about them. (*Read the first sentence aloud.*) I think the boy and the man must be Taro and Jiro-San. I guess that they are Japanese or Japanese American. Here they are again in the picture on page 162. They must spend a lot of time at the beach.

- **Pages 164–165:** Taro and Jiro-San are sweeping the beach with brooms, like Jiro-San was doing in the first picture. I can see that they are sweeping up piles of trash. They must be trying to clean up the beach. On page 165, I see Taro at home with his family.

- **Pages 166–167:** From these pictures, I think that Jiro-San must be teaching Taro about creatures that live in or near the sea. On page 170, he is telling Taro and another child to be quiet. A big turtle is swimming toward them. I wonder what will happen.

Set purpose. Model setting a purpose for reading "Turtle Bay."

MODEL From my preview, I know that this story tells about a boy and a man, Taro and Jiro-San, who are good friends. I think that Jiro-San knows a lot about sea creatures and that he is teaching Taro about them. I'll read this story both to be entertained and to learn about creatures that live in the sea.

Reread and Summarize

Have students reread and summarize "Turtle Bay" in sections, as described in the chart below.

> **Pages 161–163**
>
> **Let's reread pages 161–163 to recall what Jiro-San is like.**
>
> Summary: Jiro-San teaches Taro many things. Taro's sister Yuko thinks Jiro-San is weird because he sweeps the beach with a broom, but Taro thinks he is wise and full of secrets. Jiro-San tells Taro that some old friends are coming.
>
> ---
>
> **Pages 164–165**
>
> **Now let's reread pages 164–165 to find out why Jiro-San sweeps the beach.**
>
> Summary: Taro helps Jiro-San sweep the beach so it will be clean for his old friends. Taro is excited. He wants to find out who the old friends are.
>
> ---
>
> **Pages 166–171**
>
> **We can reread pages 166–171 to find out who Jiro-San's old friends are.**
>
> Summary: Taro and Jiro-San see dolphins, whales, and fish, but none of them are the old friends Jiro-San is waiting for. One night Yuko comes with them. Jiro-San says his friends are here at last. The children see a large turtle.
>
> ---
>
> **Pages 172–174**
>
> **Let's reread pages 172–174 to recall what happens after the turtle comes ashore.**
>
> Summary: The turtle lays eggs on the beach. Then more turtles come to lay their eggs. Yuko helps Taro and Jiro-San sweep the beach to keep it clean for the turtles. Weeks later, the baby turtles hatch and hurry down to the sea.

FLUENCY BUILDER Use *Intervention Practice Book* page 23. Call attention to the sentences on the bottom half of the page. Tell students that their goal is to read each phrase or unit smoothly. Model appropriate pace, expression, and phrasing as you read each sentence, and have students read it after you. Then have students practice by reading the sentences aloud three times to a partner.

INTERVENTION PRACTICE BOOK

page 23

Directed Reading: "The Race to the Sea," pp. 46–53

Read aloud the title, and ask students who or what they think will race to the sea. Then have students read page 46 to find out what the boy is doing at the beach. (*looking for the beach's secret*) **CHARACTERS' MOTIVATIONS**

BRIGHT SURPRISES pp. 46–53

Page 46

Ask: **What do you think the beach's secret can be?** (*Accept reasonable responses.*) **SPECULATE**

Page 47

Have students read page 47 to find out what the boy does while he looks for the secret. (*He collects litter.*) Ask: **What time of day is it? How do you know?** (*evening; sun is setting; sun is red*) **DRAW CONCLUSIONS**

Why do you think digging in the sand could be bad? (*Possible response: Maybe the secret is in the sand, and digging would hurt it.*) **SPECULATE**

Pages 48–49

Have students read pages 48–49. Remind them that the illustrations can also help them understand the story. Model using the strategy of rereading to clarify.

> **MODEL** After reading page 49 and looking at the picture, I know that the boy sees baby turtles, but I'm not sure what the secret is. I will reread page 49. (*Reread page 49 aloud, stopping after* My mom nods.) Now I see that the boy asks if this is the secret, and his mom nods. A nod means yes, so the baby turtles are the secret. ⭐(Focus Strategy) **REREAD TO CLARIFY**

Pages 50–51

Have students read page 50 to find out what the turtles do. Ask: **Why do the turtles race to the sea?** (*so the seagulls won't eat them*) **INTERPRET STORY EVENTS**

How does the boy feel when the turtles swim away? (*happy that they are safe but sad to see them go*)

Page 52

Read aloud the question on page 52. Have students read the page to find the answer. Ask: **What do you think the sea's secret might be?** (*Accept reasonable responses.*) **SPECULATE**

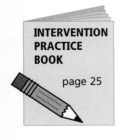

INTERVENTION PRACTICE BOOK

page 25

What was the author's purpose for writing this story? How can you tell? (*to entertain or to inform about turtles; because it is an interesting and realistic story for readers to enjoy*) ⭐(Focus Skill) **AUTHOR'S PURPOSE**

Summarize the selection. Have students think about the beach's secret and what the boy learns about it. Help them summarize the selection in three sentences.

Answers to *Think About It* Questions

1. The secret of the beach is the baby turtles in the sand. **SUMMARY**

2. Possible response: She wants him to discover the secret on his own. **INTERPRETATION**

3. After students draw their pictures, remind them that a postcard has space for only a few sentences. Suggest that they draft and revise their messages for this small space. **MAKE A POSTCARD**

AFTER

Skill Review
pages 180–181

USE SKILL CARD 6B

(Focus Skill) Author's Purpose

RETEACH **the skill.** Have students look at **side B of Skill Card 6: Author's Purpose.** Read aloud and discuss the skill reminder and diagram with them. After reading the directions, read and discuss each paragraph and set of questions with students. Point out that students might change their minds about an author's purpose as they get more information. For example, if they read Dan Author's fiction story about lost treasure, they might find that he also included facts about pirate ships from long ago. Although his main purpose is to entertain, he may also want to inform his readers about events in history.

FLUENCY BUILDER Use *Intervention Practice Book* page 23. Explain that students will practice the sentences on the bottom half of the page by reading them aloud on tape. Assign new partners. Have students take turns reading the sentences aloud to each other and then reading them on tape. After they listen to the tape, have them tell how they think they have improved their reading of the sentences. Then have them read the sentences aloud on tape a second time, with improved pacing and tone.

INTERVENTION PRACTICE BOOK

page 23

Expository Writing: Directions

Build on prior knowledge. Have students recall times that they have had to follow a set of directions. Ask whether the directions made it clear what to do first, what to do next, and so on. Point out that the steps need to be in the right order for someone to follow them correctly.

Tell students that they are going to learn how to write a set of directions. The directions will tell a friend how to see baby turtles, like the boy in "The Race to the Sea" did. Encourage students to recall events from the story that they might include in a set of directions.

Display a graphic organizer like the one shown here.

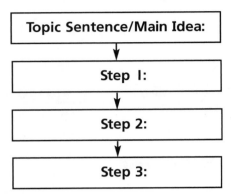

Topic Sentence/Main Idea:

↓

Step 1:

↓

Step 2:

↓

Step 3:

Construct the text. "Share the pen" with students in a collaborative group writing effort. As students dictate words and phrases, write them in the graphic organizer, guiding the process by asking questions and offering suggestions as needed.

- Remind students that their topic is how to see baby turtles. Help them compose a topic sentence that states the main idea.

- Remind students that it is important to list the steps in the correct order so the reader can carry them out. Have them identify and list three steps, such as *1. Go to the beach in the evening. 2. Sit patiently. 3. Watch the baby turtles race to the sea.*

Revisit the text. With students, reread the topic sentence and the steps. Ask: **Have we left out any steps that the reader will need to know? Are the steps in the correct order?**

- Help students use the topic sentence and steps you wrote together in the graphic organizer to develop an oral presentation on how to see baby turtles.

On Your Own

Tell a partner how to build a castle or a road in the sand. First, write a topic sentence that tells the main idea of your directions. Jot down three steps that someone should take to build a castle or road in the sand. Then use your topic sentence and three steps in your how-to talk with your partner.

Connect Spelling and Phonics

RETEACH digraphs /th/*th*, /hw/*wh*. Tell students that you will say some words in which the letters *th* stand for the /th/ sound and the letters *wh* stand for the /hw/ sound. Have volunteers write each word on the board. Work together to proofread their work.

1. when*	2. whip	3. bath*	4. cloth
5. thump	6. theft	7. thin	8. what*

***Word appears in "The Race to the Sea."**

Dictate this sentence for students to write: *Which path has a thick stick on it?*

Build and Read Longer Words

Remind students that they have learned that the letters *th* and *wh* can stand for the /th/ and /hw/ sounds. Now they will use what they have learned to help them read some longer words.

Write the word *thinner* on the board. Remind students that they can read longer words by looking for word parts that they know or by dividing a word into syllables. Point out the double consonant in the middle of the word, and draw a slash to divide the word into syllables between these two consonants. Point out the *-er* ending, and remind students that the final consonant is often doubled before adding *-er*. Have them use letter/sound associations to read *thin* and then blend the word parts to read the word *thinner*. Use appropriate strategies to help students decode the words *thistle, something, Thanksgiving, without, pathway, pathfinder,* and *bathrobe*. Encourage students to build other long words that have the /th/ sound spelled *th* and the /hw/ sound spelled *wh*. Suggest that they use a dictionary to look up words they are not sure about.

INTERVENTION ASSESSMENT BOOK

FLUENCY BUILDER Have students choose a passage from "The Race to the Sea" to read aloud to a partner. You may have students choose a passage that they found particularly interesting, or have them choose one of the following options:

- Read page 48 and the first paragraph on page 49. (From *The sun . . .* to *. . . beach.* Total: 69 words)

- Read the second paragraph on page 50 and the first paragraph on page 51. (From *No! . . .* to *. . . sea.* Total: 65 words)

Students read the selected passage aloud to their partners three times. Have students rate each of their own readings on a scale of 1 to 4. Encourage readers to note their improvement from one reading to the next by completing sentence frames such as *I know my reading improved because _____.* The partner who listens to the reading should also be encouraged to offer positive comments on the reader's improvement.

Review Vocabulary

To revisit the Vocabulary Words prior to the weekly assessment, have students listen as you read aloud each of the following sentence beginnings. Call on a volunteer to complete each sentence so that it makes sense. Alternatively, you might write the sentence beginnings on the board with the Vocabulary Words underlined, and have volunteers read aloud and complete the sentences.

1. A good way to get a **message** to someone is by _____.
2. When I see **litter**, I feel _____.
3. Some animals can be **trained** to _____.
4. It would be a mistake to wait **patiently** when _____.
5. A **wise** person probably would not _____.
6. You know people are **eager** when they _____.

You may want to display the Vocabulary Words and definitions on page 59 and have students copy them to use when they study for the vocabulary test.

Review Author's Purpose

To review author's purpose before the weekly assessment, distribute *Intervention Practice Book* page 26. Point out the title, Author's Purpose, and read aloud the directions at the top of the page. Call attention to the illustration, and explain that students can look at the notes to help them spell the terms when they complete the sentences.

You may work with students or have them work independently to read the paragraphs and complete the sentences. If students work independently, have them share and discuss their answers when they are finished. Students should be able to explain how they determined each author's purpose.

**INTERVENTION
PRACTICE
BOOK**

page 26

Review Test Prep

Ask students to turn to page 179 of the *Pupil Edition*. Call attention to the tips for answering the test questions. Tell students that paying attention to these tips can help them answer not only the test questions on this page but also other test questions like these.

**CHANGING
PATTERNS**

page 179

Have a volunteer read the first paragraph aloud. Then have students follow along as you read aloud the first test question and the tip that goes with it. Have students identify the correct choice and explain how they determined the author's purpose. Follow a similar procedure with the second question. Encourage students to tell how they might apply the tips on this page in other test situations as well.

**INTERVENTION
ASSESSMENT
BOOK**

Self-Selected Reading

Have students select their own books to read independently. They might choose books from the classroom library shelf, or you may wish to offer a group of appropriate books from which students can choose. Titles might include the following:

- *Be Careful! Turtles Ahead!* (See page 181M of the *Teacher's Edition* for a lesson plan.)

- *Turtle's Day* by Ron Hirschi. Cobblehill, 1994.

- *Parks Are to Share* by Lee Sullivan Hill. Lerner, 1997.

You may also wish to choose additional books that are the same genre as the selection or are by the same author.

After students have chosen their books, give each student a copy of My Reading Log, which can be found on page R42 in the back of the *Teacher's Edition*. Have students fill in the information at the top of the form. Then have them use the log to keep track of their reading and to record their responses to the literature.

Conduct student-teacher conferences. Arrange time for each student to confer with you individually about his or her self-selected reading. Have students bring their Reading Logs to share with you at the conference. Students might also like to choose a favorite passage to read aloud to you. Ask questions designed to stimulate discussion of the book. For example, you might ask how the student determined the author's purpose for writing. For fiction, ask where the story takes place, who the main character is, and what happens at the beginning, middle, and ending of the story.

FLUENCY PERFORMANCE Have students read aloud to you the passage from "The Race to the Sea" that they selected and practiced earlier with their partners. Keep track of the number of words each student reads correctly. Ask the student to rate his or her own performance on the 1–4 scale. If students are not happy with their oral reading, give them an opportunity to continue practicing and then to reread the passage to you.

See *Oral Reading Fluency Assessment* for monitoring progress.

LESSON 7

BEFORE

Building
Background
and Vocabulary

Use with

"Balto, the Dog Who Saved Nome"

Review Phonics: Digraphs /ch/*ch, tch*

Identify the sound. Tell students to listen for the /ch/ sound as you say the words *child* and *catch*. Then have students repeat three times: *Chuck checks the chickens and watches the chicks hatch*. Ask them to identify the words that have the /ch/ sound.

Associate letters to sound. Write on the board *Chuck checks the chickens and watches the chicks hatch*. Read the sentence aloud. Ask how the words *Chuck*, *checks*, *chickens*, and *chicks* are alike. (*begin with /ch/ sound*) Underline each *ch* and tell students that the letters *ch* usually stand for the /ch/ sound. Then underline *tch* in *watches* and *hatch*. Explain that these letters can also stand for the /ch/ sound.

Word blending. Model how to blend and read the word *watches*. Slide your hand under the letters *wa* as you elongate the sounds /wwoo/. Then blend the rest of the word /cchhiizz/. Point out that the letters *tch* at the end of a word stand for the same sound as the letters *ch* at the beginning.

Apply the skill. *Consonant Substitution* Write the following words on the board, and have students read them aloud. Make the changes necessary to form the words in parentheses. Have students read each new word.

cat (chat)	**hum** (chum)	**camp** (champ)	**not** (notch)
tip (chip)	**test** (chest)	**cart** (chart)	**dig** (ditch)

INTERVENTION
PRACTICE
BOOK

page 28

Introduce Vocabulary

PRETEACH **lesson vocabulary.** Tell students that they are going to learn six new words that they will see again when they read a selection called "Balto, the Dog Who Saved Nome." Teach each Vocabulary Word using the process shown at the right.

Use these suggestions or similar ideas to give the meaning or context.

splinters Relate to removing splinters or slivers of wood from fingers. Point out the final *-s*.

telegraph Point out the root *tele*, as in *telephone* and *television*.

trail Relate to bike or hiking trails in public parks.

guided Point out the *-ed* ending. Relate to guide dogs.

> Write the word.
> Say the word.
> Track the word and have students repeat it.
> Give the meaning or context.

drifts	This is a multiple-meaning word. Students may be more familiar with the verb than the noun. Call attention to the final *-s*.
temperature	Show a device that measures temperature.

For vocabulary activities, see Vocabulary Games on pages 2–7.

For vocabulary activities, see Vocabulary Games on pages 2–7.

AFTER
Building Background and Vocabulary

Apply Vocabulary Strategies

Use familiar word parts. Write the word *telegraph* on the board. Remind students that they can sometimes figure out the pronunciation of a word by looking for word parts that they know. Model using the strategy.

> **MODEL** I see two familiar word parts in this word. I recognize *tele* from words like *telephone* and *television*. I also know the word *graph*, which is something I make for math problems. I can blend these word parts to read the whole word.

Guide students in using a similar procedure to decode *temperature*.

RETEACH lesson vocabulary. Have students listen to the following sentences and hold up the word card that completes each rhyme. Reread the sentence aloud with the correct word choice. Then discuss how the meaning of the Vocabulary Word fits the sentence.

1. In summers and winters, watch out for sharp ___.

2. Years ago (now don't you laugh) messages went by ___.

3. You won't get lost or fail if you stay on the path or ___.

4. The trip home excited us, but our leader ___ us.

5. Shovels are good gifts when the snow is in ___.

6. Is it hot or cold? Are you sure? Let's check the ___.

FLUENCY BUILDER Use *Intervention Practice Book* page 27. Read each word in the first column aloud and have students repeat it. Then have students work in pairs to read the words in the first column aloud to each other. Follow the same procedure with each of the remaining columns. After partners have practiced reading aloud the words in each column, have them listen to each other as they practice the entire list.

INTERVENTION PRACTICE BOOK

page 27

(✦ Focus Skill) **Word Relationships**

PRETEACH **the skill.** Write *little* and *small* on the board, and read them aloud. Point out that these words have similar meanings. Tell students that having similar meanings is one way that words can be related to each other. Then have them look at **side A of Skill Card 7: Word Relationships**. Ask a student to read aloud the words under the two pictures at the top of the card. Then read aloud and discuss the sentences below the pictures. Help students think of more examples of synonyms. Follow the same procedure with the other sets of pictures.

Prepare to Read: "Balto, the Dog Who Saved Nome"

Preview. Tell students that they are going to read a selection called "Balto, the Dog Who Saved Nome," which is narrative nonfiction. Like all nonfiction, it tells about real people and real events, but the author uses a form or structure that is like a fiction story. Then preview the selection.

CHANGING PATTERNS
pages 184–198

- **Pages 184–185:** I see the title and the names of the author and illustrator. The picture shows a team of dogs pulling a dogsled through the snow. Page 184 has a photo of a man and a dog. I think the dog must be the real Balto.

- **Pages 186–187:** On page 186 I see a hand tapping a small machine. I wonder what it is. I also wonder why there is a map of Alaska on page 187. The beginning of the story is in large capital letters. I will read that part to see what I can find out. (*Read aloud the first paragraph.*) Now I know that the story takes place in Nome, Alaska. Someone is sending an urgent message, possibly using the machine in the picture.

- **Pages 188–189:** Here I see a drawing of a train and some dogs in the snow. There is also a photograph of a dogsled and driver. I think they must be going to help the people of Nome.

- **Pages 190–195:** The pictures show men and dogs going through the snow. They seem to be having a hard time. On page 194 the sled has fallen over on its side. I think the trip to Nome must be very difficult.

Set purpose. Model setting a purpose for reading "Balto, the Dog Who Saved Nome."

MODEL From my preview, I know that this is a true story about a dog named Balto who pulls a sled with other dogs to save the people of Nome, Alaska. I know that one purpose for reading nonfiction is to find out about events in history and why they were important. I'll read to find out what happened in Nome and how Balto helped.

Reread and Summarize

Have students reread and summarize "Balto, the Dog Who Saved Nome" in sections, as described in the chart below.

Pages 186–189

Let's reread pages 186–189 to recall the problem that the people of Nome faced.

Summary: The people of Nome needed medicine to treat diphtheria. The only way to get it there was by dogsled. Teams of dogs took turns carrying it.

Pages 190–193

Now let's reread pages 190–193 to find out what Balto had to do.

Summary: By the time it was Gunnar Kasson's turn to carry the medicine, it was snowing hard and the temperature was freezing. It was up to Balto, the lead dog, to find the way.

Pages 194–195

As we reread pages 194–195, let's see what challenges Balto had to overcome.

Summary: Balto led the team over smooth ice that made them slip and bumpy ice that turned the sled over many times. When the ice split apart, he led the team around the water and back to the trail.

Pages 196–198

Let's reread pages 196–198 to recall how the medicine finally got to Nome.

Summary: The storm was so bad that Gunnar Kasson's team missed the town where another dog team was waiting. Balto kept them going and got the medicine all the way to Nome. Balto became famous for what he had done.

FLUENCY BUILDER Use *Intervention Practice Book* page 27. Call attention to the sentences on the bottom half of the page. Tell students that their goal is to read each phrase or unit smoothly. Model appropriate pace, expression, and phrasing as you read each sentence, and have students read it after you. Then have students practice by reading the sentences aloud three times to a partner.

INTERVENTION PRACTICE BOOK

page 27

Directed Reading: "Help on the Trail," pp. 54–60

Page 54

Read aloud the story title and call attention to the illustration. Have students read page 54 to find out why the woman is holding up a lantern. (*Possible response: Maybe she is looking for her husband and son, who are out hunting. She hopes they get home before the storm begins.*) **DRAW CONCLUSIONS**

BRIGHT SURPRISES
pp. 54–60

Page 55

Have students read pages 55–56 to find out whether Frank and Brandon get home before the storm. Ask: **What word relationship helps you understand the sentence** *Did they go north from the ranch or south?* (*the words* north *and* south *are antonyms, or opposites*) (Focus Skill) **WORD RELATIONSHIPS**

Ask students to predict whether the dogs will find Frank and Brandon.

Pages 56–58

Have students read pages 56–58 to find out more about how dogs can find lost people. Ask: **How did Champ and Patches learn to hunt for someone who is lost?** (*They had a teacher who trained them.*) **INTERPRET STORY EVENTS**

Page 59

Have students read page 59 to find out what the dogs in the illustrations are doing. Write *someone* on the board, and model using the Use Decoding/Phonics strategy to figure out unfamiliar words.

> **MODEL** At first this looks like a difficult word, and I'm not sure how to pronounce the vowels *eo* that come together. But then I see two familiar words, *some* and *one*. I'll just blend these to pronounce the longer word. (Focus Strategy) **USE DECODING/PHONICS**

Page 60

INTERVENTION PRACTICE BOOK

page 29

Have students read page 60 to find out how Frank and Brandon are found. Ask: **How do the dogs help Frank and Brandon?** (*The dogs hunt for them and guide friends to them.*) **SUMMARIZE**

Summarize the selection. Ask students what they have learned about rescue dogs from the selection. List their responses, and have them use the list to summarize the selection. Then have students complete *Intervention Practice Book* page 29.

Answers to *Think About It* Questions

1. Dogs hunt for the Hatches. The dogs guide friends to Frank and Brandon. **SUMMARY**

2. Possible response: Dogs can smell something and then find that smell. They are better at sniffing and smelling than people are. **INTERPRETATION**

3. Encourage students to use vivid words to describe the snowstorm and Brandon's feelings. You may suggest that they brainstorm a list of descriptive words about the cold to use in their stories. **WRITE A STORY**

(Focus Skill) Word Relationships

AFTER

Skill Review
pages 204–205

USE SKILL CARD 7B

RETEACH **the skill.** Have students look at **side B of Skill Card 7: Word Relationships.** Read the skill reminder and directions with them. Ask students to look at and describe the first picture. Then have a volunteer read sentence 1 and the words below the blank. Tell students to think of a word that has the same meaning as *big* to complete the sentence. (*Possible response: large*) Follow a similar procedure with each of the remaining items. (*long; here*)

FLUENCY BUILDER Use *Intervention Practice Book* page 27. Explain that today students will practice the sentences on the bottom half of the page by reading them aloud on tape. Assign new partners. Have students take turns reading the sentences aloud to each other and then reading them on tape. After they listen to the tape, have them tell how they think they have improved their reading of the sentences. Then have them read the sentences aloud on tape a second time, with improved pacing and tone.

INTERVENTION PRACTICE BOOK

page 27

Expository Writing: Paragraph of Information

Build on prior knowledge. Point out that "Help on the Trail" includes information about how rescue dogs are trained and what they do. Tell students that they are going to learn how to write a paragraph that gives information about a topic. Suggest that they think about what information they could give on the topic of why dogs are good pets.

Explain that a paragraph of information begins with a **topic sentence** that tells the main idea that the paragraph is about. The other sentences give details that support or tell more about the main idea. Display a graphic organizer like the one shown here.

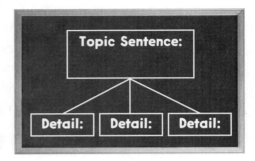

Construct the text. "Share the pen" with students in a collaborative group writing effort. As students dictate words and phrases, write them in the graphic organizer, guiding the process by asking questions and offering suggestions as needed.

- Remind students that their topic is why dogs are good pets. Help them compose a topic sentence that states the main idea.

- Have students think of three examples, or details, that support their main idea that dogs are good pets. Guide them as they compose three sentences, using these details, and add the sentences to the graphic organizer.

Revisit the text. With students, look back at the completed graphic organizer. Ask: **Do the detail sentences all support our topic sentence? Does each sentence have a subject and a verb?**

- Have students read aloud the sentences after any needed revisions have been made.

On Your Own

Write a topic sentence that tells the main idea about what kind of clothing to wear in cold weather. Think of an example that supports your main idea. Tell your information to a partner, using your topic sentence and an example.

Connect Spelling and Phonics

RETEACH digraphs /ch/ *ch, tch.* Tell students that you will say some words in which the letters *ch* stand for the /ch/ sound. Have volunteers write each word on the board. Work together to proofread their work.

1. chin*	2. much*	3. chill*	4. inch*
5. chat	6. champ*	7. branches*	8. ranch*

*Word appears in "Help on the Trail."

Dictate this sentence, and have students write it. Tell them to use *tch* to stand for the /ch/ sound: *Patches can fetch and catch.*

Build and Read Longer Words

Remind students that they have learned that the letters *ch* and *tch* can stand for the /ch/ sound. Now they will use what they have learned to help them read some longer words.

Write the word *matchbox* on the board. Remind students that they can read longer words by looking for word parts that they know or by dividing the word into syllables. Cover *match* and have students identify the smaller word *box*. Then uncover *match* and cover *box*. Tell students to use what they have learned about letters and sounds to read this smaller word. Have them blend the word parts to read the word *matchbox*. Use appropriate strategies to help students decode the words *duchess, lunchroom, patchwork, patches, scratchy,* and *chipmunk.* Encourage students to build other long words in which the letters *ch* and *tch* stand for the /ch/ sound. Suggest that they use a dictionary to look up words they are not sure about.

INTERVENTION ASSESSMENT BOOK

FLUENCY BUILDER Have students choose a passage from "Help on the Trail" to read aloud to a partner. You may have students choose passages that they found particularly interesting, or have them choose one of the following options:

- Read pages 54 and 55. (Total: 77 words)
- Read pages 56 and 57. (Total: 70 words)

Students read the selected passage aloud to their partners three times. Have students rate each of their own readings on a scale of 1 to 4. Encourage readers to note their improvement from one reading to the next by completing sentence frames such as *I know my reading improved because _____.* The partner who listens to the reading should also be encouraged to offer positive comments on the reader's improvement.

Review Vocabulary

To revisit Vocabulary Words with students prior to the weekly assessment, display a word line like the one shown here.

least surprised ——————————————————— most surprised

Have students listen to the questions and take turns indicating on the word line how surprised they would be and explaining why. If needed, ask follow-up questions to check understanding of the Vocabulary Words.

How surprised would you be if . . .

    I. you found **splinters** of cotton on the ground?

    2. a new **telegraph** station opened in your town?

    3. a group of hikers went on a **trail**?

    4. a mother animal **guided** her babies to safety?

    5. you had seen **drifts** outside when you got up this morning?

    6. the **temperature** outside stayed the same all year round?

You may want to display the Vocabulary Words and definitions on page 69 and have students copy them to use when they study for the vocabulary test.

Review Word Relationships

**INTERVENTION
PRACTICE
BOOK**

page 30

To review word relationships before the weekly assessment, distribute *Intervention Practice Book* page 30. Point out the title, Word Relationships, and read aloud the directions for item I. Have a student read aloud the word below the picture. Ask students to identify and circle the synonym for this word and then to draw a picture to show its meaning. Have students share and explain their pictures. Follow similar procedures for items 2 and 3.

Review Test Prep

Ask students to turn to page 205 of the *Pupil Edition*. Call attention to the tips for answering the test questions. Tell students that paying attention to these tips can help them answer not only the test questions on this page but also other test questions like these.

**CHANGING
PATTERNS**

page 205

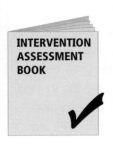

**INTERVENTION
ASSESSMENT
BOOK**

Have a volunteer read the passage aloud. Then have students follow along as you read aloud the first test question and tip. Have students identify the synonym. Then have them look back at the sentence that contains the word *soaked* and substitute their answer choice to be sure it makes sense and does not change the meaning of the sentence. Follow the same procedure with the second test question, this time having students check to see that the substituted word gives the sentence the opposite meaning. Ask students how they might apply the tips in other test situations.

Self-Selected Reading

Have students select their own books to read independently. They might choose books from the classroom library shelf, or you may wish to offer a group of appropriate books from which students can choose. Titles might include the following:

- *The Race Across Alaska* (See page 205M of the *Teacher's Edition* for a lesson plan.)

- *Dogs Don't Wear Sneakers* by Laura Numeroff. Simon and Schuster, 1996.

- *No Mail for Mitchell* by Catherine Siracusa. Random House, 1990.

You may also wish to choose additional books that are the same genre or are by the same author, or that have the same kind of text structure as the selection.

After students have chosen their books, give each student a copy of My Reading Log, which can be found on page R42 in the back of the *Teacher's Edition*. Have students fill in the information at the top of the form. Then have them use the log to keep track of their reading and to record their responses to the literature.

Conduct student-teacher conferences. Arrange time for each student to confer with you individually about his or her self-selected reading. Have students bring their Reading Logs to share with you at the conference. Students might also like to choose a favorite passage to read aloud to you. Ask questions about the book to stimulate discussion. For example, you might ask about the author's purpose for writing the story, what predictions the student made while reading, or what information the student learned from a nonfiction text.

FLUENCY PERFORMANCE Have students read aloud to you the passage from "Help on the Trail" that they selected and practiced earlier with their partners. Keep track of the number of words each student reads correctly. Ask the student to rate his or her own performance on the 1–4 scale. If students are not happy with their oral reading, give them an opportunity to continue practicing and then to read the passage to you again.

See *Oral Reading Fluency Assessment* for monitoring progress.

Use with

"Wild Shots, They're My Life"

Review Phonics: R-Controlled Vowel /är/*ar*

Identify the sound. Tell students to listen for the /är/ sound as you say the word *star*. Then have them repeat the following sentence three times: *It is hard to go far in a parked car.* Ask students to identify the four words that have the /är/ sound. (*hard, far, parked, car*)

Associate letters to sound. Write on the board and read aloud *It is hard to go far in a parked car.* Circle the words *hard, far, parked,* and *car.* Ask how these words are alike. (*the letters* ar; *the* /är/ *sound*) Underline *ar* in each of these words, and tell students that when the letters *ar* come together in a word, they often stand for the /är/ sound students hear in *hard, far, parked,* and *car.*

Word blending. Write *star* on the board. Have students repeat after you as you model how to blend and read it. Point to *st* and say /st/. Point to *ar* and say /är/. Slide your hand under the whole word, elongating the sounds, and then say the word naturally—*star.* Write these words on the board, and have students blend sounds to read them: *bar, far, car, dark, park, bark.*

INTERVENTION
PRACTICE
BOOK

page 32

Apply the skill. *Letter Substitution* Write the following words on the board, and have students read them aloud. Make the changes necessary to form the words in parentheses. Have students read each new word.

lack (lark)   **back** (bark)   **ban** (barn)   **cat** (cart)

pack (park)   **tap** (tarp)   **pat** (part)   **for** (far)

Introduce Vocabulary

PRETEACH lesson vocabulary. Tell students that they are going to learn six new words that they will see again when they read a selection called "Wild Shots, They're My Life." Teach each Vocabulary Word using the following process.

Use these suggestions or similar ideas to give the meaning or context.

curious   Demonstrate by asking many questions about a topic such as pets that students have.

collapsed   Have a student dramatize collapsing into a chair. Point out the *-ed* ending that shows the action took place in the past.

> Write the word.
> Say the word.
> Track the word and have students repeat it.
> Give the meaning or context.

marine	Tell students that some other words with the letters *mar* also have something to do with the sea, such as *marina* and *mariner*.
delicate	Give examples of delicate items, such as a bird's egg.
creature	Say simple sentences in which you first use the word *animal* and then substitute the word *creature*.
survived	Relate to the concept of people or animals who have survived a flood or fire. Point out the *-ed* ending.

Vocabulary Words

curious full of questions

collapsed fell

marine (adj.) found in the sea

delicate easily broken

creature animal

survived lived

For vocabulary activities, see Vocabulary Games on pages 2–7.

AFTER

Building Background and Vocabulary

Apply Vocabulary Strategies

Use familiar word parts. Write the word *collapsed* on the board. Remind students that they can sometimes figure out the pronunciation of a word by looking for word parts they recognize. Model using the strategy.

> **MODEL** The first thing I notice is the *-ed* ending. I know that sometimes the final e in a word is dropped before the *-ed* is added. If I cover up the *-ed*, I'm left with *collaps*. I recognize *col* as the same letters I see at the beginning of *color*, and *laps* is a familiar word. I can blend these word parts to pronounce the whole word—*collapsed*.

Guide students in using a similar procedure to decode the word *survived*. Point out that the letters *sur* are the same letters that appear at the beginning of *surprise*.

RETEACH lesson vocabulary. Have students print the Vocabulary Words neatly on cards. Tell them to cut the words apart to make letter cards and then to mix up the letters in a box. Using the word cards on page T58 as a reference, students pick out the letters to reconstruct each word. Have them tell the meaning of each word after they have spelled it.

FLUENCY BUILDER Use *Intervention Practice Book* page 31. Read each word in the first column aloud and have students repeat it. Then have students work in pairs to read the words in the first column aloud to each other. Follow the same procedure with each of the remaining columns. After partners have practiced reading aloud the words in each column, have them listen to each other as they practice the entire list.

INTERVENTION PRACTICE BOOK

page 31

Wild Shots, They're My Life/Creature Clicks **79**

BEFORE

Reading "Wild
Shots, They're
My Life"
pages 208–217

USE SKILL CARD 8A

★ (Focus Skill) **Author's Purpose**

PRETEACH **the skill.** Remind students that authors have different reasons, or purposes, for writing. Have students look at **side A of Skill Card 8: Author's Purpose.** Read aloud the sentence and four purposes at the top of the card. Tell students that authors often write for these purposes. Guide students as necessary to recall what they have learned about each purpose.

Call attention to the open book with the picture of the boy. Ask a volunteer to read aloud the text that goes with that picture. Have students identify the author's purpose and tell what text details helped them figure it out. Repeat with the other examples.

Prepare to Read: "Wild Shots, They're My Life"

Preview. Tell students that they are going to read a selection called "Wild Shots, They're My Life." Explain that this is a magazine article, a short piece of nonfiction. The author's purpose is to give information on a topic. Tell students that the author of a magazine article usually tries to present information in an interesting way. An article will often include photos with captions, and headings may divide it into sections. After discussing the genre, preview the selection.

**CHANGING
PATTERNS**
pages
208–217

- **Pages 208–209:** On these pages I see the title of the article and the name of the magazine that the article is from. A photograph shows a bird underwater looking at a person in a diving mask. I'll read the caption on page 209. (*Read the caption aloud.*)

- **Pages 210–211:** At the top of page 210, I see the author's name. I also see a small photo of a woman's face. Is she the author? Maybe the caption below the photo will tell me. (*Read the caption aloud.*) Now I know that the author is a photographer. In the big photo on pages 210–211, I see her taking a picture of a bird. I think that the smaller photo of a bird on page 211 must be that picture.

- **Pages 212–217:** The photos on these pages show different kinds of animals. I also see Tui De Roy taking pictures of animals. The headings are amusing. I think the author must present the information in this article in an entertaining way.

Set purpose. Model setting a purpose for reading "Wild Shots, They're My Life."

MODEL From my preview, I know that this selection is written by a woman who takes photos of wild animals. She gives information about her job in an entertaining way and illustrates the article with her photos. My purpose for reading will be to find out what Tui De Roy's job is like and how she took these photos.

Reread and Summarize

Have students reread and summarize "Wild Shots, They're My Life" in sections, as described in the chart below.

Pages 210–211

Let's reread pages 210–211 to recall how Tui De Roy became a photographer.

Summary: Tui De Roy grew up on the Galapagos Islands. She started taking pictures of animals there when she was a child. Now she takes wildlife photos all over the world.

Pages 212–213

Now let's reread pages 212–213 to find out how Tui De Roy photographs animals.

Summary: Tui De Roy spends a lot of time with the animals she photographs. She has adventures like chasing after a penguin chick and having to get out of the way of a huge tortoise.

Pages 214–215

As we reread pages 214–215, let's see what the heading "Into the Wash" means.

Summary: Tui De Roy had to get into the water, or "into the wash," to get a photo of an iguana in the waves.

Pages 216–217

Let's reread pages 216–217 to recall what other animals Tui De Roy has photographed.

Summary: Tui De Roy took pictures of frigate birds fighting, and even huge elephant seals. She also took a picture of a sea turtle heading back to the sea after laying its eggs. Tui De Roy likes to go back to the Galapagos now and then to meet new animal friends.

FLUENCY BUILDER Use *Intervention Practice Book* page 31. Point out the sentences on the bottom half of the page. Remind students to pay attention to the slashes and to read each phrase or unit smoothly. Model appropriate pace, expression, and phrasing as you read each sentence, and have students read it after you. Then have students practice by reading the sentences aloud three times to a partner.

INTERVENTION PRACTICE BOOK

page 31

Directed Reading: "Creature Clicks" pp. 62–68

Read aloud the title of the selection. Have students discuss the pictures and then read to find out what the people are doing. (*taking photos of animals in the wild*)
DRAW CONCLUSIONS

**BRIGHT
SURPRISES**
pp. 62–68

Pages 62–63

Ask: **What was the author's purpose for writing this article? How can you tell?** (*to inform; nonfiction article about real people and events, illustrated with photographs*) (Focus Skill) **AUTHOR'S PURPOSE**

Pages 64–65

Model using text structure and format to understand the information in the selection.

> **MODEL** I see the heading "Marine Creatures" on page 64. The heading and photographs tell me that this page tells about creatures that live in the sea. I will read to find out about these marine creatures.
> (Focus Strategy) **USE TEXT STRUCTURE AND FORMAT**

After students have read page 64, ask: **Do you think the creatures at the bottom of the ocean are as delicate as they look? Why or why not?** (*No, because they survive there without harm.*) **DRAW CONCLUSIONS**

Page 66

Read aloud the heading on page 66, and call attention to the photos. Have students read the page to find out about some yard creatures. Ask: **Why does the author say that the bug that looks like an ant is smart?** (*It is safe from birds because it looks like an ant, which birds don't eat.*) **IMPORTANT DETAILS**

Page 67

**INTERVENTION
PRACTICE
BOOK**

page 33

Have students discuss the pictures and then read page 67 to find out more about bugs. Ask: **Why do you think the dad bug carries the eggs on his back?** (*Possible response: to protect them*) **SPECULATE**

Summarize the selection. Ask students to draw pictures to show things they learned from "Creature Clicks." Have them use the pictures to help them summarize the selection. Then have students complete *Intervention Practice Book* page 33.

Answers to *Think About It* Questions

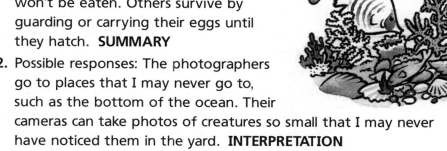

1. Possible responses: Some creatures live at the bottom of the ocean in the dark. Some bugs live in the yard and survive by looking like insects that won't be eaten. Others survive by guarding or carrying their eggs until they hatch. **SUMMARY**

2. Possible responses: The photographers go to places that I may never go to, such as the bottom of the ocean. Their cameras can take photos of creatures so small that I may never have noticed them in the yard. **INTERPRETATION**

3. Suggest that students think about what the world would look like from the perspective of the creature they have chosen to be. Have students list describing words to tell how things would look from that perspective. **WRITE A PARAGRAPH**

AFTER

Skill Review
pages 222–223

USE SKILL CARD 8B

 Focus Skill ## Author's Purpose

RETEACH **the skill.** Have students look at **side B of Skill Card 8: Author's Purpose**. Read aloud and discuss the skill reminder with them. Then read aloud the clues in the chart and discuss how they help students recognize the author's purpose. After going over the information in the chart, name several selections of different types that students have read. Guide them to identify clues and author's purpose for each selection.

FLUENCY BUILDER Use *Intervention Practice Book* page 31. Explain that today students will practice the sentences on the bottom half of the page by reading them aloud on tape. Assign new partners. Have students take turns reading the sentences aloud to each other and then reading them on tape. After they listen to the tape, have them tell how they think they have improved their reading of the sentences. Then have them read the sentences aloud on tape a second time, with improved pacing and tone.

INTERVENTION PRACTICE BOOK

page 31

Expository Writing: Summary

Build on prior knowledge. Ask students to recall a time when they told someone about information they had read. Ask whether they retold every bit of the information or just the most important ideas. Explain that when they retell information in a shorter form, they are giving a summary.

Tell students that they are going to learn how to write a summary. Their summary will retell a section of "Creature Clicks." Have a volunteer reread aloud the section titled "Marine Creatures" on page 64, while the other students follow along.

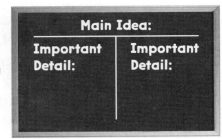

Main Idea:	
Important Detail:	Important Detail:

Display a graphic organizer like the one shown here.

Construct the text. "Share the pen" with students in a collaborative group writing effort. As students dictate words and phrases, write them in the graphic organizer, guiding the process by asking questions and offering suggestions as needed.

- Help students compose a sentence that states the main idea. Explain that this sentence should tell readers what the summary is about. For example, the main-idea sentence might tell that a sub went to the sea bottom to take photos of creatures that live there.

- Have students evaluate the importance of details in the selection and pick two that they think are most important to include in a summary. For example, one detail they might choose is that it is dark on the sea bottom, and another might be that many creatures live there.

- Help students use the main idea and important details from the chart to write a two-sentence summary of "Marine Creatures."

Revisit the text. With students, reread the summary. Ask: **Does our main-idea sentence clearly tell readers what our summary is about? Have we chosen the most important details or could we have picked better ones?**

- Have students read the completed summary aloud.

On Your Own

Reread "Yard Creatures" on pages 66–67. Write a main idea sentence and two important details from those pages. Then use your sentence and details to tell a summary of "Yard Creatures" to a partner.

Connect Spelling and Phonics

RETEACH *r*-controlled vowel /är/*ar*. Tell students that you will say some words in which the letters *ar* stand for the /är/ sound. Have volunteers write each word on the board. Work together to proofread their work.

I. jar	2. harm*	3. yarn	4. dark*
5. farm	6. part*	7. far*	8. smart*

*Word appears in "Creature Clicks."

Dictate this sentence for students to write: *The barn is not far from the park*.

Build and Read Longer Words

Remind students that they have learned that the letters *ar* can stand for the /är/ sound. Now they will use what they have learned to help them read some longer words.

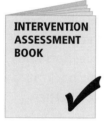

**INTERVENTION
ASSESSMENT
BOOK**

Write the word *apartment* on the board. Remind students that they can read longer words by looking for word parts they know or by dividing a word into syllables. Help students divide *apartment* into syllables. (a/part/ment) Point out that students may recognize *ment* from words like *movement* and *department*. Have them use letter/sound associations to pronounce the syllable *part,* and then blend all three syllables to read the word *apartment*. Use similar strategies to help students decode the words *harpist, carsick, starling, pardon,* and *carton*. Encourage students to build other long words in which the letters *ar* stand for the /är/ sound. Suggest that they use a dictionary to look up words they are not sure about.

FLUENCY BUILDER Have students choose a passage from "Creature Clicks" to read aloud to a partner. You may have students choose passages that they found particularly interesting, or have them choose one of the following options:

- Read page 64. (Total: 63 words)
- Read page 66. (Total: 65 words)

Students read the selected passage aloud to their partners three times. Have students rate each of their own readings on a scale of I to 4. Encourage readers to note their improvement from one reading to the next by completing sentence frames such as *I know my reading improved because* _____. The partner who listens to the reading should also be encouraged to offer positive comments on the reader's improvement.

Review Vocabulary

To revisit Vocabulary Words with students prior to the weekly assessment, display or read aloud the following sentences. Have students tell whether each statement is true or false and explain why.

1. A **curious** pet can sometimes get into trouble.
2. If your chair **collapsed** while you were sitting in it, you probably wouldn't notice.
3. A whale is an example of a **marine** animal.
4. A tomato is an example of a **creature**.
5. If you send a **delicate** item through the mail, it might get broken.
6. Animals that **survived** after a bad storm were probably the smallest and weakest ones.

You may want to display the Vocabulary Words and definitions on page 79 and have students copy them to use when they study for the vocabulary test.

Review Author's Purpose

To review author's purpose before the weekly assessment, distribute *Intervention Practice Book* page 34. Point out the title, Author's Purpose, and read aloud the directions at the top of the page. Have a volunteer read aloud the paragraph for item 1. Then read aloud each question and have students write their answers. Point out that they can look back at the paragraph or at the question for the correct spelling of words they use in their answers. Discuss how students figured out the author's purpose and what clues they used to help them. Follow the same procedure to have students complete item 2.

INTERVENTION
PRACTICE
BOOK

page 34

Review Test Prep

Ask students to turn to page 223 of the *Pupil Edition*. Call attention to the tips for answering the test questions. Tell students that paying attention to these tips can help them answer not only the test questions on this page but also other test questions like these.

CHANGING
PATTERNS

page 223

Have a volunteer read the first paragraph aloud. Then have students follow along as you read aloud the first test question and the tip that goes with it. Have students identify the correct choice and explain how they determined the author's purpose. Follow a similar procedure with the second question. Encourage students to tell how they might apply the tips on this page in other test situations as well.

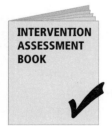

INTERVENTION
ASSESSMENT
BOOK

Self–Selected Reading

Have students select their own books to read independently. They might choose books from the classroom library shelf, or you may wish to offer a group of appropriate books from which students can choose. Titles might include the following:

- *That's My Shot* (See page 223M of the *Teacher's Edition* for a lesson plan.)
- *My Friends* by Taro Gomi. Chronicle, 1995.
- *The Night Ones* by Patricia Grossman. Harcourt, 1997.

You may also wish to choose additional books that are the same genre, that are by the same author, or that have the same kind of text structure as the selection.

After students have chosen their books, give each one a copy of My Reading Log, which can be found on page R42 in the back of the *Teacher's Edition*. Have students fill in the information at the top of the form. Then have them use the log to keep track of their reading and to record their responses to the literature.

Conduct student-teacher conferences. Arrange time for each student to confer with you individually about his or her self-selected reading. Have students bring their Reading Logs to share with you at the conference. Students might also like to choose a favorite passage to read aloud to you. Ask questions designed to stimulate discussion of the book. For example, you might ask how the student determined the author's purpose for writing. For nonfiction, you might ask what information the student learned from the text, how the author structured the text, or how illustrations or diagrams helped the student understand the topic.

FLUENCY PERFORMANCE Have students read aloud to you the passage from "Creature Clicks" that they selected and practiced earlier with their partners. Keep track of the number of words each student reads correctly. Ask the student to rate his or her own performance on the 1–4 scale. If students are not happy with their oral reading, give them an opportunity to continue practicing and then to reread the passage to you again.

LESSON 9

"Little Grunt and the Big Egg"

BEFORE
Building Background and Vocabulary

Review Phonics: *R*-controlled Vowels /ôr/*or, ore, oar, our*

Identify the sound. Tell students to listen for the /ôr/ sound as you say the words *horn* and *more*. Then have students repeat the following sentence three times: *Norm got four oars at the store.* Ask them to identify the words that have the /ôr/ sound. (*Norm, four, oars, store*)

Associate letters to sound. Write on the board and read aloud: *Norm got four oars at the store.* Underline the letters *or, our, oar*, and *ore*. Tell students that the letters *or, our, oar*, or *ore* in a word usually stand for the /ôr/ sound heard in *more*.

Word blending. Have students repeat after you as you model how to blend and read the word *store*. Slide your hand under the letters *st* as you elongate the sounds /sstt/. Next, point to the letters *ore* and say /ôr/. Slide your hand under the whole word, elongating all the sounds /ssttôôrr/, and then say the word naturally—*store*.

INTERVENTION PRACTICE BOOK

page 36

Apply the skill. *Letter Substitution* Write the following words on the board, and have students read them aloud. Make the changes necessary to form the words in parentheses. Have students read each new word.

car (core)	**stick** (stork)	**so** (soar)	**farm** (form)
mare (more)	**far** (four)	**tin** (torn)	**rare** (roar)

Introduce Vocabulary

PRETEACH **lesson vocabulary.** Tell students that they are going to learn six new words that they will see again when they read a selection called "Little Grunt and the Big Egg." Teach each Vocabulary Word using the process shown at right.

Use these suggestions or similar ideas to give the meaning or context.

> Write the word.
> Say the word.
> Track the word and have students repeat it.
> Give the meaning or context.

brunch	Explain the formation of the word from a combination of *breakfast* and *lunch*.
peaceful	Point out the word *peace* and the suffix *-ful*, meaning "full of."
omelet	Describe an omelet and ingredients that may be used.
erupting	Sketch a volcano erupting. Point out the *-ing* ending.

| lava | Compare to other melted substances, such as wax from a candle or melted cheese. |
| escape | Relate to cartoon or story characters who escape from danger. |

For vocabulary activities, see Vocabulary Games on pp. 2–7.

For vocabulary activities, see Vocabulary Games on pp. 2–7.

AFTER

Building Background and Vocabulary

Apply Vocabulary Strategies

Use familiar word parts. Write the word *peaceful* on the board. Remind students that they can sometimes figure out the pronunciation of a word by looking for word parts that they know. Model using the strategy.

> **MODEL** To figure out how to pronounce this word, I'll look for any word parts that might be familiar. I see the suffix *-ful*, which I recognize from words like *helpful* and *playful*. When I cover up *-ful*, I see the word *peace*, as in the expression *peace and quiet*. When I try blending the two parts, I pronounce the whole word, *peaceful*.

Guide students in using a similar procedure to decode the words *erupting* and *escape*.

RETEACH **lesson vocabulary.** Have students draw a picture to illustrate each Vocabulary Word. On separate strips of paper, have students write a caption for each picture. Tell them to include the Vocabulary Word in the caption. Students then exchange drawings and captions and try to match each caption with the correct picture.

Vocabulary Words

brunch a meal that comes between breakfast and lunch

peaceful calm and quiet

omelet eggs that are beaten with other ingredients and cooked

erupting blowing out lava, rocks, and gases from a volcano

lava hot, melted rock that pours from an erupting volcano

escape to get away from danger

FLUENCY BUILDER Use *Intervention Practice Book* page 35. Read each word in the first column aloud and have students repeat it. Then have students work in pairs to read the words in the first column aloud to each other. Follow the same procedure with each of the remaining columns. After partners have practiced reading aloud the words in each column, have them listen to each other as they practice the entire list.

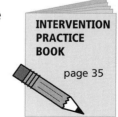

INTERVENTION PRACTICE BOOK

page 35

Little Grunt and the Big Egg/The Dinosaurs' Brunch

BEFORE

Reading "Little
Grunt and the
Big Egg"
pages 226–244

USE SKILL CARD 9A

(Focus Skill) Word Relationships

PRETEACH **the skill.** Remind students that they have learned about some ways that words may be related. Ask for examples of synonyms, antonyms, and homophones. Then have students look at **side A of Skill Card 9: Word Relationships.** Read the words in the each diagram and have students tell why the words are synonyms, antonyms, or homophones.

Ask a student to read aloud the sentence in the middle of the card. Explain multiple meanings, and guide students to identify and discuss the diagrams.

Prepare to Read: "Little Grunt and the Big Egg"

Preview. Tell students that they will read a selection called "Little Grunt and the Big Egg." Explain that it is a type of fiction called a fantasy, a story that could not happen in real life. Some fantasy stories have animal characters that talk and act like people. Other fantasy stories may have realistic characters, but their events could not happen in real life. Then preview the selection.

CHANGING PATTERNS
pages 226–244

- **Pages 226–227:** I see the title "Little Grunt and the Big Egg." The name of the author and illustrator is on a big egg. That must be the egg that the title tells about, and the boy might be Little Grunt. I wonder why he is dressed like this and why there is a volcano in the picture.

- **Pages 228–229:** On page 228 I see the same boy and some other people. I will read the first paragraph to see what I can find out. (*Read aloud the first paragraph.*) Now I know that Little Grunt and his tribe are cave dwellers who lived long, long ago. On page 229 Little Grunt finds the big egg.

- **Pages 230–231:** Little Grunt is showing the egg to his tribe. Most of them look happy about it. At the bottom of page 231 is an eggshell broken in pieces. The big egg must have hatched. I am curious to find out what came out of it.

- **Pages 232–237:** I see that a baby dinosaur hatched from the egg and is getting bigger and bigger. I think it is starting to cause problems. This looks like a funny story.

Set purpose. Model setting a purpose for reading "Little Grunt and the Big Egg."

MODEL From my preview, I know that this fantasy story tells about a boy named Little Grunt who finds a big egg that hatches into a baby dinosaur. I know that one purpose people have for reading a fantasy story is to be entertained. I'll read this story to enjoy finding out what problems the dinosaur causes for the Grunt Tribe and what they do about it.

Reread and Summarize

Have students reread and summarize "Little Grunt and the Big Egg" in sections, as described in the chart below.

Pages 228–231

Let's reread pages 228–231 to recall what happens when Little Grunt finds the big egg.

Summary: Little Grunt finds a big egg and brings it home. The tribe plans to make a big omelet, but that night the egg hatches.

Pages 232–233

Now let's reread pages 232–233 to find out what happens after the egg hatches.

Summary: A baby dinosaur hatches from the egg. The Grunt Tribe says that Little Grunt can keep him as a pet.

Pages 234–239

As we reread pages 234–239, let's see what happens when the dinosaur gets bigger.

Summary: Little Grunt names the dinosaur George. George gets so big that the cave gets crowded. He causes other problems, too. The Grunts decide to send him away.

Pages 240–243

Let's reread pages 240–243 to recall how the story ends.

Summary: One night the volcano erupts. The Grunts are trapped, but George saves them. They decide to let George live next door. They find out that George is really a female dinosaur because she is sitting on a pile of big eggs.

FLUENCY BUILDER Use *Intervention Practice Book* page 35. Call attention to the sentences on the bottom half of the page. Remind students that their goal is to read each phrase or unit smoothly. Model appropriate pace, expression, and phrasing as you read each sentence, and have students read it after you. Then have students practice by reading the sentences aloud three times to a partner.

INTERVENTION PRACTICE BOOK

page 35

Directed Reading: "The Dinosaurs' Brunch," pp. 70–77

BRIGHT
SURPRISES
pp. 70–77

Read aloud the story title. Then ask students what they think this story is about. Model as necessary:

MODEL From the title and picture, I think this story must be a fantasy about a cave boy and dinosaurs. Maybe the boy will make brunch for the dinosaurs.

Page 70

Then have students read page 70. Ask: **The word *sticks* is a multiple-meaning word. How do you know it means "twigs or branches" here instead of "stays tight to something"?** (*Possible response: because the author is telling what the trap is made of; the meaning "twigs or branches" makes sense with the other words in the sentence*) WORD RELATIONSHIPS

Pages 71–72

Tell students to read pages 71–72 to find out what is in the trap. Ask: **Why do you think the author compares the dinosaurs' roars to storms and lava erupting?** (*because the roars are loud, and storms and erupting volcanoes are loud things*) UNDERSTAND FIGURATIVE LANGUAGE

Page 73

Read aloud page 73. Ask: **What does Doris think will happen?** Model using the self-questioning strategy.

MODEL At first, I wasn't sure what Doris thinks the dinosaurs might do. I asked myself why she says that the dinosaurs do not like plants. Now I understand that she thinks these dinosaurs eat meat instead of plants. She is afraid they will eat Morris for brunch. SELF-QUESTION

Pages 74–75

Have students read page 74 to find out what Morris does. Ask: **Why does Morris make brunch for the dinosaurs?** (*He thinks they are hungry, and he doesn't want them to eat him.*) UNDERSTAND CHARACTERS' MOTIVES

Do you think Morris's plan will work? (*Accept reasonable responses.*) MAKE PREDICTIONS

Page 76

INTERVENTION
PRACTICE
BOOK

page 37

Have students read page 76 to confirm their predictions. Ask: **Why does Morris run away after the dinosaurs eat?** (*because the dinosaurs want more food*) INTERPRET STORY EVENTS

Summarize the selection. Have students work in pairs. One can be Morris and the other a dinosaur. Suggest that they take turns summarizing the story from their characters' perspectives.

Page 77

Answers to *Think About It* Questions

1. He traps two hungry dinosaurs. He makes brunch for them so that they will not eat him when he sets them free. **SUMMARY**

2. Morris is worried that the dinosaurs want to eat him, too. **INTERPRETATION**

3. Accept reasonable responses. Guide students in creating a beginning, a middle, and an end for tomorrow's scene. Encourage them to draw humorous pictures.
EXTEND THE STORY

(Focus Skill) **Word Relationships**

RETEACH the skill. Have students look at **side B of Skill Card 9: Word Relationships**. Read and discuss the skill reminder with them, and then read the directions. Have students name the animals in the pictures and read the labels.

- Have students find two pairs of synonyms (*slim, thin; large, enormous*) and tell how the meanings are the same or similar. Ask which word, *large* or *enormous*, has the stronger meaning. (*enormous*)

- Have students find a pair of antonyms (*hot, cold*) and describe how the two words are related.

- Have students find a pair of homophones. (*tail, tale*) Have them pronounce, spell, and give the meaning of each word.

- Have students find the word that has multiple meanings. (*rock*) Have them explain the two different meanings.

FLUENCY BUILDER Use *Intervention Practice Book* page 35. Explain that today students will practice the sentences on the bottom half of the page by reading them aloud on tape. Assign new partners. Have students take turns reading the sentences aloud to each other and then reading them on tape. After they listen to the tape, have them tell how they think they have improved their reading of the sentences. Then have them read the sentences aloud on tape a second time, with improved pacing and tone.

INTERVENTION PRACTICE BOOK

page 35

Little Grunt and the Big Egg/The Dinosaurs' Brunch

Expository Writing: How-To Paragraph

Build on prior knowledge. Remind students that Morris makes an omelet and some corn muffins for the dinosaurs in "The Dinosaurs' Brunch." Ask how they think Morris learned to make these things.

Tell students that they are going to learn to write a how-to paragraph telling the reader how to do something. It tells what materials will be needed and what steps to follow. Explain that students can use information from the story to tell how to make a meal for hungry dinosaurs. Discuss what Morris did: went to the store, bought eggs, and cooked an omelet.

Display a graphic organizer like the one shown here.

> **Topic Sentence/Main Idea:**
>
> **Materials Needed:**
>
> **Step 1:**
>
> **Step 2:**
>
> **Step 3:**

Construct the text. "Share the pen" with students in a collaborative group writing effort. As students dictate words and phrases, write them in the graphic organizer, guiding the process by asking questions and offering suggestions as needed.

- Remind students that their topic is how to make a meal for hungry dinosaurs. Help them compose a topic sentence that states the main idea.

- Help students develop a simple list of materials, such as eggs, a pan, and a stove.

- Tell students that it is important to list the steps in the correct order so the reader can carry them out. Work with them to write sentences describing the steps, such as buying eggs, cooking the omelet, and giving the omelet to the dinosaurs.

Revisit the text. With students, review the elements they included in the graphic organizer.

- Ask: **Are the steps in the correct order? Can we add any time-order words to make them clearer?** Make revisions as needed.

- Help students use the completed graphic organizer to develop an oral presentation on how to make a meal for hungry dinosaurs.

On Your Own

Tell a partner how to preview a book. Write a topic sentence that tells the main idea that you will talk about. List three steps that someone should do in previewing a book. Then use your topic sentence and three steps in your how-to talk with your partner.

Connect Spelling and Phonics

RETEACH *r*-controlled vowels /ôr/ *or, ore, oar, our.* Tell students that you will say four words in which the letters *or* stand for the /ôr/ sound, two words in which the spelling is *oar,* and two in which it is *our.* Identify each type before reading the word(s). Have volunteers write each word on the board. Work together to proofread.

1. fork*	2. thorns*	3. short*	4. cord*
5. roar*	6. soar	7. pour*	8. four*

*Word appears in "The Dinosaurs' Brunch."

Tell students that in this sentence *ore* will stand for the /ôr/ sound. Dictate and have students write: *He wore a hat to the store on the shore.*

Build and Read Longer Words

Remind students that they have learned that the letters *or, ore, oar,* and *our* can stand for the /ôr/ sound. Now they will use what they have learned to help them read some longer words.

INTERVENTION ASSESSMENT BOOK

Write *corncob* on the board. Remind students that they can read longer words by looking for word parts that they know or by dividing the word into syllables. Cover *corn* and have students read the smaller word *cob.* Then uncover *corn* and cover *cob.* Tell students to use what they have learned about letters and sounds to read this smaller word. Have them blend the word parts to read the word *corncob.* Use appropriate strategies to help students decode *cornhusk, border, forecast,* and *forefather.* Encourage students to build other long words in which the letters *or, ore, oar,* and *our* stand for the /ôr/ sound. Suggest that they use a dictionary to look up words they are not sure about.

FLUENCY BUILDER Have students choose a passage from "The Dinosaurs' Brunch" to read aloud to a partner. You may have students choose a passage that they found particularly interesting, or have them choose one of the following options:

- Read pages 72 and 73. (Total: 76 words)
- Read page 74 and the first two paragraphs on page 75. (Total: 84 words)

Students read the selected passage aloud to their partners three times. Have the student rate each of his or her own readings on a scale of 1 to 4. Encourage readers to note their improvement from one reading to the next by completing sentence frames such as *I know my reading improved because _____.* The partner who listens to the reading should also be encouraged to offer positive comments on the reader's improvement.

Review Vocabulary

To revisit Vocabulary Words with students prior to the weekly assessment, display a word line like the one below.

least energy ——————————————————————— most energy

Have students listen to the questions and take turns indicating on the line how much energy each action might take. Ask them to explain why they think each action would take that amount of energy. If needed, ask follow-up questions to check understanding of the Vocabulary Words.

How much energy does it take to . . .

1. eat **brunch** with your family?
2. spend a **peaceful** night?
3. make an **omelet**?
4. stop a volcano from **erupting**?
5. clean up **lava** after it cools?
6. **escape** from a hungry tiger?

You may want to display the Vocabulary Words and definitions on page 89 and have students copy them to use when they study for the vocabulary test.

Review Word Relationships

To review the focus skill before the weekly assessment, distribute *Intervention Practice Book* page 38. Point out the title, Word Relationships, and read aloud the directions at the top of the page. Explain that students will use what they have learned about word relationships to figure out how words in these sentences are related. Read aloud the first item. Guide students to use the sense of the sentence to determine the correct answer and write it in the blank. Then have a volunteer reread the sentence and completed item aloud. Follow a similar procedure for the remaining items. Discuss the two different meanings for *play* in item 4, and have students draw pictures to show the meanings.

INTERVENTION
PRACTICE
BOOK

page 38

Review Test Prep

Ask students to turn to page 255 of the *Pupil Edition*. Call attention to the tips for answering the test questions. Tell students that paying attention to these tips can help them answer not only the test questions on this page but also other test questions like these.

CHANGING
PATTERNS
page
255

Have a volunteer read the passage aloud. Then have students follow along as you read aloud the first test question and tip. Have students identify the correct choice and explain why this pronunciation makes sense in the paragraph. Now read aloud the second question and tip. Have students identify the correct choice and explain their thinking. Encourage students to tell how they might apply these tips in other test situations.

INTERVENTION
ASSESSMENT
BOOK

Self-Selected Reading

Have students select their own books to read independently. They might choose books from the classroom library shelf, or you may wish to offer a group of appropriate books from which students can choose. Titles might include the following:

- *How Fire Came to the World: A Play* (See page 255K of the *Teacher's Edition* for a lesson plan.)

- *I Took My Frog to the Library* by Eric A. Kimmel. Penguin Putnam, 1992.

- *Miss Mary Mack* by Mary Ann Hoberman. Little Brown, 2001.

You may also wish to choose additional books that are the same genre or by the same author as the selection.

After students have chosen their books, give each one a copy of My Reading Log, which can be found on page R42 in the back of the *Teacher's Edition*. Have students fill in the information at the top of the form. Then have them use the log to keep track of their reading and to record their responses to the literature.

Conduct student–teacher conferences. Arrange time for each student to confer with you individually about his or her self–selected reading. Have students bring their Reading Logs to share with you at the conference. Students might also like to choose a favorite passage to read aloud to you. Ask questions about the book to stimulate discussion. For example, you might ask about predictions the student made and confirmed while reading, what information the student learned from a nonfiction text, or how illustrations or diagrams helped the student understand the topic.

FLUENCY PERFORMANCE Have students read aloud to you the passage from "The Dinosaurs' Brunch" that they selected and practiced earlier with their partners. Keep track of the number of words the student reads correctly. Ask the student to rate his or her own performance on the 1–4 scale. If students are not happy with their oral reading, give them an opportunity to continue practicing and then to reread the passage to you.

See *Oral Reading Fluency Assessment* for monitoring progress.

Use with

"Rosie, a Visiting Dog's Story"

Review Phonics: Digraph /sh/*sh*

Identify the sound. Tell students to listen for the /sh/ sound as you say the words *show*, *share*, and *rush*. Then have students repeat twice: *She sees fish, shells, and a ship at the shop.* Ask them to identify the words with the /sh/ sound. (*she*, *fish*, *shells*, *ship*, *shop*)

Associate letters to sound. Write on the board *She sees fish, shells, and a ship at the shop.* Circle *She*, *fish*, *shells*, *ship*, and *shop*. Ask how these words are alike. (*the letters* sh; *the* /sh/ *sound*) Underline *sh* in each word. Explain that when the letters *sh* come together in a word, they usually stand for the /sh/ sound heard in *she*, *fish*, *shells*, *ship*, and *shop*.

Word blending. Model how to blend and read the word *ship*. Slide your hand under the letters *shi* as you elongate the sounds /sshhii/. Then point to the letter *p* as you say the /p/ sound. Slide your hand under the whole word and say the word naturally—*ship*. Repeat the procedure, using the words *trash*, *splash*, *shock*, and *shin*.

INTERVENTION
PRACTICE
BOOK
page
40

Apply the skill. *Consonant Substitution* Write the following words on the board, and have students read each aloud. Make the changes necessary to form the words in parentheses. Have a volunteer read aloud each new word.

bed (shed)	**back** (shack)	**fit** (fish)	**crack** (crash)
lip (ship)	**fell** (shell)	**dip** (dish)	**trap** (trash)

Introduce Vocabulary

PRETEACH **lesson vocabulary.** Tell students that they are going to learn seven new words that they will see again when they read a selection called "Rosie, a Visiting Dog's Story." Teach each Vocabulary Word by using the process shown at the right.

Use the following suggestions or similar ideas to give the meaning or context.

> Write the word.
> Say the word.
> Track the word and have students repeat it.
> Give the meaning or context.

firm	Speak in a firm manner. Invite students to imitate your firm tone.
confident	Pantomime walking or speaking in a confident way. Have students do the same.
comfortable	Relate to the word *comfort*, meaning "a pleasant condition."
approach	Ask students to approach the board.

equipment	Have students name different types of baseball equipment or playground equipment.
program	Point out that this is a multiple-meaning word. Explain that a class or course, such as a dog training class, can be called a program.
appointment	Relate to an appointment with a dentist.

For vocabulary activities, see Vocabulary Games on pp. 2–7.

AFTER

Building Background and Vocabulary

Vocabulary Words

firm stern or commanding

confident sure of one-self; certain

comfortable at ease in mind or body

approach to come close to

equipment the things needed or used for a particular purpose

program structured course of activities or training

appointment arrangement for a meeting at a specific time

Apply Vocabulary Strategies

Use spelling patterns. Write the word *equipment* on the board. Tell students that they can sometimes figure out a word's pronunciation by looking for familiar spelling patterns. Model using the strategy.

> **MODEL** I have seen the spelling pattern *qu* in words I know, such as *quick* and *quit.* I have also seen the spelling pattern *ment* in the word *department.* I can use these familiar spelling patterns to pronounce the word *equipment.*

Guide students in using a similar procedure to decode the word *approach*, relating the letter pattern *oa* to words such as *boat* and *soap.* Similarly, help them use the letter patterns *oi*, as in *join* and *point*, and *ment*, as in *department* and *equipment*, to read the word *appointment.*

RETEACH lesson vocabulary. Provide a set of word cards for each student or pair of students. Read aloud or write on the board the meaning of one of the Vocabulary Words and the first letter in that word. Students match the correct word card to the definition. Continue until students have matched all the words.

FLUENCY BUILDER Use *Intervention Practice Book* page 39. Read each word in the first column aloud and have students repeat it. Then have students work in pairs to read the words in the first column aloud to each other. Follow the same procedure with each of the remaining columns. After partners have practiced reading aloud the words in each column, have them listen to each other as they practice the entire list.

INTERVENTION PRACTICE BOOK
page 39

Decode Long Words

PRETEACH **the skill.** Ask students what they do to figure out long words. Students might mention looking for word parts or letter patterns they know, using letter sounds, and breaking a word into syllables.

Have students look at **side A of Skill Card 10: Decode Long Words**. Read the sentences at the top. Have students take turns reading aloud the steps in the boxes. Guide them in following the steps to decode each word on the card. Have students use each decoded word in a sentence. Point out that each word has one word part added to the root word, but some words, such as *unlocking,* have more than one part added to the root word.

Prepare to Read: "Rosie, a Visiting Dog's Story"

Preview. Tell students that they are going to read a selection called "Rosie, a Visiting Dog's Story." Explain that this is a personal narrative, a true story about something the author has done. The author of a personal narrative usually writes in the first person, using the words *I, me, my,* and *mine,* and tells his or her thoughts and feelings. Then preview the selection.

CHANGING PATTERNS
pp. 258–274

- **Pages 258–259:** On page 259 I see the title, "Rosie, a Visiting Dog's Story," and the names of the author and the photographer. I guess the dog in the photographs is Rosie. Maybe the woman with Rosie is the author.

- **Pages 260–261:** Rosie looks different in the photo on page 261 than in the other photos. She looks like a puppy. I think the author probably tells about Rosie when she was a puppy.

- **Page 262:** It looks like the woman in the photographs on this page is training Rosie. When I read the words under the photos, I see that the woman is teaching Rosie to sit, get down, and stay.

- **Page 263:** On this page I see Rosie sitting with an elderly man. I wonder who the man is and why Rosie is sitting with him.

- **Pages 264–265:** On page 265 Rosie is making friends with a young man in a wheelchair. Maybe Rosie is trained to visit people who are elderly, ill, or injured in order to cheer them up.

Set purpose. Model setting a purpose for reading "Rosie, a Visiting Dog's Story."

MODEL From my preview, I see that the author tells how Rosie was trained to be a visiting dog. One important purpose for reading nonfiction is to learn about a topic, but nonfiction is also read for enjoyment. I'll read to learn about visiting dogs and to enjoy getting to know Rosie.

Reread and Summarize

Have students reread and summarize "Rosie, a Visiting Dog's Story" in sections, as described in the chart below.

Pages 258–260

Let's reread pages 258–260 to recall why Rosie is special.

Summary: Rosie is a working dog. Her job is to visit people who need cheering up.

Pages 261–263

Now let's reread pages 261–263 to find out about Rosie's early training.

Summary: Rosie learned many lessons at puppy kindergarten and at home with the author.

Pages 264–267

As we reread pages 264–267, let's see what new skills Rosie had to learn in the visiting dog program.

Summary: Rosie learned how to be patient and gentle with different kinds of people and in different situations.

Pages 268–274

Let's reread pages 268–274 to recall what happened after Rosie's training was done.

Summary: Rosie visited a children's hospital and a nursing home. She cheered up many people and showed that she was a good visiting dog.

FLUENCY BUILDER Use *Intervention Practice Book* page 39. Point out the sentences on the bottom half of the page. Remind students to pay attention to the slashes and to read each phrase or unit smoothly. Model appropriate pace, expression, and phrasing as you read each sentence, and have students read it after you. Then have students practice by reading the sentences aloud three times to a partner.

INTERVENTION PRACTICE BOOK
page 39

BEFORE

Making Connections
pages 276–277

Pages 78–79

Page 80

Page 81

Directed Reading: "A Special Pup," pp. 78–84

Read the title of the story aloud. Ask students to look at the illustrations to see if they can identify the special pup. Have students read pages 78–79 to find out why the pup is special. Ask: **Who is the special pup, and why is he special?** (*Flash; because he is being trained to help someone who can't see; because he is gentle, friendly, and smart*) **SYNTHESIZE**

BRIGHT SURPRISES pp. 78–84

Read the first sentence on page 80 aloud. Then have students read the rest of the page to find out where Flash travels and why. Ask: **Why is it important for Flash to go to new places?** (*Possible response: so he will be a good working dog; so he will be comfortable in many places*) **SPECULATE**

Have students read the first paragraph on page 81 to find what the boy wishes. Ask: **How did you figure out the long word *thinking*?** (*Possible response: by noticing the word part -ing at the end of the word and by sounding out the root word*) (Focus Skill) **DECODE LONG WORDS**

Model the strategy of using context to determine word meaning.

> **MODEL** When I looked at the root word *think*, I used the wrong vowel sound and said the word *thanking*. That sounds like a real word I know, but it does not make sense in the sentence. I looked at the word again and figured out that it was *thinking*. That sounds right and makes sense in the sentence. (Focus Strategy) **USE CONTEXT TO CONFIRM MEANING**

Have students predict what else Flash will do during his training. Then have them read the rest of the page to confirm their predictions.

Pages 82–83

Have students read pages 82–83 to find out what happens when the boy takes Flash to school. Ask: **What does Sharon tell her brother about being a good trainer?** (*Possible responses: She tells him he has to be firm and confident. She tells him to remember to tell Flash when he is doing a good job.*) **SUMMARIZE**

How do you know the boy enjoys taking Flash to school with him? (*Possible response: He says that maybe he will have a special pup like Flash one day.*) **CHARACTERS' EMOTIONS**

Summarize the selection. Have pairs of students make a poster that advertises for working-dog trainers. Have them refer to the story to include all the skills a working dog needs to learn. Then have students complete *Intervention Practice Book* page 41.

INTERVENTION PRACTICE BOOK

page 41

Answers to *Think About It* Questions

1. Flash has to have a lot of training so he can be a good working dog and help someone who can't see. **SUMMARY**

2. Possible response: When he helps someone who can't see, Flash will have to be comfortable in all the kinds of places that person might go, such as work, the store, or the airport. **INTERPRETATION**

3. Suggest that students make a schedule with blocks of time for each activity. While planning their training, they should consider the skills Flash needs. **MAKE A PLAN**

AFTER

Skill Review
pages 278–279

USE SKILL CARD 10B

(Focus Skill)  **Decode Long Words**

RETEACH the skill. Have students look at **side B of Skill Card 10: Decode Long Words.** Read the skill reminder and directions with them. Then have students look at the first set of word parts. Explain that these are parts of a long word that has already been divided into syllables. Have students identify smaller words, word parts, or letter patterns that they know. Ask a volunteer to blend the sounds of the word parts to say a word that makes sense. Continue similarly to have students read each of the remaining words.

Now read the directions below the line with students. After they have divided the words into parts, ask volunteers to read the words aloud and explain how they decoded them.

FLUENCY BUILDER Use *Intervention Practice Book* page 39. Explain that students will practice the sentences on the bottom half of the page by reading them aloud on tape. Assign new partners. Have students take turns reading the sentences aloud to each other and then reading them on tape. After they listen to the tape, have them tell how they think they have improved their reading of the sentences. Then have them read the sentences aloud on tape a second time, with improved pacing and tone.

INTERVENTION PRACTICE BOOK
page 39

Expository Writing: How-To Essay

Build on prior knowledge. Ask students to recall writing a personal narrative for a writing test in Theme 1. Have them share their thoughts about preparing for and taking such a test. Remind them that writing for a test usually must be completed in a certain amount of time. Write this prompt on the board: *You have a friend who is about to take a writing test. Write a two-paragraph essay. Explain to your friend how to do a good job on a writing test.*

Work with students to analyze the prompt. Have them circle words that identify the general topic, the type of writing they will do, the audience, and any other important information.

Point out that students have just taken the first step in doing a good job on a writing test, analyzing the prompt. Work with them to create and complete a graphic organizer listing steps for writing for a test.

| Analyze the prompt. |
| Plan your time. Decide how many minutes to spend on each step in the writing process. |
| Prewrite. Make a list or graphic organizer. |
| Draft. Write your essay, using your graphic organizer. |
| Revise and proofread. |

Construct the text.

"Share the pen" with students in a collaborative group writing effort. As students dictate words and phrases, write them on the board or chart paper, guiding the process by asking questions and offering suggestions as needed.

Guide students in using the information in the completed graphic organizer to write a how-to essay.

- Remind students that their ideas need to be organized into two paragraphs, perhaps telling about analyzing the prompt and planning the time in the first paragraph and about the writing process in the second paragraph.

- As you revise the essay together, ask **Does the writing sound smooth and connected? Do we need to add transition words to help the reader move from one idea to the next?**

- Have students read the completed how-to essay aloud.

On Your Own

You are writing a message for new students. Think of a task that students do in your classroom, such as watering plants. Write a paragraph to tell new classmates how to do this task.

Connect Spelling and Phonics

RETEACH digraph /sh/*sh.* Tell students that you will say some words in which the letters *sh* stand for the /sh/ sound. Have volunteers write each word on the board. Work together to proofread their work.

1. she*   2. rush   3. short   4. Sharon*
5. wish*   6. shut   7. shops*   8. flash*

*Word appears in "A Special Pup."

Dictate the following sentence and have students write it: *The fish in the shop splash in the big dish.*

Build and Read Longer Words

Remind students that they have learned that the letters *sh* in a word usually stand for the /sh/ sound. Now they will use what they have learned to help them read some longer words.

Write the word *shimmery* on the board. Remind students that they know many words that have *y* added at the end, such as *rainy* and *sandy.* Cover the *y* with your hand and guide students in breaking the root word into syllables. (*shim/mer*) Have a volunteer sound out each syllable and blend the sounds to say the root word. Then uncover the *y* and guide students in pronouncing the whole word. Use appropriate strategies to help students decode the words *accomplish*, *shortstop*, *dishwasher*, *slushy*, and *sharpen.* Encourage students to build other long words with the digraph *sh.* Suggest that they use a dictionary to look up words they are not sure about.

INTERVENTION
ASSESSMENT
BOOK

FLUENCY BUILDER Have students choose a passage from "A Special Pup" to read aloud to a partner. You may have students choose passages that they found particularly interesting, or have them choose one of the following options:

- Read page 80. (Total: 75 words)
- Read page 82. (Total: 70 words)

Students read the selected passage aloud to their partners three times. Have students rate each of their own readings on a scale of 1 to 4. Encourage readers to note their improvement from one reading to the next by completing sentence frames such as *I know my reading has improved because* _____. The partner who listens to the reading should also be encouraged to offer positive comments on the reader's improvement.

Review Vocabulary

To revisit Vocabulary Words with students prior to the weekly assessment, display a word line like the one shown here.

very pleased ——————————————————— **not pleased at all**

Have students listen to the questions and take turns indicating on the word line how pleased they would be. Ask them to explain why they would be pleased or displeased in each instance. If needed, ask follow-up questions to check understanding of the Vocabulary Words.

How pleased would you be if . . .

1. your principal speaks to you in a **firm** voice?
2. you are **confident** your team will win?
3. you feel **comfortable** in a new place?
4. some of your friends **approach** you?
5. your birthday present is sports **equipment**?
6. your mother signs you up for a special science **program**?
7. your dentist says you need another **appointment** next week?

You may want to display the Vocabulary Words and definitions. Students can copy them to use when they study for the vocabulary test.

Review Decode Long Words

To review the focus skill before the weekly assessment, distribute *Intervention Practice Book* page 42. Call attention to the title, and read the directions with students. Point out the list of four words. Remind students that they may be able to read long words like these by looking for smaller parts. Guide them in breaking the first word into smaller parts and writing the parts in the boxes. (*ex/tend/ed*) Tell them to use the word parts to help them read the long word. Have a student read the long word aloud. Follow the same procedure with the other words. Have volunteers read aloud the sentences at the bottom of the page and confirm whether the words make sense.

**INTERVENTION
PRACTICE
BOOK**

page 42

Review Test Prep

Ask students to turn to page 279 of the *Pupil Edition*. Call attention to the tips for answering the test questions. Tell students that paying attention to these tips can help them answer not only the test questions on this page but also other test questions like these.

**CHANGING
PATTERNS**

page 279

Have students follow along as you read aloud each test question and tip. Ask volunteers to identify the last syllable of *intelligent* (*gent*) and name another word they know with that spelling pattern. (*Possible response: gentle*) Then have students read aloud each answer choice for item 2 and explain which strategy is most helpful for decoding *pathways* and why. Ask students how they might apply the tips in other test situations.

**INTERVENTION
ASSESSMENT
BOOK**

Self-Selected Reading

Have students select their own books to read independently. They might choose books from the classroom library shelf, or you may wish to offer a group of appropriate books from which students can choose. Titles might include the following:

- *Everyone Can Help.* (See page 279K of the *Teacher's Edition* for a lesson plan.)

- *What's Claude Doing?* by Dick Gackenbach. Houghton Mifflin, 1986.

- *What Is a Reptile?* by Susan Kuchalla. Troll Communications, 1982.

You may also wish to choose additional books that are the same genre, that are by the same author, or that have the same kind of text structure as the selection.

After students have chosen their books, give each student a copy of My Reading Log, which can be found on page R42 in the back of the *Teacher's Edition*. Have students fill in the information at the top of the form. Then have them use the log to keep track of their reading and to record their responses to the literature.

Conduct student-teacher conferences. Arrange time for each student to meet with you individually about his or her self-selected reading. Have students bring their Reading Logs to share with you at the conference. Students might also like to choose a favorite passage to read aloud to you. Ask questions designed to stimulate discussion of the book. For example, you might ask what information the student learned from a nonfiction text, how the author structured the text, or how illustrations or diagrams helped the student understand the topic.

FLUENCY PERFORMANCE Have students read aloud to you the passage from "A Special Pup" that they selected and practiced earlier with their partners. Keep track of the number of words the student reads correctly. Ask the student to rate his or her own performance on the 1–4 scale. If students are not happy with their oral reading, give them an opportunity to continue practicing and then to reread the passage to you.

See *Oral Reading Fluency Assessment* for monitoring progress.

LESSON 11

BEFORE

Building Background and Vocabulary

Use with

"The Stories Julian Tells"

Review Phonics: Vowel Diphthongs /ou/ *ou*, ow

Identify the sound. Tell students to listen for the /ou/ sound as you say the words *now* and *shout*. Then have them repeat the following sentence three times: *The brown cow makes loud sounds.* Ask students to identify the four words that have the /ou/ sound. (*brown, cow, loud, sounds*)

Associate letters to sound. Write this sentence on the board and read it aloud: *The brown cow makes loud sounds.* Underline the letters *ou* in *loud* and *sound*. Tell students that the vowel combination *ou* usually stands for the /ou/ sound in *loud*. Then underline *ow* in *brown* and *cow*. Explain that the letters *ow* often stand for the /ou/ sound, too.

Word blending. Write *out* on the board and have students read it aloud. Add *sh* to *out*. Model blending the sounds to read *shout*. Slide your hand under the letters as you elongate the sounds /sshhoutt/. Then say the word naturally.

Apply the skill. *Letter Substitution* Write the following words on the board, and have students read them aloud. Make the changes necessary to form the words in parentheses. Have students read each new word.

INTERVENTION PRACTICE BOOK

page 44

clan (clown)	**or** (our)	**fell** (foul)	**pond** (pound)
den (down)	**part** (pout)	**tan** (town)	**hand** (hound)

Introduce Vocabulary

Tell students that they are going to learn six new words that they will see again when they read a selection called "The Stories Julian Tells." Teach each Vocabulary Word using the following process.

Use these suggestions or similar ideas to give the meaning or context.

> Write the word.
> Say the word.
> Track the word and have students repeat it.
> Give the meaning or context.

beyond	Have a student walk beyond a certain point in the classroom.
collection	Give a familiar example, such as a collection of baseball cards. Point out the root word *collect*.
mustache	Draw a face on the board. Add a mustache.
seriously	Point out the suffix *-ly*, meaning "in a way." Demonstrate speaking seriously, or in a serious way.
fastened	Clip papers and tell students that you fastened them together. Point out the *-ed* ending that shows past action.

cartwheel Point out the smaller words that make up the compound word. Use a small doll to demonstrate turning a cartwheel, pointing out the similarity to a wheel rolling.

For vocabulary activities, see Vocabulary Games on pages 2–7.

For vocabulary activities, see Vocabulary Games on pages 2–7.

Vocabulary Words

beyond past

collection similar items chosen to save

mustache something, usually hair, between the nose and lips

seriously thoughtfully

fastened attached

cartwheel handspring that turns sideways

Building Background and Vocabulary

AFTER
Building Background and Vocabulary

Apply Vocabulary Strategies

Use familiar word parts. Write the word *cartwheel* on the board. Remind students that they can sometimes figure out the pronunciation of a word by looking for word parts they recognize. Model using the strategy.

> **MODEL** I'll look for familiar word parts to see if they can help me pronounce this word. I cover up *wheel*, which is a word I know, and I see the word *cart*. I also know this shorter word. I can blend these word parts to pronounce the whole word: *cartwheel*.

Guide students in using a similar procedure to decode the words *collection*, *seriously*, and *fastened*. Point out the familiar word part *-tion*, the suffix *-ly*, and the word endings *-ed* and *-en*.

RETEACH lesson vocabulary. Have students listen to each of the following sentences. Tell them to hold up the word card that completes each rhyme. Reread the sentence aloud with the correct word choice. Then discuss how the meaning of the Vocabulary Word fits the sentence.

1. Go to the pond. /Then go past, or _____.

2. If you go in that direction, /you'll find rocks for your _____.

3. Under his nose, quick as a flash, /Richie had a milk _____.

4. Some people act mysteriously. /Some act thoughtfully, or _____.

5. We worked until the last end /had been pasted and _____.

6. You kick up your heel /when you do a _____.

FLUENCY BUILDER Use *Intervention Practice Book* page 43.
Read each word in the first column aloud and have students repeat it. Then have students work in pairs to read the words in the first column aloud to each other. Follow the same procedure with each of the remaining columns. After partners have practiced reading aloud the words in each column, have them listen to each other as they practice the entire list.

INTERVENTION
PRACTICE
BOOK

page 43

BEFORE

Reading "The
Stories Julian
Tells"
pages 284–296

USE SKILL CARD 11A

(Focus Skill) Sequence

PRETEACH the skill. Ask whether students ever put their shoes on first and then their socks. Have them tell why doing things in this order would not make sense. Then have students look at **side A of Skill Card 11: Sequence.** Read aloud and discuss the introductory sentences. Then read the directions, and have students follow along as you read the paragraph to them. Explain that the underlined words are clue words that will help them understand when events took place.

Tell students to pay attention to the underlined clue word as a volunteer rereads the first sentence aloud. Ask when the events occurred and how students know. (*today; clue word* today) Continue similarly with the second and third sentences. After a volunteer reads the last sentence aloud, ask the order in which these events happened: giving Grandma the apples, making the apple pie.

Call attention to the pictures. Have students tell the correct sequence of the events shown. Tell them that they can look back at the paragraph to remind themselves of the sequence.

Prepare to Read: "The Stories Julian Tells"

Preview. Tell students that they are going to read a selection called "The Stories Julian Tells." Explain that this selection is realistic fiction, a story about characters who are like people in real life. After discussing the genre, preview the selection.

CHANGING PATTERNS
pages 284–296

- **Pages 284–285:** I see a kite made of newspaper. A boy and girl are flying it. Above them I see the title of the selection and the names of the author and illustrators.

- **Pages 286–287:** Here is another title, "Gloria, Who Might Be My Best Friend." A boy and girl are watching workers unload a moving van. The girl must be Gloria. I will read the first paragraph to find out more. I think the boy must be Julian. I wonder whether he and Gloria will become friends.

- **Pages 288–291:** In the big picture the boy is looking at the girl as if he's not sure about something. In the smaller picture on page 289, the boy and girl are looking at a bird's nest together, and they are both smiling. They seem to be having a good time in the pictures on pages 290–291.

Set purpose. Model setting a purpose for reading "The Stories Julian Tells."

MODEL From my preview, I know that this story is about a boy who isn't sure he wants a girl for a friend, even though they seem to have fun together. I know that readers often read fiction for the purpose of enjoying a good story. I'll enjoy reading to find out if Julian and Gloria become good friends.

Reread and Summarize

Have students reread and summarize "The Stories Julian Tells" in sections, as described in the chart below.

Pages 286–287

Let's reread page 286 to recall how Julian meets Gloria.

Summary: Julian is feeling lonely. He meets Gloria, who is moving into a house in his neighborhood.

Pages 288–291

Now let's reread pages 288–291 to find out how Julian and Gloria get along.

Summary: Julian decides he likes Gloria because she doesn't laugh at him for falling when he tries to do a cartwheel. They have fun doing things together. Gloria is going to show Julian how to use a kite to make wishes.

Pages 292–295

As we reread pages 292–295, let's see how Gloria and Julian make their wishes.

Summary: Gloria and Julian write their wishes on pieces of paper and tie them onto the tail of the kite. One of Julian's wishes is that Gloria will be his best friend. Gloria says their wishes will come true if the wind takes them all.

Page 296

Let's reread page 296 to recall how the story ends.

Summary: When they bring the kite down, the wind has taken all their wishes. Julian is happy because he is pretty sure he and Gloria will be friends.

FLUENCY BUILDER Use *Intervention Practice Book* page 43. Point out the sentences on the bottom half of the page. Remind students to pay attention to the slashes and to read each phrase or unit smoothly. Model appropriate pace, expression, and phrasing as you read each sentence, and have students read it after you. Then have students practice by reading the sentences aloud three times to a partner.

INTERVENTION PRACTICE BOOK

page 43

Directed Reading: "A New Best Friend," pp. 86–92

Read the title aloud. Have students read page 86 to find out who needs a new best friend and why. (*Howard; because his best friend, Rick, is moving away*) **DRAW CONCLUSIONS**

BRIGHT SURPRISES
pp. 86–92

Page 86

Pages 87–88

Ask: **Who does Beth think Howard should have as a new best friend?** Model using the strategy of reading ahead.

> **MODEL** On page 87 I read that Howard frowns when Beth says he can get a new best friend. I decided to read ahead to see who Beth thinks might be Howard's new best friend. I found out that she thought of Jack and Norman, but they don't get along with Howard's dog Bow Wow. **READ AHEAD**

Ask: **Do Beth and Bow Wow get along? How do you know?** (*Yes; they play together.*) **DRAW CONCLUSIONS**

Page 89

Tell students to pay attention to the sequence of events as they read page 89. Ask: **What happens before Beth and Howard continue talking about who his new best friend might be?** (*Howard and Beth take turns shooting baskets.*) **How do you know the events happen in this order?** (*The author tells about events in the order that they happen.*) **SEQUENCE**

Page 90

Have students read page 90 to find out who else Beth suggests. Ask: **Why wouldn't any of the people Beth names be good best friends for Howard?** (*They don't like the same things that Howard likes.*) **SUMMARIZE**

Page 91

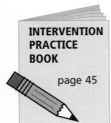

INTERVENTION
PRACTICE
BOOK

page 45

Ask students to predict who Howard's new best friend will be. Have them read page 91 to confirm their predictions. Ask: **Why will Beth make a good best friend for Howard?** (*Possible response: She likes the same things he likes; she is nice; they have fun together.*) **CONFIRM PREDICTIONS/MAIN IDEA**

Summarize the selection. Have pairs of students make paper-bag puppets of Howard and Beth and use them to retell the story. Make sure they use action words from the story to bring the main events to life.

Answers to *Think About It* Questions

1. Howard's best friend, Rick, went to a new town. Now Beth will be Howard's new best friend. **SUMMARY**

2. Possible response: At first Howard does not think that a girl could be his best friend. **INTERPRETATION**

3. Remind students to write the letter using the first-person point of view, as if they were Howard. **WRITE A LETTER**

AFTER

Skill Review
pages 302–303

USE SKILL CARD 11B

(Focus Skill) Sequence

Have students look at **side B of Skill Card 11: Sequence**. Read aloud and discuss the skill reminder with them, and then have a volunteer read the paragraph aloud. Ask students to take turns finding and reading aloud the sentences that tell what happens first, what happens next, what happens then, and what happens last. Have students identify the time-order words in the paragraph.

Now read aloud the next set of directions. Have students work with partners to create sequence diagrams. Remind them to write one event in each box to show the sequence.

After students have completed their sequence diagrams, have them display and explain their work.

FLUENCY BUILDER Use *Intervention Practice Book* page 43. Explain that today students will practice the sentences on the bottom half of the page by reading them aloud on tape. Assign new partners. Have students take turns reading the sentences aloud to each other and then reading them on tape. After they listen to the tape, have them tell how they think they have improved their reading of the sentences. Then have them read the sentences aloud on tape a second time, with improved pacing and tone.

INTERVENTION PRACTICE BOOK

page 43

Persuasive Writing: Writing an Opinion and Reasons

Build on prior knowledge. Tell students that they are going to learn how to write a persuasive paragraph, or a paragraph that persuades the reader to agree with the writer's opinion. Point out that some people, like Howard and Beth in "A New Best Friend," think it is fun to play basketball. Other people, like Chuck in the story, do not agree. Explain that students need to think of reasons to help persuade readers that playing basketball is fun.

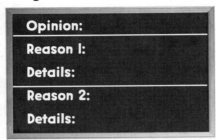

Opinion:

Reason I:

Details:

Reason 2:

Details:

Display a graphic organizer like the one shown here.

Construct the text. "Share the pen" with students in a collaborative group writing effort. As students dictate words and phrases, write them in the graphic organizer, guiding the process by asking questions and offering suggestions as needed.

- Help students compose a sentence that states the opinion they want to express in their paragraph.

- Have students suggest reasons why playing basketball is fun. Explain that they should also give details to support their reasons. For example, if they give as a reason that basketball is an exciting game, details might include that players are always running and jumping and that the score changes often.

Revisit the text. Reread with students their opinion sentence and the details they listed.

- Ask: **Do these reasons all support our opinion? Can we add any details to persuade the reader to agree with this opinion?**

- Have students read aloud the completed opinion sentence, reasons, and details.

On Your Own

Choose your favorite art or music activity, such as drawing, working with clay, singing, or dancing. Write a sentence giving your opinion of this activity. Then write two reasons that support your opinion. Under each reason, write at least one detail.

Connect Spelling and Phonics

RETEACH vowel diphthongs /ou/*ou, ow*. Tell students that you will say some words in which the letters *ou* stand for the /ou/ sound. Have volunteers write each word on the board. Work together to proofread their work.

1. shouted*
2. loud*
3. sprout
4. ground
5. unwound*
6. without*
7. bounded*
8. proud

*Word appears in "A New Best Friend."

Tell students that in this sentence the letters *ow* will stand for the /ou/ sound. Dictate the following sentence and have students write it: *How did a brown cow get to the crowded town?*

Build and Read Longer Words

Remind students that they have learned that the letters *ou* or *ow* can stand for the /ou/ sound. Now they will use what they have learned to help them read some longer words.

Write the word *shouting* on the board. Remind students that they can read longer words by looking for word parts they know or by dividing a word into syllables. Underline the familiar ending *-ing*. Cover *-ing* and point out the familiar word part *shout*. Then uncover the rest of the word and have students blend the two parts to read the word *shouting*. Use appropriate strategies to help students decode the words *crowded, loudly, cowhand, downhill, foundation, groundhog*, and *southwest*. Encourage students to build other long words in which the /ou/ sound is spelled either *ou* or *ow*. Suggest that they use a dictionary to look up words they are not sure about.

INTERVENTION
ASSESSMENT
BOOK

FLUENCY BUILDER Have students choose a passage from "A New Best Friend" to read aloud to a partner. You may have students choose passages that they found particularly interesting, or have them choose one of the following options:

- Read page 88 and the first paragraph on page 89. (Total: 97 words)

- Read pages 90 and 91. (Total: 94 words)

Students read the selected passage aloud to their partners three times. Have students rate each of their own readings on a scale of 1 to 4. Encourage readers to note their improvement from one reading to the next by completing sentence frames such as *I know my reading improved because* _____. The partner who listens to the reading should also be encouraged to offer positive comments on the reader's improvement.

Review Vocabulary

To revisit Vocabulary Words with students prior to the weekly assessment, display a word line like the one shown here.

not unusual at all ——————————————— very unusual

Have students listen to the following questions and take turns indicating on the word line how unusual each event would be. Have them explain their reasons. If needed, ask follow-up questions to check students' understanding of the Vocabulary Words.

How unusual would it be if . . .

  1. a baseball player hit a ball **beyond** the end of the field?
  2. someone had a raindrop **collection**?
  3. everyone woke up tomorrow morning with a **mustache**?
  4. your teacher spoke **seriously** to the class?
  5. a girl **fastened** a bracelet on her wrist?
  6. a cat did a **cartwheel**?

You may want to display the Vocabulary Words and definitions on page 109 and have students copy them to use when they study for the vocabulary test.

 Sequence

To review the focus skill before the weekly assessment, distribute *Intervention Practice Book* page 46. Point out the title, Sequence, and read aloud the introductory sentence. Ask volunteers to read aloud the four sentences that are not in time order. Then read the directions with students and have them complete the sequence diagram.

Review Test Prep

Ask students to turn to page 303 of the *Pupil Edition*. Call attention to the tips for answering the test questions. Tell students that paying attention to these tips can help them answer not only the test questions on this page but also other test questions like these.

**CHANGING
PATTERNS**
page 303

Read the directions to students, and have a volunteer read the paragraph aloud. Then have students follow along as you read aloud the first test question and the tip that goes with it. Have students identify the correct choice and explain how they used time-order clues to determine the sequence. Follow a similar procedure with the second question. Encourage students to tell how they might apply the tips on this page in other test situations as well.

**INTERVENTION
PRACTICE
BOOK**
page 46

**INTERVENTION
ASSESSMENT
BOOK**

Self-Selected Reading

Have students select their own books to read independently. They might choose books from the classroom library shelf, or you may wish to offer a group of appropriate books from which students can choose. Titles might include the following:

- *I Wish . . .* (See page 303M of the *Teacher's Edition* for a lesson plan.)

- *Wyatt the Whale* by Dan Slottje. Armstrong, 1994.

- *The Big Balloon Race* by Eleanor Coerr. HarperCollins, 1984.

You might also like to choose additional books that are the same genre as the selection or by the same author.

After students have chosen their books, give each one a copy of My Reading Log, which can be found on page R42 in the back of the *Teacher's Edition*. Have students fill in the information at the top of the form. Then have them use the log to keep track of their reading and to record their responses to the literature.

Conduct student-teacher conferences. Arrange time for each student to confer with you individually about his or her self-selected reading. Have students bring their Reading Logs to share with you at the conference. Students might also like to choose a favorite passage to read aloud to you. Ask questions about the book to stimulate discussion. For example, you might ask the student to describe the sequence of events in the story. For nonfiction, you might ask what information the student learned from the text, how the author structured the text, or how illustrations or diagrams helped the student understand the topic.

FLUENCY PERFORMANCE Have students read aloud to you the passage from "A New Best Friend" that they selected and practiced earlier with their partners. Keep track of the number of words the student reads correctly. Ask the student to rate his or her own performance on the 1–4 scale. If students are not happy with their oral reading, give them an opportunity to continue practicing and then to reread the passage to you.

See *Oral Reading Fluency Assessment* for monitoring progress.

Use with

"The Talent Show"

Review Phonics: *R*-controlled Vowels /ûr/*er, ir, ur*

Identify the sound. Tell students to listen for the /ûr/ sound as you say the words *her, shirt,* and *hurt.* Then have them repeat the following sentence three times: *The girl turned and twirled her curls.* Ask students to identify the words that have the /ûr/ sound. (*girl, turned, twirled, her, curls*)

Associate letters to sound. Write this sentence on the board and read it aloud: *The girl turned and twirled her curls.* Underline the letters *ir, ur,* and *er* in *girl, turned, twirled, her,* and *curls.* Tell students that the letters *er, ir,* and *ur* can stand for the /ûr/ sound they hear in *burn.*

Word blending. Have students repeat after you as you model how to blend and read the word *girl.* Slide your hand under the letters as you elongate the sounds /ggûûrrll/. Then say the word naturally—*girl.*

Apply the skill. *Letter Substitution* Write the following words on the board, and have students read them aloud. Make the changes necessary to form the words in parentheses. Have students read each new word.

INTERVENTION
PRACTICE
BOOK

page 48

barn (burn)	**hard** (herd)	**dart** (dirt)	**farm** (firm)
gargle (gurgle)	**torn** (turn)	**fast** (first)	**clock** (clerk)

Introduce Vocabulary

PRETEACH lesson vocabulary. Tell students that they are going to learn seven new words that they will see again when they read a selection called "The Talent Show." Teach each Vocabulary Word using the process shown at the right.

Use these suggestions or similar ideas to give the meaning or context.

gym	Example: your school gym.
perform	Have students pantomime a musician performing on stage.
prefer	Have students tell which of two colors or foods they prefer.
recite	Demonstrate how you can recite a familiar short poem.
enjoying	Point out the *-ing* ending. Ask students to show the expressions they might have on their faces if they were enjoying a show or a game.
billions	Give examples of things that might number in the billions, such as grains of sand on a beach.

> Write the word.
> Say the word.
> Track the word and have students repeat it.
> Give the meaning or context.

roam   Show how you might walk if you wanted to roam about. Contrast with rushing.

For vocabulary activities, see Vocabulary Games on pages 2–7.

Apply Vocabulary Strategies

Use spelling patterns. Write *perform* on the board. Tell students that they can sometimes figure out how to pronounce a word by using the sounds that letters stand for. Model using the strategy.

MODEL To figure out how to pronounce this word, I'll break it into syllables between the two consonants that come together: *per/form*. I know that the letters *er* can stand for the /ûr/ sound, so I pronounce this as /pûr/. I also know that the letters *or* can stand for the /ôr/ sound. When I blend the sounds of the two syllables, I get /pûr fôrm/.

Guide students in using a similar procedure to decode the word *prefer*.

RETEACH lesson vocabulary. Have students listen to each of the following sentences. Tell them to hold up the word card that completes each rhyme. Reread the sentence aloud with the correct word choice. Then discuss how the meaning of the Vocabulary Word fits the sentence.

1. The teacher told Tim to play ball in the _____.
2. The stage lights get warm when actors _____.
3. Dogs bark, and cats purr. Which do you _____?
4. Try to get the words right when you have to _____.
5. Some chores are annoying, but this one I'm _____.
6. There used to be millions, and now there are _____!
7. I like to wander home when I've been out to _____.

Vocabulary Words

gym large room used for indoor sports

perform to take part in a public show

prefer to like better than something else

recite to repeat from memory

enjoying having a good time; taking pleasure in

billions a very, very large number of things

roam to wander; to move around without a purpose

FLUENCY BUILDER Use *Intervention Practice Book* page 47. Read each word in the first column aloud and have students repeat it. Then have students work in pairs to read the words in the first column aloud to each other. Follow the same procedure with each of the remaining columns. After partners have practiced reading aloud the words in each column, have them listen to each other as they practice the entire list.

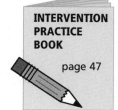

INTERVENTION PRACTICE BOOK

page 47

⭐ (Focus Skill) **Prefixes and Suffixes**

PRETEACH **the skill.** Tell students that they are going to learn more about parts that are added to words to change the meanings. Have students look at **side A of Skill Card 12: Prefixes and Suffixes.** Read aloud and discuss the bulleted sentences and the illustrations.

Point out the trains with the word parts. Ask a volunteer to identify the word parts in the first picture and put them together to say a word. Explain that the prefix *dis-* means "not," and guide students to see how adding the prefix changes the meaning of the root word. Follow a similar procedure with the other words, explaining that *-er* means "one who," *un-* means "not," and *-ful* means "filled with."

Prepare to Read: "The Talent Show"

Preview. Tell students that they are going to read a selection called "The Talent Show." Explain that this is realistic fiction, with characters, a setting, and events like those in real life. After discussing the genre, preview the selection.

CHANGING PATTERNS
pages
306–320

- **Pages 306–307:** Across the top I see the title and the names of the author and illustrator. In the illustration I see children raising their hands and a woman with smiley-face earrings. I think the setting is a school and the woman is the children's teacher.

- **Pages 308–309:** I see two girls at home. One is lying on pillows with a paper on her lap. I can read the words "Bee Poem" on the paper. The other girl is holding a mop and pail. She looks unhappy.

- **Pages 310–311:** Now the girl who had the mop and pail is seeing a picture in her mind as the other girl talks to her. The girl is imagining herself in a bee costume tripping over the pail and dropping the mop. She is performing for an audience of other children, who are all laughing. I remember that the title of this story is "The Talent Show." I think these girls may be planning to perform in a talent show.

- **Pages 312–313:** Here I see the girl who had the mop eating with her family. She has her arms crossed and looks unhappy.

Set purpose. Model setting a purpose for reading "The Talent Show."

MODEL From my preview, I think that this story is about two girls who are planning to be in a talent show. One girl seems happy about it, but I think the girl with the mop is not very happy. I wonder why. I know that readers often read fiction for the purpose of being entertained. I'll enjoy reading to find out why this girl is unhappy and what she does about it.

Reread and Summarize

Have students reread and summarize "The Talent Show" in sections, as described in the chart below.

Pages 306–309

Let's reread pages 306–309 to recall how Beany and Carol Ann make plans for the talent show.

Summary: Beany's class is going to have a talent show. Carol Ann writes a poem that she and Beany will recite. Carol Ann says she will be the queen bee, and Beany will be the worker bee.

- -

Pages 310–313

Now let's reread pages 310–313 to see how Beany feels about her part in the talent show.

Summary: Beany is worried about making mistakes. She tells her family she is not having fun. Her mother suggests doing cartwheels instead.

- -

Pages 314–317

We can reread pages 314–317 to find out what Beany's dad tells her.

Summary: Beany and her dad watch the stars together. Her dad tells her that some things should just be enjoyed.

- -

Pages 318–320

Let's reread pages 318–320 to recall how Beany solves her problem.

Summary: Beany tells Carol Ann she doesn't want to do the bee poem. Instead, Beany does cartwheels and enjoys being in the talent show.

FLUENCY BUILDER Use *Intervention Practice Book* page 47. Point out the sentences on the bottom half of the page. Remind students to pay attention to the slashes and to read each phrase or unit smoothly. Model appropriate pace, expression, and phrasing as you read each sentence, and have students read it after you. Then have students practice by reading the sentences aloud three times to a partner.

INTERVENTION PRACTICE BOOK

page 47

Directed Reading: "Star Time," pp. 94–101

Read the title aloud. Ask students where they think the story takes place. (*at a camp*) Have them read the letter on page 94. Ask: **How did you figure out the meaning of the word** *campers*? (*from the meanings of the root word* camp *and the suffix* -er) (Focus Skill) **PREFIXES AND SUFFIXES**

BRIGHT
SURPRISES
pp. 94–101

Page 94

What is Kirsten's problem? (*She has to perform in a show, but she would rather study stars.*) **STORY ELEMENTS**

Pages 95–96

Have students read pages 95–96 to find out if Kirsten thinks of something to do. Then point out the items in Kirsten's gym bag in the illustration on page 96, and discuss how they are used for stargazing. Ask: **Do you think Kirsten's idea has something to do with things in her gym bag? Why or why not?** (*Possible response: yes; because she went to get the gym bag after she spent some time thinking about what she could do, and she has it with her while she talks to Gilbert*) **SPECULATE**

Page 97

Tell students to read page 97 to find out about Kirsten's idea. Model using the strategy of creating mental images.

> **MODEL** In the illustration on page 97, I see Kirsten showing Gilbert the pattern of a dragon in the stars. The pattern looks to me like a wavy line. I close my eyes and create a picture of a dragon in my mind. In my mental picture, the wavy line is the dragon's back. (Focus Strategy) **CREATE MENTAL IMAGES**

Pages 98–99

Have students read page 98–99 to find out what Kirsten and Gilbert do in the talent show. You may wish to explain that Pegasus is an imaginary winged horse and that an archer is someone with a bow and arrow. Ask: **What do the other campers think of Kirsten and Gilbert's act? How can you tell?** (*They like it a lot. They clap and clap.*) **CHARACTERS' EMOTIONS**

Page 100

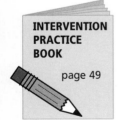

INTERVENTION
PRACTICE
BOOK

page 49

Point out that Kirsten is writing another letter to her parents after the talent show. After students have read the letter, ask: **How have Kirsten's feelings about camp changed?** (*At first she was unhappy and wanted to quit, but now she is happy and likes camp.*) **COMPARE AND CONTRAST**

Summarize the selection. Have students complete the story map on *Intervention Practice Book* page 49.

Answers to *Think About It* Questions

1. Possible response: Kirsten wants to look at stars in the sky. She does not want to be in the talent show. She solves her problem by showing star patterns in the talent show. **SUMMARY**

2. When Gilbert growls, it reminds her of a star pattern she knows. **INTERPRETATION**

3. Posters should be vibrant and inviting. **MAKE A POSTER**

Skill Review
pages 328–329

USE SKILL CARD 12B

(Focus Skill) Prefixes and Suffixes

RETEACH **the skill.** Have students look at **side B of Skill Card 12: Prefixes and Suffixes.** Read aloud and discuss the skill reminder with them. Then read the directions and go over the charts that show the meanings of the prefixes and suffixes. Call on volunteers to read aloud the five numbered sentences. After each sentence is read, have students identify the underlined word, the root word, and any prefixes or suffixes that have been added. Have them tell the meanings of the new words formed by adding the prefixes and suffixes.

FLUENCY BUILDER Use *Intervention Practice Book* page 47. Explain that today students will practice the sentences on the bottom half of the page by reading them aloud on tape. Assign new partners. Have students take turns reading the sentences aloud to each other and then reading them on tape. After they listen to the tape, have them tell how they think they have improved their reading of the sentences. Then have them read the sentences aloud on tape a second time, with improved pacing and tone.

INTERVENTION PRACTICE BOOK

page 47

Persuasive Writing: Speech

Build on prior knowledge. Remind students that writing is one way to persuade others to do something or to agree with the writer's ideas. Another way to persuade is by giving a speech. Explain that it is

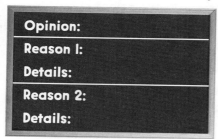

important for a speaker to stay focused on the topic because listeners cannot go back and reread parts of the speech that they did not understand.

Tell students that they are going to learn how to stay focused on the topic as they write a speech that Kirsten might give to persuade other campers to learn about the stars. Explain that writing a persuasive speech is like writing a persuasive paragraph, except that the audience will listen to the speech instead of reading it. Display a graphic organizer like the one shown here.

Construct the text. "Share the pen" with students in a collaborative group writing effort. As students dictate words and phrases, write them in the graphic organizer, guiding the process by asking questions and offering suggestions as needed.

- Help students compose a sentence that states the opinion they want to express in their speech.

- Encourage students to discuss the topic of learning about the stars. Then help them list reasons and details from their discussion as sentences that they can use in their persuasive speech. Remind them to stay on the topic expressed in the opinion sentence.

Revisit the text. With students, reread the sentences they wrote. Ask: **Do all of the reasons and details support the opinion sentence? Can we add any others to help persuade the listeners?**

- Students can use the opinion, reasons, and details from the graphic organizer to develop and give a brief speech.

On Your Own

Choose a topic that you think other students your age would like to learn about. Write a sentence giving your opinion. Then jot down at least one reason that you think students would enjoy learning about this topic. Use what you wrote to give a persuasive speech to one or two classmates.

Connect Spelling and Phonics

RETEACH *r-controlled vowels /ûr/er, ir, ur.* Tell students that you will say some words in which the letters *ir* stand for the /ûr/ sound. Have volunteers write each word on the board. Work together to proofread.

I. first*	2. girl*	3. twirled*	4. dirt*
5. shirt	6. bird	7. firm	8. stir

*Word appears in "Star Time."

Tell students that you will read a sentence in which the letters *er* will stand for the /ûr/ sound. Dictate the sentence and have students write it: *Gilbert sees the lantern and the pattern.*

Build and Read Longer Words

Remind students that they have learned that the letters *er, ir,* or *ur* can stand for the /ûr/ sound. Now they will use what they have learned to help them read some longer words.

INTERVENTION ASSESSMENT BOOK

Write the word *birdhouse* on the board. Remind students that they can read longer words by looking for word parts they know or by dividing a word into syllables. Cover *bird* and model using letter/sound associations to read the word *house*. Then uncover *bird* and cover *house*. Have students use letter/sound associations to pronounce *bird*. Then uncover the whole word and have students blend the two smaller words to read the compound word *birdhouse*. Use appropriate strategies to help students decode the words *cowgirl, curler, herself, stirring, purring, blurry, occur, personal, emergency,* and *dirty.* Encourage students to build other long words in which the letters *er, ir,* or *ur* stand for the vowel sound /ûr/. Suggest that they use a dictionary to look up words they are not sure about.

FLUENCY BUILDER Have students choose a passage from "Star Time" to read aloud to a partner. You may have students choose passages that they found particularly interesting, or have them choose one of the following options:

- Read page 95. (Total: 79 words)
- Read page 97. (Total: 82 words)

Students read the selected passage aloud to their partners three times. Have them rate each of their own readings on a scale of I to 4. Encourage readers to note their improvement from one reading to the next by completing sentence frames such as *I know my reading improved because _____.* The partner who listens to the reading should also be encouraged to offer positive comments on the reader's improvement.

Review Vocabulary

To revisit Vocabulary Words prior to the weekly assessment, have students listen as you read aloud each of the following sentence beginnings. Call on a volunteer to complete each sentence so that it makes sense. Alternatively, you might write the sentence beginnings on the board with the Vocabulary Words underlined, and have volunteers read aloud and complete the sentences.

1. A **gym** is different from a playground because _____.
2. If I could **perform** in a circus, I would _____.
3. Some people **prefer** cold weather because _____.
4. In order to **recite** well, you need to _____.
5. A child who is not **enjoying** a game might _____.
6. You can't have **billions** of pets because _____.
7. A good place to **roam** is _____.

You may want to display the Vocabulary Words and definitions on page 119 and have students copy them to use when they study for the vocabulary test.

INTERVENTION PRACTICE BOOK

page 50

Review Prefixes and Suffixes

To review the focus skill before the weekly assessment, distribute *Intervention Practice Book* page 50. Point out the title, Prefixes and Suffixes, and read the directions aloud. Give help as needed as students read the words in the first column, identify the prefix or suffix and its meaning, and then write the meaning of the new word in the third column.

Review Test Prep

Ask students to turn to page 329 of the *Pupil Edition*. Call attention to the tips for answering the test questions. Tell students that paying attention to these tips can help them answer not only the test questions on this page but also other test questions like these.

CHANGING PATTERNS

page 329

Ask a volunteer to read the paragraph aloud. Read the directions to students, and have them follow along as you read aloud the first test question and the tip that goes with it. Have students identify the correct choice and explain how they figured out the meaning of the new word. Remind them to try the meaning in the sentence to check that it makes sense. Follow a similar procedure with the second question. Encourage students to tell how they might apply the tips on this page in other test situations as well.

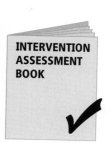

INTERVENTION ASSESSMENT BOOK

Self-Selected Reading

Have students select their own books to read independently. They might choose books from the classroom library shelf, or you may wish to offer a group of appropriate books from which students can choose. Titles might include the following:

- *Stacy's Surprise* (See page 329M of the *Teacher's Edition* for a lesson plan.)

- *So That's How the Moon Changes Shape* by Allan Fowler. Children's Press, 1991.

- *Our Stars* by Ann Rockwell. Harcourt, 1999.

You might also like to choose additional books that are the same genre as the selection or by the same author.

After students have chosen their books, give each one a copy of My Reading Log, which can be found on page R42 in the back of the *Teacher's Edition*. Have students fill in the information at the top of the form. Then have them use the log to keep track of their reading and to record their responses to the literature.

Conduct student-teacher conferences. Arrange time for each student to confer with you individually about his or her self-selected reading. Have students bring their Reading Logs to share with you at the conference. Students might also like to choose a favorite passage to read aloud to you. Ask questions designed to stimulate discussion of the book. For example, you might ask the student to describe the sequence of events in the story or to tell where the story takes place and who the characters are.

FLUENCY PERFORMANCE Have students read aloud to you the passage from "Star Time" that they selected and practiced earlier with their partners. Keep track of the number of words the student reads correctly. Ask the student to rate his or her own performance on the 1–4 scale. If students are not happy with their oral reading, give them an opportunity to continue practicing and then to read the passage to you again.

See *Oral Reading Fluency Assessment* for monitoring progress.

LESSON 13

"Centerfield Ballhawk"

BEFORE

Building
Background
and Vocabulary

Review Phonics: Long Vowel /ō/o-e

Identify the sound. Tell students to listen for the /ō/ sound as you say the word *stone*. Then have them repeat the following sentence three times: *Hope can hop home.* Ask them to identify the words that have the /ō/ sound. (*Hope, home*)

Associate letters to sound. Write this sentence on the board: *Hope can hop home.* Circle the words *Hope* and *home*, and point out the CVCe pattern. Tell students that words with CVCe usually have a long vowel sound. Have them listen for the long o vowel sound in *Hope* and *home*. Ask how *hop* is different from *Hope*. (*no final* e, *short vowel sound*)

Word blending. Have students repeat after you as you model how to blend and read the word *home*. Slide your hand under the letters as you elongate the sounds /hhōōmm/. Then say the word naturally—*home*.

Apply the skill. *Vowel Substitution* Write the following words on the board, and have students read them aloud. Make the changes necessary to form the words in parentheses. Have students read each new word.

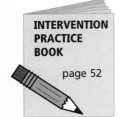

INTERVENTION
PRACTICE
BOOK

page 52

hop (hope)	**rod** (rode)	**mop** (mope)	**not** (note)
tot (tote)	**rob** (robe)	**slop** (slope)	**cod** (code)

Introduce Vocabulary

PRETEACH **lesson vocabulary.** Tell students that they are going to learn six new words that they will see again when they read a selection called "Centerfield Ballhawk." Teach each Vocabulary Word using the following process.

Use these suggestions or similar ideas to give the meaning or context.

> Write the word.
> Say the word.
> Track the word and have students repeat it.
> Give the meaning or context.

outfielder   Draw a diagram of a baseball field and show where the outfielders play.

concentrate   Give examples of times when students need to concentrate, such as during a test or while listening to directions.

depend   Suggest a simple memory aid: *You can depend on a friend.*

ballhawk   Point out the two smaller words that make up this compound word. Tell students that a hawk is a bird that swoops down swiftly to catch its prey.

vanish	Give the example of an illusion in which an object seems to disappear, or vanish.
fault	Relate to familiar phrases such as *It's not my fault*.

For vocabulary activities, see Vocabulary Games on pages 2–7.

Apply Vocabulary Strategies

Use familiar word parts. Write the word *ballhawk* on the board. Remind students that they can sometimes figure out the pronunciation and the meaning of a word by looking for shorter words or syllables that they know. Model using the strategy.

> **MODEL** When I look closely at this long word, I see two short words that I know—*ball* and *hawk*. I can blend these to read the longer word. Since I know that a hawk is a type of large bird that hunts for prey, I can figure out that a ballhawk is someone who goes after a ball the way a hawk goes after its prey—swiftly and accurately.

Guide students in using a similar procedure to decode *outfielder*.

PRETEACH lesson vocabulary. Write the letters of the Vocabulary Words on small squares of construction paper. If possible, use a different color for each word. Place the letters for each word in a separate envelope, and write a clue sentence on the front. Students figure out the correct word from the clue and put the letters together to form that word. Have students refer to the word cards on page T93 to help them spell the words.

Vocabulary Words

outfielder a baseball player whose position is in the outfield

concentrate to pay close attention

depend to rely

ballhawk a baseball player who always seems to get to the ball and catch it

vanish to go suddenly out of sight; disappear

fault responsibility for a mistake; blame

FLUENCY BUILDER Use *Intervention Practice Book* page 51. Read each word in the first column aloud and have students repeat it. Then have students work in pairs to read the words in the first column aloud to each other. Follow the same procedure with each of the remaining columns. After partners have practiced reading aloud the words in each column, have them listen to each other as they practice the entire list.

INTERVENTION PRACTICE BOOK

page 51

BEFORE

Reading
"Centerfield
Ballhawk"
pages 332–348

USE SKILL CARD 13A

(Focus Skill) Sequence

PRETEACH the skill. Remind students that sequence is the order in which events happen. Have students look at **side A of Skill Card 13: Sequence.**

Read aloud the directions at the top. Ask a volunteer to read aloud the story while the other students follow along. Have students identify the time-order clues and discuss the order of events. Then read with students the second set of directions. Students can work with partners to complete it. Have students share and discuss their work.

Prepare to Read: "Centerfield Ballhawk"

Preview. Tell students that they are going to read a realistic fiction story called "Centerfield Ballhawk," with characters, a setting, and events that are like those in real life. After discussing the genre, preview the selection.

CHANGING PATTERNS
pages 332–348

- **Pages 332–333:** On page 333 I see the title and the names of the author and illustrator. In the illustration a man is holding a baseball and talking to a boy. I will read the first paragraph on page 333 to find out who they are. (*Read paragraph aloud.*) Now I know how the car window got broken. I wonder how José will try to make his father proud.

- **Pages 334–335:** Here is José playing in a baseball game. From the way the ball looks on page 335, I think he got a hit. I can also see the score of the game. I wonder whether José plays for the Mudders or the Bulls.

- **Pages 336–339:** On pages 336–337 I see José making a catch in the outfield and people cheering. Now the score is 7–2. On page 338 José is at bat, but on page 339, a player on the other team is making a catch and the score is tied.

- **Pages 340–343:** On pages 340–341 I see José making a diving catch. He must be a good fielder. On pages 342–343 he seems to be comforting a teammate who looks sad. I also see his dad calling to him. I wonder what José and his dad will say to each other and whether his dad is still disappointed in him for breaking the car window.

Set purpose. Model setting a purpose for reading "Centerfield Ballhawk."

MODEL From my preview, I know that this story is about a boy named José who plays baseball and who wants to make his dad proud of him. I know that one purpose for reading fiction is for enjoyment. I'll enjoy reading to find out what happens in the game and if José makes his father proud.

Reread and Summarize

Have students reread and summarize "Centerfield Ballhawk" in sections, as described in the chart below.

Pages 332–335

Let's reread pages 332–335 to recall why José wants to become a better batter.

Summary: José thinks his father will be proud of him if he becomes a better hitter. He hits a home run for his team. A player on the other team hits the ball, and José runs back to catch it.

Pages 336–339

Now let's reread pages 336–339 to find out if José makes the catch and whether he gets another hit.

Summary: José makes a great catch but makes outs in his next two times at bat. Now the score is tied. A player on the other team hits the ball.

Pages 340–343

We can reread pages 340–343 to find out if José's team wins the game.

Summary: José makes another great catch, but his team ends up losing the game. José thinks his father will never be proud of him because he got only one hit.

Pages 344–348

Let's reread pages 344–348 to recall what José's father tells him.

Summary: José's father tells him not to worry about his hitting because he is a great outfielder. José realizes he doesn't have to be a great hitter to make his father proud of him.

FLUENCY BUILDER Use *Intervention Practice Book* page 51. Point out the sentences on the bottom half of the page. Remind students to pay attention to the slashes and to read each phrase or unit smoothly. Model appropriate pace, expression, and phrasing as you read each sentence, and have students read it after you. Then have students practice by reading the sentences aloud three times to a partner.

INTERVENTION PRACTICE BOOK

page 51

Directed Reading: "Coach Ben" pp. 102–108

BEFORE

Making
Connections
pages 352–353

**BRIGHT
SURPRISES**
pp. 102–108

Page 102

Read the title of the story aloud. Have students read page 102 to find out who Ben is. (*the first-base player*) Ask: **Why do you think the story is called "Coach Ben"?** (*Possible response: Maybe Ben helps the other players the way a coach would.*) **SPECULATE**

Pages 103–104

Have students read pages 103–104 to find out if the Reds get a hit. Ask: **How does Ben help Jeff?** (*Possible response: by encouraging him and letting him know that the other players will do their part*) **DRAW CONCLUSIONS**

If students can't understand how Ben knows that the batter is planning to hit rather than bunt, model the thinking: **Ben knows the batter lets the first pitch go by because he is waiting for a pitch that he can hit. That means this batter is hoping to score**, not just tie the game.

Page 105

Have students read page 105 to find out what happens when the pop-up is hit. Model using the Summarize strategy:

> **MODEL** A lot is going on in this game. Summarizing as I read can help me keep track of story events. To summarize this part of the story, I might say: Ben can't catch the pop-up, so the Reds score two runs. Ben says it's his fault and tells Jeff they can still win. (Focus Strategy) **SUMMARIZE**

Page 106

After students read page 106, ask: **What time-order words and phrases help you understand the sequence of events?** (*Possible responses: next, now, first, then, after that*) (Focus Skill) **SEQUENCE**

Pages 107–108

Have students read pages 107–108 to find out how the game ends. Ask: **Why do you think the Tans were able to win the game?** (*Accept reasonable responses.*) **MAIN IDEA**

Why do Jeff and Tim think Ben is special? (*He helps them play like a team; he is a good friend.*) **CHARACTERS' EMOTIONS**

Summarize the selection. Have students work with partners to write an article for the camp's newsletter that gives a summary of the last inning of the game. Then have students complete *Intervention Practice Book* page 53.

**INTERVENTION
PRACTICE
BOOK**

page 53

Answers to *Think About It* Questions

1. Possible responses: Ben gives the team good advice. He makes the team feel good. **SUMMARY**

2. Possible response: Ben tells Jeff to wait for the pitch he can hit. He helps Jeff believe that he can get a hit. **INTERPRETATION**

3. Tell students to express the feelings that they think Jeff had that day. Remind them to use details from the story in their diary entries. **WRITE A DIARY ENTRY**

AFTER

Skill Review
pages 354–355

USE SKILL CARD 13B

(Focus Skill) Sequence

RETEACH the skill. Have students look at **side B of Skill Card 13: Sequence.** Read aloud and discuss the skill reminder with them. Then ask a student to read the first sentence. Ask students to identify the clue word in the sentence and tell which event happened first. Point out the diagram that shows the sequence. Follow a similar procedure with the second sentence. Explain to students that two or more events often take place at the same time. Authors use clue words like *as* and *while* to show that two things are happening at the same time.

Now read the directions with students. Explain that they should draw diagrams like the first one, with the arrow pointing from the first event to the second event. Then have them read the sentences and complete their diagrams.

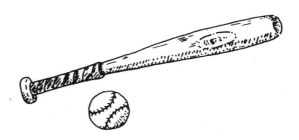

FLUENCY BUILDER Use *Intervention Practice Book* page 51. Explain that students will practice the sentences on the bottom half of the page by reading them aloud on tape. Assign new partners. Have students take turns reading the sentences aloud to each other and then reading them on tape. After they listen to the tape, have them tell how they think they have improved their reading of the sentences. Then have them read the sentences aloud on tape a second time, with improved pacing and tone.

INTERVENTION PRACTICE BOOK

page 51

Expository Writing: Persuasive Letter

Build on prior knowledge. Have students recall the topics they wrote about in their persuasive paragraph and speech. Tell them that now they are going to learn how to write a persuasive letter. Remind them that the setting for "Coach Ben" is a summer camp. Suggest that they write a letter that Ben might write to persuade his friend Scott to come to summer camp.

Display a graphic organizer like this. You may also wish to show a return address, greeting, and closing in the proper letter format.

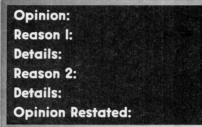

Opinion:
Reason 1:
Details:
Reason 2:
Details:
Opinion Restated:

Construct the text. "Share the pen" with students in a group writing effort. As students dictate, complete the graphic organizer, guiding the process by asking questions and offering suggestions as needed.

- Help students compose a sentence that states Ben's opinion. Remind them that the audience is a friend, so they should use language appropriate to a friendly letter.

- Have students suggest reasons why Scott might enjoy camp. Explain that they should also give details to support their reasons. For example, if one of their reasons is that the campers get to play baseball, details might include that there are good ballplayers at camp and the games are exciting. With students, develop the reasons and details into complete sentences.

- Encourage students to vary their wording as they restate Ben's opinion in a sentence at the end of the letter.

Revisit the text. With students, look over the sentences that you wrote together. Ask: **Would the reasons and details we listed persuade you to go to camp? Are there any others we could add?**

- Have students check the sentences for correct capitalization and punctuation.

- Students can read the sentences aloud in an oral version of the letter.

On Your Own

In "Coach Ben," Ben persuades his friends to play like a team. Suppose you wanted to write a letter to your classmates to persuade them to work together and help each other. Write a sentence stating your opinion. Read your statement to a partner. Tell your partner two good reasons for your opinion, and give details to support or explain your reasons.

Connect Spelling and Phonics

RETEACH **long vowel /ō/o-e.** Tell students that you will say some words in which the letters o–e stand for the /ō/ sound. Have volunteers write each word on the board. Work together to proofread their work.

I. home*	2. dove*	3. hose	4. hope*
5. rose	6. joke	7. stone	8. stole*

*Word appears in "Coach Ben."

Dictate the following sentence and have students write it: *I hope he rode home.*

Build and Read Longer Words

Remind students that they have learned that the CVCe pattern *o-e* can stand for the long *o* vowel sound. Now they will use what they have learned to help them read some longer words.

Write the word *wishbone* on the board. Remind students that they can read longer words by looking for word parts they know or by dividing a word into syllables. Cover *bone* and have students read the word *wish*. Then uncover *bone* and cover *wish*. Have students use letter/sound associations to pronounce *bone*. Uncover the whole word and have students blend the two smaller words to read the compound word *wishbone*. Use similar strategies to help students decode the words *bathrobe, telephone, stethoscope, periscope, homesick*, and *voter*. Encourage students to build other long words with the long *o* vowel sound spelled *o-e*. Suggest that they use a dictionary to look up words they are not sure about.

**INTERVENTION
ASSESSMENT
BOOK**

FLUENCY BUILDER Have students choose a passage from "Coach Ben" to read aloud to a partner. You may have students choose passages that they found particularly interesting, or have them choose one of the following options:

- Read page 102. (Total: 81 words)
- Read page 105. (Total: 85 words)

Students read the selected passage aloud to their partners three times. Have students rate each of their own readings on a scale of 1 to 4. Encourage readers to note their improvement from one reading to the next by completing sentence frames such as *I know my reading improved because _____* . The partner who listens to the reading should also be encouraged to offer positive comments on the reader's improvement.

Review Vocabulary

To revisit Vocabulary Words with students prior to the weekly assessment, display or read aloud the following sentences. Have students tell whether each statement is true or false, and explain why.

1. An **outfielder** may run a long way to catch a fly ball.
2. You make more mistakes when you **concentrate** on what you are doing.
3. Pets **depend** on people for food and care.
4. To become a **ballhawk**, you probably have to practice a lot.
5. The best way to make an elephant **vanish** is to wash it with soap and water.
6. If you borrow your brother's ball and lose it, it's your brother's **fault**.

You may want to display the Vocabulary Words and definitions on page 129 and have students copy them to use when they study for the vocabulary test.

Review Sequence

To review the focus skill before the weekly assessment, distribute *Intervention Practice Book* page 54. Point out the title, Sequence, and read the directions aloud. Students may work with partners to complete the sequence diagram, or you may prefer to guide them through the activity. If students work on their own, have them share and discuss their completed diagrams with the group. Ask how the time-order words in the story helped them understand the sequence of events.

INTERVENTION PRACTICE BOOK

page 54

Review Test Prep

Ask students to turn to page 355 of the *Pupil Edition*. Call attention to the tips for answering the test questions. Tell students that paying attention to these tips can help them answer not only the test questions on this page but also other test questions like these.

CHANGING PATTERNS

page 355

Read the directions to students. Then ask a volunteer to read the paragraph aloud. Have students follow along as you read aloud the first test question and the tip that goes with it. Have students identify the correct choice and explain how they determined which event happened first. Follow a similar procedure with the second question. Encourage students to tell how they might apply the tips on this page in other test situations as well.

INTERVENTION ASSESSMENT BOOK

Self-Selected Reading

Have students select their own books to read independently. They might choose books from the classroom library shelf, or you may wish to offer a group of appropriate books from which students can choose. Titles might include the following:

- *Making the Right Moves* (See page 355M of the *Teacher's Edition* for a lesson plan.)
- *Owen* by Kevin Henkes. HarperCollins, 1993.
- *Tom's Fish* by Nancy Coffelt. Harcourt, 1994.

You might also like to choose additional books that are the same genre or are by the same author as the selection.

After students have chosen their books, give each one a copy of My Reading Log, which can be found on page R42 in the back of the *Teacher's Edition*. Have students fill in the information at the top of the form. Then have them use the log to keep track of their reading and to record their responses to the literature.

Conduct student-teacher conferences. Arrange time for each student to confer with you individually about his or her self-selected reading. Have students bring their Reading Logs to share with you at the conference. Students might also like to choose a favorite passage to read aloud to you. Ask questions designed to stimulate discussion of the book. For example, you might ask the student to describe the sequence of events in the story or to tell where the story takes place and who the characters are.

FLUENCY PERFORMANCE Have students read aloud to you the passage from "Coach Ben" that they selected and practiced earlier with their partners. Keep track of the number of words each student reads correctly. Ask the student to rate his or her own performance on the 1–4 scale. If students are not happy with their oral reading, give them an opportunity to continue practicing and then to reread the passage to you again.

See *Oral Reading Fluency Assessment* for monitoring progress.

Use with

"Ramona Forever"

Review Phonics: Long Vowel /ī/*i-e, ie*

Identify the sound. Tell students to listen for the /ī/ sound as you say the word *fine*. Then have them repeat the following sentence three times: *Sid tries to ride his bike.* Ask students to identify the words that have the /ī/ sound. (*tries, ride, bike*)

Associate letters to sound. Write on the board *Sid tries to ride his bike.* Circle *Sid* and *his*, and ask how they are alike. (*CVC, short* i) Remind students that the vowel in a word with the CVC pattern usually stands for a short vowel sound. Then underline *ride* and *bike*. Ask how these words are different from *Sid* and *his*. (CVC*e pattern*) Remind students that the vowel in a word with the CVC*e* pattern usually stands for the long vowel sound. Have students listen for the long *i* vowel sound as they repeat *ride* and *bike*. Then underline *ie* in *tries*, and explain that *ie* can also stand for the long *i* vowel sound.

Word blending. Model how to blend the word *ride*. Slide your hand under the letters *ri* as you elongate the sounds /rrīī/. Then point to the letter *d* as you say /d/. Slide your hand under the whole word and say the word naturally—*ride*. Repeat the procedure, using the word *tries*.

Apply the skill. *Letter Substitution* Write the following words on the board, and have students read each aloud. Make the changes necessary to form the word in parentheses. Have a volunteer read aloud each new word.

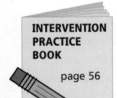

INTERVENTION
PRACTICE
BOOK

page 56

sit (site)	**pin** (pine)	**din** (dine)	**drips** (dries)
rip (ripe)	**kit** (kite)	**dome** (dime)	**trees** (tries)

Introduce Vocabulary

PRETEACH **lesson vocabulary.** Tell students that they are going to learn seven new words that they will see again when they read a selection called "Ramona Forever." Teach each Vocabulary Word using the process shown at the right.

Use these suggestions or similar ideas to give the meaning or context.

> Write the word.
> Say the word.
> Track the word and have students repeat it.
> Give the meaning or context.

glanced   Demonstrate glancing at something. Point out the -*ed* ending.

comfort   Give examples of things or people that may be a comfort to someone, such as a teddy bear or a grandparent.

longed	Explain that *long* is a multiple-meaning word. Example: *He longed for a bike for a long time.* Point out the *-ed* ending.
contagious	Give an example of a contagious illnesses, such as a cold.
prescription	Talk about the doctor writing a prescription that you take to the pharmacy to get medicine.
attention	Demonstrate giving a child attention.
unexpected	Point out the prefix *un-*, the *-ed* ending, and the root word *expect*. Discuss how the prefix changes the meaning.

For vocabulary activities, see Vocabulary Games on pages 2–7.

For vocabulary activities, see Vocabulary Games on pages 2–7.

Vocabulary Words

glanced took a quick look

comfort someone or something that makes you feel better

longed wanted very much

contagious able to be spread by contact

prescription a doctor's written instructions for taking medicine

attention thoughtful care or kindness

unexpected not expected; surprising

AFTER
Building Background and Vocabulary

Apply Vocabulary Strategies

Identify multiple-meaning words. Write on the board *She longed to see her mother.* Tell students that when a word has more than one meaning, they can often figure out the meaning from the way the word is used. Model using the strategy.

> **MODEL** I'm not sure what *longed* means in this sentence. When I cover up the *-ed* ending, I see the word *long*, but the meaning "not short" doesn't make sense here. I know that *long* can also be a verb that means "want very much." The *-ed* ending tells me the action took place in the past. The meaning "wanted very much" makes sense.

RETEACH lesson vocabulary. Have students take turns pantomiming scenes that illustrate the meaning of a Vocabulary Word. The other students guess the word and hold up the correct word card. (See page T93 for a copying master for the word cards.)

FLUENCY BUILDER Using *Intervention Practice Book* page 55, read each word in the first column aloud and have students repeat it. Then have students work in pairs to read the words in the first column aloud to each other. Follow the same procedure with each of the remaining columns. After partners have practiced reading aloud the words in each column, have them listen to each other as they practice the entire list.

INTERVENTION PRACTICE BOOK

page 55

★ (Focus Skill) **Prefixes and Suffixes**

PRETEACH **the skill.** Ask students to tell the difference between the words *cover* and *uncover*. (*They have opposite meanings. Uncover has the prefix un-.*) Tell students that they are going to learn more about prefixes and suffixes. Have them look at **side A of Skill Card 14: Prefixes and Suffixes.** Read aloud the definition of a prefix, and ask students to explain the example. Do the same with the definition of a suffix. Then read aloud the direction line above the prefix and suffix charts, and go over the charts with students. Call on volunteers to read aloud the four new words and identify the prefix or suffix in each word. Have students demonstrate their understanding of the new words by responding to items 1–4.

Prepare to Read: "Ramona Forever"

Preview. Tell students that they are going to read a realistic fiction story called "Ramona Forever." Have students recall what they have learned about realistic fiction. If necessary, remind them that the characters, settings, and events are like people, places, and events in real life. Then preview the selection.

CHANGING PATTERNS
pages 358–380

- **Pages 358–359:** I see the title, "Ramona Forever," and the names of the author and illustrator. The girl sitting on the steps must be Ramona. She looks like she might be unhappy about something. I wonder why. I will read the paragraph on page 359 to find out more. (*Read the paragraph aloud.*)

- **Pages 360–361:** Here I see Ramona's mom patting Ramona on the head. Ramona's dad is carrying a bag. I think maybe they are leaving for the hospital where the new baby will be born.

- **Pages 362–363:** In this picture Ramona and her sister are hugging each other and smiling, but I see a tear on Ramona's face. I think Ramona might be worried because her mom is gone, and her big sister is making her feel better.

Set purpose. Model setting a purpose for reading "Ramona Forever."

MODEL From my preview, I see that this story is about a girl named Ramona and her family. One purpose for reading realistic fiction is for enjoyment. I will read to enjoy this story and find out how Ramona feels about having a new baby in the family.

Reread and Summarize

Have students reread and summarize "Ramona Forever" in sections, as described below.

Pages 360–365

Let's reread pages 360–365 to recall what happens when it is time for the Quimby family's new baby to be born.

Summary: Ramona is sad and worried when her mother and dad are at the hospital. Her big sister Beezus helps her feel better. When their father comes home, he tells them that they have a new sister named Roberta.

Pages 366–369

Now let's reread pages 366–369 to find out what happens when Ramona and Beezus go to visit their mother and the new baby in the hospital.

Summary: Ramona is excited about seeing her new sister, but a nurse tells her she is too young. She has to wait in the lobby while her father and Beezus visit Mrs. Quimby and the baby.

Pages 370–375

As we reread pages 370–375, let's think about how Ramona feels.

Summary: Ramona feels itchy, worried, and angry. A doctor talks to her and writes a prescription for attention. She feels better when her father gives her a big hug and kiss.

Pages 376–380

Let's reread pages 376–380 to recall what happens when Ramona finally meets her new baby sister.

Summary: Ramona is glad when her mother and Roberta come home. She decides she's happy to be herself and not a little baby like Roberta anymore.

FLUENCY BUILDER Use *Intervention Practice Book* page 55. Call attention to the sentences on the bottom half of the page. Remind students that their goal is to read each phrase or unit smoothly. Model appropriate pace, expression, and phrasing as you read each sentence, and have students read it after you. Then have students practice by reading the sentences aloud three times to a partner.

INTERVENTION PRACTICE BOOK

page 55

Directed Reading: "Room to Share," pp. 110–117

Pages 110–111

Have students read the title of the story aloud. Ask them to read pages 110–111 to find out who Mike will share his room with. (*Grandpa Ike*) Ask: **How do you think Mike feels about sharing his room?** (*unhappy, but willing to do it for the family*) **CHARACTERS' EMOTIONS**

**BRIGHT
SURPRISES**
pp. 110–117

Pages 112–113

Have students read pages 112–113 to find out what happens when Grandpa Ike comes. Ask: **Does Mike really mean it when he says, "Me, too" after Grandpa says he'll like being Mike's roommate?** (*Possible response: No, he's just being polite.*) **SYNTHESIZE**

How can you tell that Mike's feelings are changing? (*Possible responses: He winks back at Grandpa Ike; he thinks maybe sharing his room won't be so bad after all.*) **DRAW CONCLUSIONS**

Discuss how students might have figured out the word *bedtime* on page 113. Write the word on the board, and model the strategy of using decoding/phonics.

> **MODEL** At first I'm not sure how to pronounce this word, but when I take another look at it, I see two smaller, familiar words— *bed* and *time*. I know how to pronounce *bed*, and I know the *i* in *time* has the long *i* vowel sound because the word has the CVCe pattern. I put the two words together and get *bedtime*. (Focus Strategy) **USE DECODING/PHONICS**

Pages 114–115

Have students predict from the illustration on pages 114–115 what Grandpa Ike is doing. Then have them read page 114 to find out whether their predictions are right. Ask: **What is Grandpa Ike doing?** (*making a tent from a blanket so he and Mike can pretend to be camping*) **STORY EVENTS**

How did you figure out the meaning of the word *unpacked*? (*The prefix un- means "not," or "the opposite of," so unpacked is the opposite of packed.*) (Focus Skill) **PREFIXES AND SUFFIXES**

Page 116

Have students read page 116 to find out how Mike's feelings have changed. (*At the beginning of the story, he did not want to share his room, but now he is happy to share it with Grandpa Ike.*) **SUMMARIZE**

**INTERVENTION
PRACTICE
BOOK**

page 57

How can you tell that Grandpa Ike knows Mike might have been unhappy about sharing his room? (*He says, "It's too bad you had to share your room."*) **DRAW CONCLUSIONS**

Summarize the selection. Have small groups of students summarize the story by acting it out. Encourage students to take the roles of Mike, Mom, Grandpa Ike, and the narrator.

Answers to *Think About It* Questions

1. Grandpa does not let Mike's baby sisters into the room. He sets up a tent and a tiny TV. He has snacks, and he tells Mike family stories. **SUMMARY**

2. Possible response: Mike is telling Grandpa he is glad to have a roommate, but that is not how he really feels. **INTERPRETATION**

3. Before students write, have them list the things Grandpa Ike and Mike did together. Remind students that a thank-you note should be shorter than a letter. **WRITE A THANK-YOU NOTE**

AFTER

Skill Review
pages 386–387

USE SKILL CARD 14B

(Focus Skill) Prefixes and Suffixes

RETEACH **the skill.** Have students look at **side B of Skill Card 14: Prefixes and Suffixes.** Read aloud and discuss the skill reminder with them. Then read the directions. Tell students that they can use the meanings of the prefixes and suffixes shown in the chart to figure out the meanings of the underlined words in sentences 1–4. Have students take turns reading aloud the sentences and identifying the picture that answers each question. Then have students identify the prefix or suffix in the underlined word and explain how they figured out the word's meaning.

FLUENCY BUILDER Use *Intervention Practice Book* page 55. Explain that students will practice the sentences on the bottom half of the page by reading them aloud on tape. Assign new partners. Have students take turns reading the sentences aloud to each other and then reading them on tape. After they listen to the tape, have them tell how they think they have improved their reading of the sentences. Then have them read the sentences aloud on tape a second time, with improved pacing and tone.

INTERVENTION PRACTICE BOOK

page 55

Persuasive Writing: Support an Opinion

Build on prior knowledge. Point out that students often talk about why they like or do not like stories they have read. Explain that an opinion about a story is called a review. Tell students that they are going to write their opinion about "Room to Share."

Display a graphic organizer like the one shown here.

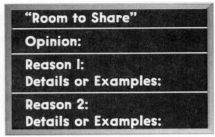

"Room to Share"
Opinion:
Reason 1: **Details or Examples:**
Reason 2: **Details or Examples:**

Construct the text. "Share the pen" with students in a collaborative group writing effort. As students dictate words and phrases, write them in the graphic organizer, guiding the process by asking questions and offering suggestions as needed.

- Help students compose a sentence that states their opinion of "Room to Share."

- Have students state reasons for their opinion and details to support the reasons. For example, one reason for liking the story might be that it has a happy ending. Details might include that Mike has fun with Grandpa Ike and that Grandpa Ike enjoys his visit.

Revisit the text. Go back and read the opinion sentence in the graphic organizer together. Ask: **Does this sentence state our opinion clearly?**

- Then read the reasons and details. Ask: **Do these reasons and details support our opinion in a strong and clear way? Is there anything we need to add? Is there any extra information that we do not need?**

- If appropriate for the sentences students have composed, ask: **Can we use a subject pronoun to take the place of a noun in any of our sentences?**

- Have students use the opinion sentence, reasons, and details from the graphic organizer to develop an oral review of "Room to Share."

On Your Own

Think of a TV show that you like or dislike. Write a sentence giving your opinion of the show. Write a reason for your opinion and one or more details or examples to support your reason. Then use your opinion sentence, reason, and details to give a partner an oral review of the TV show.

Connect Spelling and Phonics

RETEACH **long vowel /ī/ *i-e, ie.*** Tell students that you will say some words in which the letters *i-e* stand for the /ī/ sound. Have volunteers write each word on the board. Work together to proofread their work.

1. liked*	2. hide	3. size*	4. smile*
5. dive	6. fine*	7. time*	8. wide*

***Word appears in "Room to Share."**

Tell students that in the following sentence, the letters *ie* stand for the long *i* vowel sound. Dictate the sentence, and have students write it: *It's no lie that the pie fell on my tie.*

Build and Read Longer Words

Remind students that they have learned that the letters *ie* and *i-e* can stand for the /ī/ sound. Now they will use what they have learned to help them read some longer words.

Write the word *pineapple* on the board. Remind students that they can read longer words by looking for smaller words in a longer word or by looking for familiar spelling patterns. Cover *pine* and point out the familiar word *apple*. Then cover *apple*, and have students use letter/sound associations to pronounce *pine*. Have students blend the word parts to say the word *pineapple*. Similarly, use appropriate strategies to help students decode the words *lifetime, prescribe, lively, untied, horseflies, turnpike, provide*. Encourage students to build other long words in which the letters *ie* or *i-e* stand for the long *i* vowel sound. Suggest that they use a dictionary to look up words they are not sure about.

INTERVENTION
ASSESSMENT
BOOK

FLUENCY BUILDER Have students choose a passage from "Room to Share" to read aloud to a partner. You may have students choose a passage that they found particularly interesting, or have them choose one of the following options:

- Read page 112 and the first two paragraphs on page 113. (Total: 89 words)

- Read pages 114 and 115. (Total: 96 words)

Students read the selected passage aloud to their partners three times. Have students rate each of their own readings on a scale of 1 to 4. Encourage readers to note their improvement from one reading to the next by completing sentence frames such as *I know my reading improved because* _____. The partner who listens to the reading should also be encouraged to offer positive comments on the reader's improvement.

Review Vocabulary

To revisit Vocabulary Words with students prior to the weekly assessment, have students demonstrate understanding by answering questions such as the following:

1. What might someone notice if he or she **glanced** out your classroom window?
2. What might be a **comfort** to you if you were having a bad day?
3. What is something you **longed** for that turned out the way you hoped it would?
4. What **contagious** illness or illnesses can you remember having?
5. How do you feel when your doctor gives you a **prescription**?
6. Do you think getting **attention** from a teacher helps students learn? Why or why not?
7. Tell about something **unexpected** that happened lately. How did you feel?

You may want to display the Vocabulary Words and definitions on page 139 and have students copy them to use when they study for the vocabulary test.

Review Prefixes and Suffixes

To review the focus skill before the weekly assessment, distribute *Intervention Practice Book* page 58. Point out the title, Prefixes and Suffixes, and ask students to explain what the charts show. Read aloud the direction line. Explain that students can use the meanings of prefixes and suffixes shown in the chart to figure out the meanings of the underlined words in sentences 1–4. Tell them to use markers or colored pencils to follow the directions that sentences 1–4 give them. You may choose to guide students through the page, or have them work independently and then share and explain their work.

INTERVENTION
PRACTICE
BOOK

page 58

Review Test Prep

Ask students to turn to page 387 of the *Pupil Edition*. Call attention to the tips for answering the test questions. Tell students that paying attention to these tips can help them answer not only the test questions on this page but also other test questions like these.

CHANGING
PATTERNS
page 387

Have a volunteer read the paragraph aloud. Then have students follow along as you read aloud the first test item and the tip that goes with it. Have students identify the correct choice and explain how they figured out the meaning of the word. Follow a similar procedure with each of the other items. Encourage students to tell how they might apply the tips on this page in other test situations as well.

INTERVENTION
ASSESSMENT
BOOK

Self-Selected Reading

Have students select their own books to read
independently. They might choose books from the
classroom library shelf, or you may wish to offer a
group of appropriate books from which students can
choose. Titles might include the following:

- *Who Needs a Baby?* (See page 387M of
  the *Teacher's Edition* for a lesson plan.)

- *Dinosaur Babies* by Lucille Recht Penner.
  Random House, 1991.

- *My New Kitten* by Joanna Cole.
  Morrow/Avon, 1995.

After students have chosen their books, give each
student a copy of My Reading Log, which can be
found on page R42 in the back of the *Teacher's
Edition*. Have students fill in the information at the
top of the form. Then have them use the log to
keep track of their reading and to record their
responses to the literature.

Conduct student-teacher conferences. Arrange time for each student to
confer with you individually about his or her self-selected reading. Have
students bring their Reading Logs to share with you at the conference.
Students might also like to choose a favorite passage to read aloud to you.
Ask questions designed to stimulate discussion of the book. For example,
you might ask where the story takes place, who the main character is, and
what happens at the beginning, middle, and end of the story.

FLUENCY PERFORMANCE Have students read aloud to you
the passage from "Room to Share" that they selected and practiced
earlier with their partners. Keep track of the number of words the
student reads correctly. Ask the student to rate his or her own
performance on the 1–4 scale. If students are not happy with their oral
reading, give them an opportunity to continue practicing and then to
reread the passage to you.

See *Oral Reading Fluency Assessment* for monitoring progress.

Use with

"Sayings We Share: Proverbs and Fables"

Review Phonics: Long Vowel /ā/a-e

Identify the sound. Tell students to listen for the /ā/ sound as you say the word *rake*. Then have them repeat three times: *Jake and Pam made cake.* Ask them to identify the words with the /ā/ sound.

Associate letters to sound. Write on the board: *Jake and Pam made cake.* Underline *Pam* and point out the CVC pattern. Remind students that words with the CVC pattern usually have a short vowel sound. Then circle the words *Jake*, *made*, and *cake*, and point out the CVCe pattern. Tell students that words with CVCe usually have a long vowel sound. Have them listen for the long *a* vowel sound in *Jake*, *made*, and *cake*.

Word blending. Have students repeat after you as you model how to blend and read the word *made*. Slide your hand under the letters as you elongate the sounds /mmāā/. Point to *d* and say /d/. Then say the word naturally—*made*.

Apply the skill. *Letter Substitution* Write these words on the board, and have students read each aloud. Change as needed to form the word in parentheses. Have a volunteer read aloud each new word.

INTERVENTION
PRACTICE
BOOK

page 60

mat (mate)	**fad** (fade)	**tap** (tape)	**glad** (glade)
at (ate)	**pan** (pane)	**man** (mane)	**Sam** (same)

Introduce Vocabulary

PRETEACH **lesson vocabulary.** Tell students that they are going to learn six new words that they will see again when they read a selection called "Sayings We Share." Teach each Vocabulary Word using the process below.

Use these suggestions or similar ideas to give the meaning or context.

> Write the word.
> Say the word.
> Track the word and have students repeat it.
> Give the meaning or context.

summoned Demonstrate by calling a student up to your desk.

fortunate Give examples of times when people are fortunate, such as winning a game of chance. Relate to the word *fortune*.

generation Explain that all students in the class were born around the same time and are members of the same generation; their parents are members of a different generation.

persistently Demonstrate behaving persistently by asking a series of "why" questions. Point out the suffix *-ly*.

faithful	Relate to a dog and its master. Point out the suffix *-ful*.
illuminated	Demonstrate by turning all the lights off and then on.

For vocabulary activities, see Vocabulary Games on pages 2–7.

For vocabulary activities, see Vocabulary Games on pages 2–7.

Vocabulary Words

summoned called to come

fortunate lucky

generation people who grow up at about the same time

persistently repeatedly, without giving up

faithful loyal

illuminated lit up; made brighter

Apply Vocabulary Strategies

Use synonyms/antonyms. Write this sentence on the board: **The morning sun <u>illuminated</u> the bedroom, so Rory <u>darkened</u> the room by pulling down the shades.**

Tell students that they can sometimes figure out the meaning of a word by looking for a synonym or antonym in the sentence or another sentence nearby. Model using the strategy.

> **MODEL** I don't know what the word *illuminated* means, but from reading the sentence I know that Rory did not want the room to be illuminated, so he did something that darkened it. I know that *darkened* means "made dark," so it makes sense that *illuminated* means "made light." *Illuminated* is the opposite of *darkened*, so the words are antonyms.

Guide students in looking for a synonym to figure out the meaning of *persistently* in the following sentence: *The squirrel returned <u>persistently</u> to the bird feeder, even though we repeatedly chased it away.* (repeatedly)

RETEACH lesson vocabulary. Have students print the Vocabulary Words neatly on cards. Tell them to cut the words apart to make letter cards and then mix the letters in a box. Using the word cards on page T94 as a reference, students pick out the letters to reconstruct each word. Have them tell the meaning of each word after they have completed it.

FLUENCY BUILDER Using *Intervention Practice Book* page 59, read each word in the first column aloud and have students repeat it. Then have students work in pairs to read the words in the first column aloud to each other. Follow the same procedure with each of the remaining columns. After partners have practiced reading aloud the words in each column, have them listen to each other as they practice the entire list.

INTERVENTION PRACTICE BOOK

page 59

★Focus Skill Narrative Elements

PRETEACH the skill. Have students recall the basic elements of a story—characters, setting, and plot. Then have them look at **side A of Skill Card 15: Narrative Elements**. Briefly read and discuss the questions in the two boxes at the top of the story map. Then read aloud the part of the story map that deals with the plot. Have students identify the problem and resolution in several stories they have read. Call attention to the picture story, and have volunteers read aloud the dialogue. Refer students back to the diagram and have them answer the questions to identify the characters, setting, problem, and resolution in the picture story.

Prepare to Read: "Sayings We Share"

Preview. Tell students that they are going to read a selection called "Sayings We Share: Proverbs and Fables." Explain that proverbs are short sayings that give advice and that fables are very short stories. Tell students that a fable teaches a lesson about life. Its characters are often animals that act like people. After discussing the genre, preview the selection.

CHANGING PATTERNS
pages 390–403

- **Pages 390–391:** On page 390 I see the title and the names of the author and illustrator. The picture shows a man catching fish with his hands. On page 391 I see the heading Proverbs. I think this section might explain what proverbs are and the picture might illustrate a proverb.

- **Pages 392–394:** There is a heading, Vietnamese Proverbs, on page 392. This page is not written in paragraphs. These short sayings must be proverbs from the country of Vietnam. I think the people in the picture on page 393 must be Vietnamese. I see more proverbs under the heading Other Well-Known Proverbs on page 394.

- **Pages 395–399:** From the heading Fables and the way the text is arranged on page 395, I guess that this page gives information about fables. The Greek fable "The Hare and the Tortoise" begins on page 396. I can see that it is a very short story because it ends on the next page. Another fable, "The Young Rooster," begins on page 398. I can tell from the titles and the illustrations that both fables have animal characters.

Set purpose. Model setting a purpose for reading "Sayings We Share."

MODEL From my preview, I know that this selection is a collection of proverbs and fables from different parts of the world that teach lessons about life. One purpose for reading is to enjoy and another is to learn. I think I will read this selection to enjoy the stories and to learn the lessons they teach.

Reread and Summarize

Have students reread and summarize "Sayings We Share" in sections, as described below.

Pages 391–394

Let's reread pages 391–394 to recall how we learn from proverbs.

Summary: Proverbs are common sayings that teach us about life and how to be a good person. Proverbs from many different cultures use different words to express very similar ideas.

Pages 395–397

Now let's reread pages 395–397 to find out about fables.

Summary: Fables are short tales. A fable may have a moral that tells what the story teaches. "The Hare and the Tortoise" is a fable told by Aesop long ago. Even though Tortoise is slow, she wins her race with Hare.

Pages 398–399

As we reread pages 398–399, let's see what the next fable teaches.

Summary: "The Young Rooster" is an American fable. At first the Rooster does not crow loudly enough to make the sun come up, but he learns to crow very loudly. The moral is that failure may prepare the way for success.

Pages 400–403

Let's reread pages 400–403 to recall what the other fables are about.

Summary: In "The Dog and the Wolf," a wolf thinks a dog is fortunate to be taken care of by its master until the wolf finds out that the master keeps the dog on a chain. The characters in "Two Mice" are a hard-working mouse and a lazy mouse. The fable teaches that it is better to work before taking time for pleasure.

FLUENCY BUILDER Use *Intervention Practice Book* page 59. Point out the sentences on the bottom half of the page. Remind students that their goal is to read each phrase or unit smoothly. Model appropriate pace, expression, and phrasing as you read each sentence, and have students read it after you. Then have students practice by reading the sentences aloud three times to a partner.

INTERVENTION PRACTICE BOOK

page 59

Making Connections
pages 404–405

Directed Reading: "The Lazy Horse" pp. 118–124

BRIGHT SURPRISES pp. 118–124

Pages 118–119

Tell students that this story is a fable. Have them read the title aloud. Then have them read pages 118–119 to find out what the horse's life is like. Ask: **What does the author mean when she says that the horse did not recognize his good luck?** (*The horse had a good life and everything he needed, but he did not know how lucky he was.*) **AUTHOR'S VIEWPOINT**

Pages 120–121

Have students read pages 120–121 to find out what the horse sees in the kitchen. (*the man taking care of the dog*) Ask: **What is the problem in this story?** (*The horse wishes he could live in the house like the dog.*) (Focus Skill) **NARRATIVE ELEMENTS**

Tell students that you can use clues from the story to make a guess about what might happen next. Model using the strategy of making and confirming predictions.

> **MODEL** I know from what I've read so far and from the pictures that the horse thinks the dog has a better life than he does and he is angry about that. The horse thinks he deserves to be treated like the dog. I predict that the horse will try to go in the house. (Focus Strategy) **MAKE AND CONFIRM PREDICTIONS**

Pages 122–123

Ask students to read pages 122–123 to find out whether your prediction is correct. Ask: **What happens when the horse goes in the house?** (*He tries to act like a dog, but he is so big that he breaks things.*) **CAUSE/EFFECT**

INTERVENTION PRACTICE BOOK

page 61

How do the horse and the man solve their problem? (*The horse learns to pull a cart, which is something the dog can't do, and he makes the man proud of him.*) **What is the theme of this story?** (*Be happy to be yourself and do the things that you can do.*) (Focus Skill) **NARRATIVE ELEMENTS**

Summarize the selection. Have students work with partners or in small groups to make simple puppets that represent characters in the fables. Then have them perform puppet shows to summarize the fables.

Answers to *Think About It* Questions

1. He was trying to behave like a dog. **SUMMARY**
2. Responses will vary. **INTERPRETATION**
3. Tell students to think about how the horse behaved when he was angry and then to think about how he acted when he pulled the cart. As they write the dialogue, remind them to consider each animal's point of view as they comment on the events. Also remind students that the dog lives in the house and the chickens live in the barn. **WRITE A DIALOGUE**

AFTER

Skill Review
pages 406–407

USE SKILL CARD 15B

(Focus Skill) ★ **Review Narrative Elements**

RETEACH **the skill.** Have students look at **side B of Skill Card 15:** **Narrative Elements.** Read aloud the skill reminder and directions. Call on volunteers to take turns reading the story aloud, with each student reading a paragraph. After students have read the story and the moral, have them read and respond to each of the questions. (*Possible responses: 1. He can't get out of the net. 2. The mouse cuts the net with his sharp teeth. 3. Even someone small and weak can help others.*)

FLUENCY BUILDER Use *Intervention Practice Book* page 59. Explain that students will practice the sentences on the bottom half of the page by reading them aloud on tape. Assign new partners. Have students take turns reading the sentences aloud to each other and then reading them on tape. After they listen to the tape, have them tell how they think they have improved their reading of the sentences. Then have them read the sentences aloud on tape a second time, with improved pacing and tone.

> **INTERVENTION PRACTICE BOOK**
>
> page 59

Persuasive Writing: Opinion, Reasons, and Details

Build on prior knowledge. Ask students to recall what they have learned about persuasive writing. Tell them that now they are going to learn about doing persuasive writing when they take a writing test.

Remind students that the first thing they should do when they take a writing test is to read and analyze the prompt. Write this prompt on the board: *"The Hare and the Tortoise" teaches the moral that slow and steady wins the race. Write to persuade your classmates to take their time and not rush through their work. Include reasons and details to persuade readers to share your opinion. (45 minutes)*

Have students identify the **writing form** (*persuasive writing*), the **topic** (*taking your time is better than rushing*), the **audience** (*your classmates*), and any **special instructions**. (*include reasons and details*)

Point out that students would have 45 minutes to write this paragraph. Discuss how they would budget their time. Write numbers on the board to show that 10 minutes for prewriting, 25 minutes for drafting, and 10 minutes for revising and proofreading add up to a total of 45 minutes.

Display a graphic organizer like this one.

Opinion:	
Reasons:	Details:

Construct the text. "Share the pen" with students in a collaborative group effort. As students dictate words and phrases, write these in the organizer. Guide the process by asking questions and offering suggestions as needed.

- Point out that this is the prewriting step of the writing process. To give an idea of the time constraint in a test situation, set a timer and allow 10 minutes for this step.

Revisit the text. Go back and reread the prompt together. Ask: **Can we use the opinion, reasons, and details in our chart to carry out the instructions in this prompt?**

- Help students use the opinion, reasons, and details from the graphic organizer to develop an oral presentation.

On Your Own

Family members and teachers often give young people good advice. Think of a piece of advice that has helped you. Write three or four sentences to persuade your classmates to follow this advice. Give reasons and examples to persuade your readers to share your opinion.

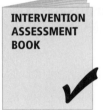

AFTER

Spelling Lesson
pages 407G–407H

Connect Spelling and Phonics

RETEACH **long vowel /ā/ *a-e*.** Tell students that you will say some words in which the letters *a-e* stand for the /ā/ sound. Have volunteers write each word on the board. Work together to proofread their work.

I. rake	2. game	3. shake*	4. gate*
5. made*	6. plate*	7. mane*	8. came*

*Word appears in "The Lazy Horse."

Dictate the following sentence and have students write it: *Jane will take a cake to the game.*

Build and Read Longer Words

Remind students that they have learned that the letters *a-e* can stand for the /ā/ sound. Now they will use what they have learned to help them read some longer words.

Write the word *lateness* on the board. Remind students that they can read longer words by looking for familiar word parts. Underline the familiar word part *-ness*, which means "the condition of being." Then cover *-ness* and blend the sounds to read the word *lateness*. Point out the long *a* sound in *late*. Have students read the word *lateness*. Use appropriate strategies to help students decode the words *cupcake*, *safely*, *arrange*, *escape*, *makeup* and *rattlesnake*. Encourage students to build other long words in which the letters *a-e* stand for the long *a* vowel sound. Suggest that they use a dictionary to look up words they are not sure about.

INTERVENTION ASSESSMENT BOOK

FLUENCY BUILDER Have students choose a passage from "The Lazy Horse" to read aloud to a partner. You may have students choose passages that they found particularly interesting, or have them choose one of the following options:

- Read pages 118 and 119. (Total: 91 words)
- Read page 122 and the first two paragraphs on page 123. (From *The horse . . .* to *. . . cannot."* Total: 89 words)

Students read the selected passage aloud to their partners three times. Have students rate each of their own readings on a scale of I to 4. Encourage readers to note their improvement from one reading to the next by completing sentence frames such as *I know my reading improved because* _____. The partner who listens to the reading should also be encouraged to offer positive comments on the reader's improvement.

Review Vocabulary

To revisit Vocabulary Words with students prior to the weekly assessment, display or read aloud the following sentences. Have students tell whether each statement is true or false and explain why.

1. A **generation** is one person.
2. If you do something **persistently**, you do it over and over.
3. When the king **summoned** his subjects, he wanted them to go away.
4. A **faithful** friend will stay with you in good times and bad times.
5. You would be **fortunate** if you won a free trip.
6. The fireworks **illuminated** the night sky.

Correct responses: 1. False, 2. True, 3. False, 4. True, 5. True, 6. True

You may want to display the Vocabulary Words and definitions on page 149 and have students copy them to use when they study for the vocabulary test.

INTERVENTION
PRACTICE
BOOK

page 62

Focus Skill Review Narrative Elements

To review the focus skill before the weekly assessment, distribute *Intervention Practice Book* page 62. Point out the title, Narrative Elements, and read the directions aloud. You may choose to guide students through the activity, or have them complete it with a partner and then share and discuss their work with the group.

Review Test Prep

Ask students to turn to page 407 of the *Pupil Edition*. Call attention to the tips for answering the test questions. Tell students that paying attention to these tips can help them answer not only the test questions on this page but also other test questions like these.

CHANGING
PATTERNS
page 407

INTERVENTION
ASSESSMENT
BOOK

Read the directions to students, and have them follow along as you read the story aloud. Ask a volunteer to read aloud the first test question and the tip that goes with it. Have students tell how they would answer the question. Then read aloud the second question, answer choices, and tip. Have students identify the correct choice and explain how they determined the answer. Encourage students to tell how they might apply the tips on this page in other test situations as well.

Self-Selected Reading

Have students select their own books to read independently. They might choose books from the classroom library shelf, or you may wish to offer a group of appropriate books from which students can choose. Titles might include the following:

- *Apollo: To the Moon* (See page 407K of the *Teacher's Edition* for a lesson plan.)

- *Johnny Appleseed* by Patsy Jensen. Troll, 1997.

- *The Little Red Hen* by Byron Barton. HarperCollins, 1993

After students have chosen their books, give each student a copy of My Reading Log, which can be found on page R42 in the back of the *Teacher's Edition*. Have students fill in the information at the top of the form. Then have them use the log to keep track of their reading and to record their responses to the literature.

Conduct student-teacher conferences. Arrange time for each student to confer with you individually about his or her self-selected reading. Have students bring their Reading Logs to share with you at the conference. Students might also like to choose a favorite passage to read aloud to you. Ask questions about the book to stimulate discussion. For example, you might ask which character the student liked best, when and where the story takes place, or how the student feels about the story problem and its resolution.

FLUENCY PERFORMANCE Have students read aloud to you the passage from "The Lazy Horse" that they selected and practiced earlier with their partners. Keep track of the number of words the student reads correctly. Ask the student to rate his or her own performance on the 1–4 scale. If students are not happy with their oral reading, give them an opportunity to continue practicing and then to reread the passage to you again.

See *Oral Reading Fluency Assessment* for monitoring progress.

BEFORE

Building
Background
and Vocabulary

Use with

"Papa Tells Chita a Story"

Review Phonics: Vowel Variants /o͞o/*u-e, ue, ui, ew*

Identify the sound. Tell students to listen for the /o͞o/ sound as you say the words *flute, true, fruit,* and *flew.* Then have students repeat this sentence three times: *June drew a blue suit.* Ask them to identify the words that have the /o͞o/ sound they hear in *flute.* (*June, drew, blue, suit*)

Associate letters to sound. On the board, write *June drew a blue suit.* Underline *u* and *e* in *June*, and tell students that these letters can stand for the /o͞o/ sound they hear in *June.* Follow a similar procedure for the letters *ew* in *drew*, *ue* in *blue*, and *ui* in *suit.* Point out that the letters *u-e, ue, ew,* and *ui* all can stand for the /o͞o/ sound.

Word blending. Have students repeat after you as you model how to blend the word *suit.* Slide your hand under the letters *sui* as you elongate the sounds /sso͞o/. Next, include the letter *t*, saying /sso͞o/–/t/, /sso͞ot/. Then say the word naturally—*suit.*

Apply the skill. *Letter Substitution* Write the following words on the board, and have students read each aloud. Make the changes necessary to form the words in parentheses. Have students read aloud each new word.

tone (tune)	**day** (dew)	**tree** (true)	**fret** (fruit)
role (rule)	**stay** (stew)	**clay** (clue)	**sit** (suit)

INTERVENTION
PRACTICE
BOOK

page 64

Introduce Vocabulary

PRETEACH **lesson vocabulary.** Tell students that they are going to learn seven new words that they will see again when they read a selection called "Papa Tells Chita a Story." Teach each Vocabulary Word by using the process shown at the right.

Use these suggestions or similar ideas to give the meaning or context.

colonel	Explain that a colonel is an important person in an army.
soldier	Relate to soldiers that students may have seen on TV.
urgent	Compare examples of urgent messages (*Come quick! I need help!*) and messages that are not urgent (*Call me when you have time*).
brambles	Pantomime walking through a patch of brambles. Point out the *s* at the end of this plural noun.

> Write the word.
>
> Say the word.
>
> Track the word and have students repeat it.
>
> Give the meaning or context.

stumbling	Demonstrate stumbling. Point out the *-ing* ending.
outstretched	Demonstrate outstretched arms. Point out the *-ed* ending.
weary	Show how a weary person might act.

For vocabulary activities, see Vocabulary Games on pp. 2–7.

For vocabulary activities, see Vocabulary Games on pp. 2–7.

AFTER

Building Background and Vocabulary

Apply Vocabulary Strategies

Use familiar word parts. Write the word *outstretched* on the board. Remind students that they can sometimes figure out the meaning of a word by looking for word parts that they know. Model using the strategy.

> **MODEL** I see the familiar word ending *-ed,* which shows that an action happened in the past. I cover it up and I'm left with *outstretch.* *Out* is another familiar word part. I cover that up, too, and now I see *stretch.* I know that word, and now I'll put all three parts back together to read the whole–*outstretched.*

Guide students in using a similar procedure to decode the word *stumbling.* After covering *-ing,* point out that the final *e* was dropped from the root word before *-ing* was added. Divide *stumble* into syllables.

RETEACH **lesson vocabulary.** Have students draw an illustration for each Vocabulary Word. On separate strips of paper, students should write a caption for each picture, using the Vocabulary Word. Students then exchange drawings and captions and try to match each caption with the correct picture.

Vocabulary Words

colonel a person with a certain rank, or position, in an army

soldier a person who serves in an army

urgent in need of immediate action or attention; pressing

brambles prickly plants or bushes

stumbling moving in an unsteady way

outstretched extended; stretched forward

weary tired

FLUENCY BUILDER Use *Intervention Practice Book* page 63. Read each word in the first column aloud and have students repeat it. Then have students work in pairs to read the words in the first column aloud to each other. Follow the same procedure with each of the remaining columns. After partners have practiced reading aloud the words in each column, have them listen to each other as they practice the entire list.

INTERVENTION PRACTICE BOOK

page 63

BEFORE

Reading
"Papa Tells Chita
a Story"
pages 16–29

USE SKILL CARD 16A

(Focus Skill) **Summarize**

PRETEACH the skill. Tell students that summarizing means retelling a story in a shorter way. Have students look at **side A of Skill Card 16: Summarize.** Read and discuss with them the introductory sentences at the top of the card. Then read the direction line aloud. After giving students time to read the paragraph silently, ask a volunteer to read it aloud. Read the next set of directions and the sentence frame with students, and guide them in completing the one-sentence summary. You may wish to complete the sentence interactively on the board and then have students write it on their papers.

Call attention to Check Your Summary at the bottom of the page. Have students read aloud and answer each question.

Prepare to Read: "Papa Tells Chita a Story"

Preview. Tell students that they are going to read a story called "Papa Tells Chita a Story." Explain that this selection is historical fiction, which tells about events that happened or could have happened in the past. The story is fiction because the author makes up some of the characters, events, and details. After talking about the genre, preview the selection.

ON YOUR MARK
pages 16–29

- **Pages 16–17:** On these pages I see the title, "Papa Tells Chita a Story," and the names of the author and illustrator. I think the man in the picture is Papa, and the little girl is Chita. At the bottom of page 17, I see a smaller title, "Papa Time, Chita Time." The story or its introduction must begin here. I'll read this section to find out.

- **Page 18:** I see that the story continues on page 18. I also see two headings. I'll read what it says under the first heading, "A Story, a Story." The next heading is "Brave Papa." I think the story that Papa tells Chita begins here.

- **Page 19:** The picture on page 19 shows a soldier on a horse, waving his sword at a big snake. This must be an illustration of Papa's story about the days when he was a brave soldier.

- **Pages 20–23:** These pages show the same soldier and a huge alligator. I guess this is also part of Papa's story. It looks exciting!

Set Purpose. Model setting a purpose for reading "Papa Tells Chita a Story."

MODEL From my preview, I know that Chita is a little girl who asks her father to tell her a story about his days as a soldier. I think it will be exciting to read the story that Papa tells Chita. I know that readers often read fiction to be entertained. I'll read to find out the exciting things Papa did.

Reread and Summarize

Have students reread and summarize "Papa Tells Chita a Story" in sections, as described in the chart below.

Pages 17–18

Let's reread pages 17–18 to recall what Papa's story is about.

Summary: Chita asks her father to tell a story about his days as a brave soldier in the Spanish War.

Pages 19–23

Now let's reread pages 19–23 to find out what dangers Papa faced.

Summary: On his way to deliver a secret message, Papa escaped from a big snake and an alligator.

Pages 24–25

As we reread pages 24–25, let's see what happened to Papa when he fell asleep.

Summary: Papa slept in an eagle's nest, but the eagle came back and chased him away.

Pages 26–28

Let's reread pages 26–28 to recall how Papa's story ends.

Summary: Papa delivered the urgent message. Chita looks at Papa's medal and asks if the story is true. Papa says that some of it is true and some is not.

FLUENCY BUILDER Use *Intervention Practice Book* page 63. Point out the sentences on the bottom half of the page. Remind students to pay attention to the slashes and to read each phrase or unit smoothly. Model appropriate pace, expression, and phrasing as you read each sentence and have students read it after you. Then have students practice by reading the sentences aloud three times to a partner.

INTERVENTION
PRACTICE
BOOK

page 63

Directed Reading: "The Bravest Soldier," pp. 126–133

BEFORE

Making Connections
pages 32–33

Pages 126–127

Read the title of the story aloud. Call attention to the two young men in the illustration. Have students read pages 126–127. Ask: **Who are the characters in the picture, and where are they going?** (*Tom Andrews and his friend Rube Jones; they are leaving home to become soldiers.*) **IMPORTANT DETAILS**

BRIGHT SURPRISES
pp. 126–133

Page 128

Have students read page 128. Ask: **Why doesn't Rube think he is a true soldier?** (*He does not like camping in the dark forest; he may be scared.*) **CHARACTERS' EMOTIONS**

Model using the strategy of rereading to clarify.

> **MODEL** I don't remember for sure why Rube thinks he is not a true soldier. I will go back and reread the paragraph that begins with the sentence *Rube did not think he was a true soldier.* Now I remember that Rube doesn't like the dark forest and probably is scared about going into battle. (Focus Strategy) **REREAD TO CLARIFY**

Pages 129–131

Remind students to take time to look at the illustrations as they read pages 129 through 131 to find out what happens to Tom and Rube when their training ends. Ask: **What important events take place after Tom and Rube finish their training?** (*Possible response: They carry supplies to the next camp. There they find that all the soldiers are sick. They are picked to take a message that a doctor is needed*) (Focus Skill) **SUMMARIZE**

Page 132

Have students read page 132 to find out whether Tom and Rube succeed in delivering the message. Ask: **How does the message get delivered?** (*Possible response: Rube takes it the rest of the way by himself after Tom gets hurt.*) **STORY EVENTS**

Ask: **Why does Tom say that Rube is the bravest soldier?** (*because Rube did what he had to do, even though he was scared*) **CAUSE/EFFECT**

INTERVENTION PRACTICE BOOK

page 65

Summarize the selection. Have students make up certificates that the colonel might give Tom and Rube for their bravery. Tell students to include details from the story about what each of the young soldiers did. Then have students complete *Intervention Practice Book* page 65.

Answers to *Think About It* Questions

1. He has to march a long way even when he is tired. He is given the jobs of delivering supplies and an important message. **SUMMARY**

2. Possible response: He is scared but confident that his friend will be able to deliver the message by himself. **INTERPRETATION**

3. Accept reasonable responses. **WRITE A STORY**

AFTER

Skill Review
pages 34–35

USE SKILL CARD 16B

★(Focus Skill) Summarize

RETEACH the skill. Have students look at **side B of Skill Card 16: Summarize.** Read the skill reminder and directions with them.

Ask volunteers to read the summary aloud. Explain that a student might write a paragraph like this to summarize a longer story about some soldiers who are chased by a bear. Point out that the writer included the important story events but also some details that are not as important.

After students have copied the paragraph, read the next set of directions with them. You may wish to have students read each sentence aloud, discuss whether it tells an important event or unimportant detail, and decide as a group whether to underline it or cross it out. Then read the next direction line and have students write the new summary on their papers. Alternatively, students may work through the process with partners and then share their new summaries with the group.

Finally, call attention to the questions at the bottom of the card. Students should recognize that the new summary is better because it is shorter and includes only the most important information.

FLUENCY BUILDER Use *Intervention Practice Book* page 63. Explain that students will practice the sentences on the bottom half of the page by reading them aloud on tape. Assign new partners. Have students take turns reading the sentences aloud to each other and then reading them on tape. After they listen to the tape, have them tell how they think they have improved their reading of the sentences. Then have them read the sentences aloud on tape a second time, with improved pacing and tone.

INTERVENTION PRACTICE BOOK

page 63

Expository Writing: Paragraph That Compares

Build on prior knowledge. Ask how many students have or would like to have pet dogs. Then ask how many have or would like to have pet cats. Tell students that you want them to think about ways in which dogs and cats are alike. Explain that they are going to write a paragraph that compares, or tells how two things are alike.

Construct the text. "Share the pen" with students in a collaborative group writing effort. As students dictate words and phrases, write them in the organizer, guiding the process by asking questions and offering suggestions as needed.

Guide students in using the completed graphic organizer to write a paragraph that compares.

	Examples of Similarities	
dogs	have fur are good pets have four legs have tails like people need care and attention	cats

- Help students develop an interesting topic sentence that tells what two things the paragraph will compare.

- Suggest that students present the similarities in a logical way. In the example shown on this page, for instance, they might first compare the physical characteristics (fur, four legs, tails) and then tell how the animals are alike in their relationships with people (good pets, like people, need care and attention).

- Help students write a concluding sentence that restates the main point of the paragraph.

Revisit the text. As you work with students to revise the paragraph, encourage them to make their writing more interesting. Ask: **Can we use *and* or *but* to combine short, choppy sentences into longer sentences? Can we add interesting adjectives?**

- Have students read the completed paragraph aloud.

On Your Own

Write a paragraph that compares two things. Pick two things that are alike in several ways, such as a bike and a scooter, or a bird and a butterfly. Remember to begin your paragraph with a topic sentence and to restate the main point in the last sentence.

Connect Spelling and Phonics

RETEACH vowel variants /o͞o/*u-e, ue, ui, ew.* Tell students that you will say some words in which the letters *ew* stand for the /o͞o/ sound. Have volunteers write each word on the board. Work together to proofread their work.

I. dew*   2. flew   3. grew*   4. crew
5. blew   6. threw   7. stew   8. Andrews*

*Word appears in "The Bravest Soldier."

Tell students that in the following sentence, the letters *ue* stand for the /o͞o/ sound. Dictate this sentence and have students write it: *Sue made a clue with blue glue.*

Build and Read Longer Words

Remind students that they have learned that the letters *u-e, ue, ui,* and *ew* can stand for the /o͞o/ sound. Now they will use what they have learned to help them read some longer words.

Write the word *suitcase* on the board. Remind students that they can read longer words by looking for word parts that they know or by dividing the word into syllables. Cover *suit* and ask a volunteer to identify the shorter word *case.* Then uncover *suit* and cover *case.* Remind students that they can use what they have learned about letters and sounds to help them read this shorter word. Uncover the whole word and have students pronounce it. Use appropriate strategies to help students decode the words *blueberry, fruitcake, stewing, newest, screwdriver,* and *newscast.* Encourage students to build other long words in which the letters *u-e, ue, ui,* and *ew* stand for the /o͞o/ sound. Suggest that they use a dictionary to look up words they are not sure about.

INTERVENTION ASSESSMENT BOOK

FLUENCY BUILDER Have students choose a passage from "The Bravest Soldier" to read aloud to a partner. You may have students choose passages that they found particularly interesting, or have them choose one of the following options:

- Read page 128 and the first paragraph on page 129. (Total: 92 words)

- Read page 132. (Total: 100 words)

Students read the selected passage aloud to their partners three times. Have students rate each of their own readings on a scale of 1 to 4. Encourage readers to note their improvement from one reading to the next by completing sentence frames such as *I know my reading improved because_____.* The partner who listens to the reading should also be encouraged to offer positive comments on the reader's improvement.

Review Vocabulary

To revisit Vocabulary Words with students prior to the weekly assessment, display a word line like the one shown here.

least surprised ——————————————— most surprised

Have students listen to the following questions and take turns indicating on the word line how surprised they would be. Ask them to explain why they would or would not be surprised in each instance. If needed, ask follow-up questions to check understanding of the Vocabulary Words.

How surprised would you be if . . .

1. you met a **colonel** who was younger than you?
2. you heard that a teacher in your school had been a **soldier**?
3. your mother said playing games was more **urgent** than doing your homework?
4. you got a scratch from walking through **brambles**?
5. a baby taking her first steps was **stumbling**?
6. your friend had his arms **outstretched** and his hands in his pockets?
7. someone was **weary** after working hard all day?

You may want to display the Vocabulary Words and definitions on page 159 and have students copy them to use when they study for the vocabulary test.

 Review Summarize

To review the focus skill before the weekly assessment, distribute *Intervention Practice Book* page 66. Read the directions with students. Review what students have learned about writing a summary. Then have them read the story and identify important information and unimportant details. Tell students to write on the lines a short summary of the story in their own words. Remind them to tell the information in the same order as the story. Students should read their summaries aloud and discuss them with the group.

**INTERVENTION
PRACTICE
BOOK**

page 66

Review Test Prep

Ask students to turn to page 35 of the *Pupil Edition*. Call attention to the tips for answering the test questions. Tell students that these tips can help them answer not only the test questions on this page but also other test questions like these.

**ON YOUR
MARK**

p. 35

Have students follow along as you read aloud the first test question and tip. Ask a volunteer to identify the choice that gives the writer's own idea or opinion. Discuss why that choice does not belong in a good summary. Then have a student read aloud the second test item and tip. Remind students to think about what they have learned about writing a summary before they begin writing one on a test.

**INTERVENTION
ASSESSMENT
BOOK**

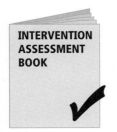

Self-Selected Reading

Have students select their own books to read independently. They might choose books from the classroom library shelf, or you may wish to offer a group of appropriate books from which students can choose. Titles might include the following:

- *Rebecca's Story.* (See page 35M of the *Teacher's Edition* for a lesson plan.)

- *Shy Charles* by Rosemary Wells. Penguin Putnam, 2001.

- *Paul Bunyan and His Blue Ox* by Patsy Jensen. Troll Communications, 1999.

You may also wish to choose additional books that are of the same genre, that are by the same author, or that have the same kind of text structure as the selection.

After students have chosen their books, give each student a copy of My Reading Log, which can be found on page R42 in the back of the *Teacher's Edition*. Have students fill in the information at the top of the form. Then have them use the log to keep track of their reading and to record their responses to the literature.

Conduct student-teacher conferences. Arrange time for each student to confer with you individually about his or her self-selected reading. Have students bring their Reading Logs to share with you at the conference. Students might also like to choose a favorite passage to read aloud to you. Ask questions about the book to stimulate discussion. For example, you might ask where the story took place, who the main character was, and what happened at the beginning, middle, and end of the story.

FLUENCY PERFORMANCE Have students read aloud to you the passage from "The Bravest Soldier" that they selected and practiced earlier with their partners. Keep track of the number of words the student reads correctly. Ask the student to rate his or her own performance on the 1–4 scale. If students are not happy with their oral reading, give them an opportunity to continue practicing and then to reread the passage to you.

See *Oral Reading Fluency Assessment* for monitoring progress.

Use with

"Coyote Places the Stars"

Review Phonics: Long Vowel /ē/ *ee, ea*

Identify the sound. Tell students to listen for the /ē/ sound as you say the words *need* and *seat*. Then have students repeat this sentence three times: *Jean and Jen got beets and beans.* Ask them to identify the words that have the /ē/ sound they hear in *need* and *seat*. (*Jean, beets, beans*)

Associate letters to sound. Write on the board *Jean and Jen got beets and beans.* Point out the CVC pattern and short *e* vowel sound in *Jen.* Underline *ea* in *Jean* and *beans*, and tell students that the letters *ea* together in a word often stand for /ē/, the long *e* vowel sound. Follow a similar procedure with *ee* in *beets.* Point out the CVVC pattern, noting that two vowels that come together in a word often stand for a long vowel sound. Then have students read the sentence aloud.

Word blending. Have students repeat after you as you model the word *beets.* Slide your hand under the letters *bee* as you elongate the sounds /bbēē/. Next, point to the *t* and say /t/. Slide your hand again, elongating /bbēētt/. Point to *s* and say /s/. Slide your hand under the whole word, elongating /bbēēttss/, and then say it naturally—*beets.*

Apply the skill. *Vowel Substitution* Write these words on the board, and have students read each aloud. Make the changes needed to form the words in parentheses. Have a volunteer read aloud each new word.

INTERVENTION
PRACTICE
BOOK

page 68

red (reed)	**bed** (bead)	**set** (seat)	**met** (meat)
step (steep)	**net** (neat)	**sped** (speed)	**Ned** (need)

Introduce Vocabulary

PRETEACH lesson vocabulary. Tell students that they are going to learn seven new words that they will see again when they read a selection called "Coyote Places the Stars." Teach each Vocabulary Word using the following process.

Use these suggestions or similar ideas to give the meaning or context.

canyon	Relate to the Grand Canyon.
pride	Relate to the word *proud.*
swiftly	Demonstrate moving swiftly. Point out the *-ly* that shows how an action is performed.
skillful	Explain that certain skills are needed to play a sport or to make or repair something. Point out the suffix *-ful.*

> Write the word.
>
> Say the word.
>
> Track the word and have students repeat it.
>
> Give the meaning or context.

feast	Point out the letters *ea* that stand for the /ē/ sound. Relate to Thanksgiving or a family meal.
gazing	Gaze out the window.
arranged	Demonstrate by arranging items on your desk. Point out the *-ed* ending that shows past action.

For vocabulary activities, see Vocabulary Games on pages 2–7.

For vocabulary activities, see Vocabulary Games on pages 2–7.

Apply Vocabulary Strategies

Use prefixes and suffixes. Write the word *skillful* on the board. Remind students that they can sometimes figure out the pronunciation of a word by looking for word parts that they know. Model using the strategy.

> **MODEL** I recognize the suffix *-ful* from words like *helpful* and *playful*. When I cover it up, I see the word *skill*, which I know. I can blend these word parts to say the whole word— *skillful*.

Guide students in using a similar procedure to decode *swiftly*.

RETEACH lesson vocabulary. Have students illustrate each Vocabulary Word. On separate strips of paper, students should write a caption for each picture, using the Vocabulary Word. Students then exchange drawings and captions and try to match each caption with the correct picture. Some words, such as *skillful*, *pride*, *arranged*, might lend themselves to a series of illustrations that relate to one topic. Students should write the caption for each picture in the series on a separate strip of paper.

Vocabulary Words

canyon a narrow valley with steep sides

pride a feeling of happiness and satisfaction about doing something well

swiftly very quickly

skillful showing skill; showing a talent for doing something well

feast a special celebration with a large amount of food

gazing looking with a long, steady stare

arranged put in some kind of order

FLUENCY BUILDER Using *Intervention Practice Book* page 67, read each word in the first column aloud and have students repeat it. Then have students work in pairs to read the words in the first column aloud to each other. Follow the same procedure with each of the remaining columns. After partners have practiced reading aloud the words in each column, have them listen to each other as they practice the entire list.

INTERVENTION PRACTICE BOOK

page 67

BEFORE

Reading "Coyote Places the Stars" *pages 38–50*

USE SKILL CARD 17A

★ Focus Skill **Compare and Contrast**

PRETEACH **the skill.** Hold up two sheets of paper of different sizes and colors. Ask students how these two objects are alike. (*both are paper; used to write or draw on*) Tell students that they have just compared two things. Then ask how they are different. (*size, color*) Tell students that now they have contrasted the two papers. Have students look at **side A of Skill Card 17: Compare and Contrast**. Read aloud and discuss the definitions. Call attention to the pictures, and have students compare and contrast the two fish. Read aloud the statement about the Venn diagram, and then have students look at the diagram and read aloud the information in it. Point out that the part of the diagram where the two ovals overlap shows how the fish are alike, while the separate parts of the ovals show how the fish are different.

Prepare to Read: "Coyote Places the Stars"

Preview. Tell students that they are going to read a Native American tale called "Coyote Places the Stars." Explain that a tale is a story that has been told over and over and passed down through time. Some tales, including "Coyote Places the Stars," tell how something in nature came to be the way it is. Then preview the selection.

ON YOUR MARK
pages 38–50

- **Pages 38–39:** I see the title, "Coyote Places the Stars." Under it I see that this tale is retold and illustrated by Harriet Peck Taylor. I know that the storyteller is retelling a tale first told by Native Americans long ago. In the picture I see Coyote looking up at the moon and stars.

- **Pages 40–41:** Here I see Coyote in the daytime. He looks like he is having fun chasing a butterfly. The scene is painted in bright, happy colors.

- **Page 42–43:** On pages 42–43 Coyote looks like he is standing on the moon in the night sky. He has a bow and arrows. I see stars in the sky, with arrows hitting some of them. I think Coyote must have shot the arrows. I wonder why. I think it will be fun to read about Coyote and the stars.

Set Purpose. Model setting a purpose for reading "Coyote Places the Stars."

MODEL From my preview I think that Coyote will be an interesting character to read about. I know that one purpose for reading is to enjoy a story. I will enjoy reading to find out why Coyote shoots arrows at the stars.

Reread and Summarize

Have students reread and summarize "Coyote Places the Stars" in sections, as described below.

Pages 40–41

Let's reread pages 40–41 to recall how Coyote gets to the moon.

Summary: Coyote shoots arrows from his bow to make a ladder to the moon.

Pages 42–43

Now let's reread pages 42–43 to find out how Coyote places the stars.

Summary: Coyote shoots arrows at the stars to move them around. He makes pictures of all his animal friends.

Pages 44–47

As we reread pages 44–47, let's see why Coyote calls the animals.

Summary: Coyote calls all the animals to come and see the star pictures he has made of them.

Pages 48–50

Let's reread pages 48–50 to recall what the animals do.

Summary: The animals give a feast for Coyote. To this day, you can see the star pictures that Coyote made.

FLUENCY BUILDER Use *Intervention Practice Book* page 67. Point out the sentences on the bottom half of the page. Remind students that their goal is to read each phrase or unit smoothly. Model appropriate pace, expression, and phrasing as you read each sentence, and have students read it after you. Then have students practice by reading the sentences aloud three times to a partner.

INTERVENTION PRACTICE BOOK

page 67

Directed Reading: "Many Moons Ago" pp. 134–140

Page 134

Have students read the title of the tale aloud. Then have them read page 134 to find out why it was dark all the time. (*because a mean man kept the sun, moon, and stars hidden in three bags*) Ask: **How does the author contrast animals in those days with animals today?** (*Animals then could sing and tell stories. Some could play tricks.*)

**Bright
Surprises**
pp. 134–140

(Focus Skill) **COMPARE AND CONTRAST**

Pages 135–136

Have students read pages 135–136 to find out about Raven's plan. Ask: **Why do you think Raven pretends to be a baby?** (*It is part of his plan to get the sun, moon, and stars back so it won't be dark all the time.*) **CHARACTERS' MOTIVATIONS**

Pages 137–138

Ask students to read pages 137–138 to find out what Raven does to carry out his plan. Model the strategy of summarizing.

> **MODEL** Raven cries until the man gives him the bag of stars. Raven opens the bag, and the stars go up in the sky. Raven cries some more, and the man gives him another bag. Raven lets the moon out of the bag, and then he cries some more.
> (Focus Strategy) **SUMMARIZE**

Ask: **What do you think will happen next?** (Possible response: *The man will give Raven the third bag, and Raven will let the sun out.*) **MAKE PREDICTIONS**

Page 139

Have students read page 139 to confirm their predictions. Ask: **Why is Raven proud?** (*because he put the stars, moon, and sun back in the sky where they belong*) **CHARACTERS' EMOTIONS**

**INTERVENTION
PRACTICE
BOOK**

page 69

What things in nature does this story explain? (Accept reasonable responses.) **STORY EVENTS**

Summarize the selection. Have pairs of students make a movie poster for the story. Have them illustrate their favorite part of the story and write a brief plot summary underneath.

Answers to *Think About It* Questions

1. Raven tricked the man and woman into giving him the stars, the moon, and the sun. He put them into the sky so that everyone could have heat and light. **SUMMARY**

2. Possible response: Raven wanted the man and woman to keep trying to find a way to make him happy, such as giving him the bags. **INTERPRETATION**

3. Before students begin drawing, remind them to look for details in the selection that describe the two scenes. Encourage them to check their sentences for proper capitalization and punctuation. **DRAW PICTURES/WRITE SENTENCES**

AFTER

Skill Review
pages 58–59

USE SKILL CARD 17B

(Focus Skill) Compare and Contrast

RETEACH **the skill.** Have students look at **side B of Skill Card 17: Compare and Contrast**. Read aloud and discuss the skill reminder with them. Have students identify the pictures and read the directions. You may wish to draw the Venn diagram on the board and fill it in as a group as students compare and contrast the carrot and the lettuce. (Possible responses: *Carrot: orange, long and thin*; *Lettuce: green, round and full*; *Both: vegetables, good to eat*)

FLUENCY BUILDER Be sure students have copies of *Intervention Practice Book* page 67. Explain that today students will practice the sentences on the bottom half of the page by reading them aloud on tape. Assign new partners. Have students take turns reading the sentences aloud to each other and then reading them on tape. After they listen to the tape, have them tell how they think they have improved their reading of the sentences. Then have them read the sentences aloud on tape a second time, with improved pacing and tone.

INTERVENTION PRACTICE BOOK

page 67

Expository Writing: Sentences that Contrast

Build on prior knowledge. Have students recall that they contrast when they tell how things are different from each other. Tell students that they are going to write sentences that contrast a bear and a rabbit.

Display a graphic organizer like the one shown here.

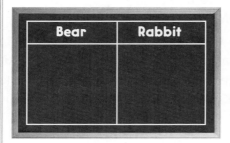

Bear	Rabbit

Construct the text. "Share the pen" with students in a collaborative group writing effort. As students dictate words and phrases, write them in the graphic organizer, guiding the process by asking questions and offering suggestions as needed.

- Have students list specific differences between bears and rabbits, such as large and small size and small and long ears.

- Help students use the information in their graphic organizer to construct several sentences that contrast the two animals.

Revisit the text. With students, reread the sentences you wrote. Ask: **Do our sentences clearly state how the two animals are different from each other?**

- Point out that using a variety of sentence types makes writing more interesting. Ask: **Can we make some of our sentences longer or shorter, or use different kinds of sentences?**

- Ask: **Have we used adjectives that tell what kind to describe color, shape, and size?**

- After revising, have students read the sentences aloud.

On Your Own

Think of two objects that are different colors, shapes, or sizes. List ways that they are different. Then use your list to write sentences that contrast the two objects.

Connect Spelling and Phonics

RETEACH long vowel /ē/ee, ea. Tell students that you will say some words in which the letters *ee* stand for the long *e* vowel sound. Have volunteers write each word on the board. Work together to proofread their work.

I. three*	2. sleep*	3. need	4. feel*
5. feed*	6. deepest*	7. tree	8. jeep

*Word appears in "Many Moons Ago."

Tell students that the letters *ea* stand for the long *e* vowel sound in the following sentence. Dictate the sentence, and have students write it: *In my dream I sit by a stream.*

Build and Read Longer Words

Remind students that they have learned that the letters *ee* and *ea* can stand for the /ē/ sound. Now they will use what they have learned to help them read some longer words.

Write the word *dreaming* on the board. Remind students that they can read longer words by looking for familiar word parts that they know. Cover *-ing* and identify the CVVC pattern in *dream*. Ask students to identify the letters that stand for the long *e* vowel sound. Uncover the whole word, and have students blend the word parts to form the word *dreaming*. Use similar strategies to help students decode the words *weekly*, *beeper*, *speaker*, *speedy*, and *beanbag*. Encourage students to build other long words in which the letters *ee* or *ea* stand for the long *e* vowel sound. Suggest that they use a dictionary to look up words they are not sure about.

INTERVENTION
ASSESSMENT
BOOK

FLUENCY BUILDER Have students choose a passage from "Many Moons Ago" to read aloud to a partner. You may have students choose passages that they found particularly interesting, or have them choose one of the following options:

- Read page I37. (Total: 93 words)
- Read page I38. (Total: 90 words)

Students read the selected passage aloud to their partners three times. Have students rate each of their own readings on a scale of I to 4. Encourage readers to note their improvement from one reading to the next by completing sentence frames such as *I know my reading improved because* _____. The partner who listens to the reading should also be encouraged to offer positive comments on the reader's improvement.

Review Vocabulary

To revisit the Vocabulary Words prior to the weekly assessment, have students demonstrate their understanding of the words by answering questions such as the following:

1. What might you notice if you were **gazing** up at the sky?
2. What animals do you know of that run **swiftly**?
3. What is something you would take **pride** in doing?
4. When have you **arranged** something? How and why did you do it?
5. What would you most like to eat at a **feast**?
6. Where might you see a **canyon**?
7. Tell about something you are **skillful** at.

Correct responses: Accept responses that reflect an understanding of the Vocabulary Words.

You may want to display the Vocabulary Words and definitions on page 169 and have students copy them to use when they study for the vocabulary test.

Review Compare and Contrast

To review the focus skill before the weekly assessment, distribute *Intervention Practice Book* page 70. Point out the title, Compare and Contrast, and read the directions to students. Call attention to the pictures, and have students tell what each shows. You may choose to guide students through the page, or have them work independently and then share and explain their work.

INTERVENTION PRACTICE BOOK

page 70

Review Test Prep

Ask students to turn to page 59 of the *Pupil Edition*. Call attention to the tips for answering the test questions. Tell students that paying attention to these tips can help them answer not only the test questions on this page but also other test questions like these.

ON YOUR MARK

page 59

Have a volunteer read the paragraph aloud. Read aloud the directions and then have students follow along as you read the first test item and the tip that goes with it. Have students identify the correct choice and explain how they figured it out. Follow a similar procedure with the second item. Encourage students to tell how they might apply the tips on this page in other test situations as well.

INTERVENTION ASSESSMENT BOOK

Self-Selected Reading

Have students select their own books to read
independently. They might choose books from the
classroom library shelf, or you may wish to offer a
group of appropriate books from which students can
choose. Titles might include the following:

- *Phaeton and the Chariot of the Sun.* (See
  page 59M of the *Teacher's Edition* for a
  lesson plan.)

- *Dogs in Space* by Nancy Coffelt. Harcourt
  Brace, 1993.

- *We Got Here Together* by Kim R. Stafford.
  Harcourt Brace, 1987.

After students have chosen their books, give each
student a copy of My Reading Log, which can be
found on page R42 in the back of the *Teacher's
Edition*. Have students fill in the information at the
top of the form. Then have them use the log to
keep track of their reading and to record their
responses to the literature.

Conduct student-teacher conferences. Arrange time for each student to
confer with you individually about his or her self-selected reading. Have
students bring their Reading Logs to share with you at the conference.
Students might also like to choose a favorite passage to read aloud to you.
Ask questions about the book to stimulate discussion. For example, you
might ask the student to compare and contrast the characters, setting, or
plot of a story with others in a story that he or she has read.

FLUENCY PERFORMANCE Have students read aloud to you
the passage from "Many Moons Ago" that they selected and practiced
earlier with their partners. Keep track of the number of words each
student reads correctly. Ask the student to rate his or her own performance on the 1–4 scale. If students are not happy with their oral reading,
give them an opportunity to continue practicing and then to reread the
passage to you again.

See *Oral Reading Fluency Assessment* for monitoring progress.

Use with

"Why Mosquitoes Buzz in People's Ears"

Review Phonics: Long Vowel /ā/ai, ay

Identify the sound. Tell students to listen for the /ā/ sound as you say the words *mail* and *day*. Then have students repeat this sentence three times: *Ray may play on the trail in the rain.* Ask them to identify the words that have the /ā/ sound they hear in *mail* and *day*. (*Ray, may, play, trail, rain*)

Associate letters to sound. Write on the board *Ray may play on the trail in the rain.* Underline *ay* in *Ray, may,* and *play,* and tell students that the letters *ay* together in a word usually stand for the long *a* vowel sound. Follow a similar procedure with *ai* in *trail* and *rain.* Point out the CVVC pattern, and remind students that two vowels that come together in a word often stand for a long vowel sound. Then have students read the sentence aloud.

Word blending. Have students repeat after you as you model how to blend the word *rain.* Slide your hand under the letters *rai* as you elongate the sounds /rrāā/. Next, point to the letter *n* and say /n/. Slide your hand under the whole word, elongating all the sounds /rrāānn/, and then say the word naturally—*rain.*

INTERVENTION
PRACTICE
BOOK

page 72

Apply the skill. *Letter Substitution* Write the following words on the board, and have students read them aloud. Make the changes necessary to form the words in parentheses. Have students read each new word.

we (way)	**see** (say)	**plow** (play)	**how** (hay)
grin (grain)	**man** (main)	**pal** (pail)	**now** (nail)

Introduce Vocabulary

PRETEACH **lesson vocabulary.** Tell students that they are going to learn six new words that they will see again when they read a selection called "Why Mosquitoes Buzz in People's Ears." Teach each Vocabulary Word, using the process shown at the right.

Use the following suggestions or similar ideas to give the meaning or context.

satisfied	Have students smile to show they are satisfied.
duty	Give examples, such as a mail carrier's duty to deliver the mail.
council	Relate to meetings of town or city officials.
mischief	Give examples of mischief in school, such as hiding another student's belongings.

> Write the word.
> Say the word.
> Track the word and have students repeat it.
> Give the meaning or context.

nonsense Point out the word *sense* and the prefix *non-* , meaning "no."

tidbit Point out the word *bit*. Relate to the idea of a little bit or tiny bit of something.

For vocabulary activities, see Vocabulary Games on pp. 2–7.

Vocabulary Words

satisfied having one's needs or desires fulfilled

duty job or responsibility

council meeting called to find answers

mischief behavior that causes problems for others

nonsense words or ideas that are foolish and have no real meaning

tidbit small piece of something

AFTER

Building Background and Vocabulary

Apply Vocabulary Strategies

Use syllabication. Write the word *nonsense* on the board. Remind students that they can sometimes figure out how to pronounce a word by dividing it into syllables. Model using the strategy.

MODEL **I see the consonants *ns* between the vowels *o* and *e*. I know that I can divide a word into syllables between two consonants: *non-sense*. In the first syllable I see the CVC pattern. I know that the vowel in a syllable with this pattern has the short vowel sound, so this is pronounced /non/. When I cover up this syllable, I see the familiar word *sense*. I then look at the entire word and blend the syllables to say it.**

Guide students in using a similar procedure to decode the words *tidbit* and *council*, pointing out the vowel pair *ou* and the /s/ spelled with a *c* in *council*. Then model dividing *duty* into syllables, first dividing between *t* and *y* and trying the short *u* sound. Point out that this does not sound like a word that makes sense. Then divide the word correctly, and use the long *u* sound to pronounce it.

RETEACH **lesson vocabulary.** Have students use word cards and sorting pockets to sort the Vocabulary Words in different ways. For example, have them sort the words into nouns and adjectives and share their results. (All are nouns except for *satisfied*.) Then have them sort by the number of syllables in each word and again share their results. (All have two syllables except for *satisfied*.)

FLUENCY BUILDER Use *Intervention Practice Book* page 71. Read each word in the first column aloud and have students repeat it. Then have students work in pairs to read the words in the first column aloud to each other. Follow the same procedure with each of the remaining columns. After partners have practiced reading aloud the words in each column, have them listen to each other as they practice the entire list.

⭐(Focus Skill) Summarize

PRETEACH the skill. Remind students that summarizing is a way of retelling a story. Have them look at **side A of Skill Card 18: Summarize** and read the sentence about the web. Ask volunteers to read aloud and explain the items in the web. Then call attention to the picture and caption at the bottom of the card. Have a student read the caption aloud. Discuss how, when, and why students might summarize. Point out that a summary can be oral or written.

Prepare to Read: "Why Mosquitoes Buzz in People's Ears"

Preview. Tell students that they are going to read a folktale from Africa called "Why Mosquitoes Buzz in People's Ears." Remind them that a folktale is a story from long ago. Its main purpose is to entertain, but it may also teach a lesson. Then do a preview.

ON YOUR MARK
pp. 62–82

- **Pages 62–63:** On these pages, I see the title and subtitle. The words *retold by* before the author's name tell me that Verna Aardema is writing down a tale that has been told many times before. The pictures are by Leo and Diane Dillon. On page 63 I see a mosquito buzzing in a person's ear, as in the story title.

- **Pages 64–67:** The story begins on page 65 with the words ONE MORNING. I will read the first paragraph to see if I can find out what the story is about. On page 64, the mosquito is talking to an iguana with its foot over its ear, as if it doesn't want to listen. Across both pages is an unhappy iguana with two sticks coming out of its head. I wonder why the sticks are there.

- **Pages 66–67:** These pages show a snake, the iguana, a rabbit, and some birds. This story seems to have a variety of animal characters.

- **Pages 68–69:** On page 68 a big owl is holding a baby owl. The round red face behind it must be the sun. On page 69, the sun gets smaller and lower, as if it is setting. The little animals in the bottom corner of page 69 look sad and scared. I wonder why.

- **Pages 70–71:** A lot of different animals seem to be talking about something. The background is black, like night.

Set purpose. Model setting a purpose for reading "Why Mosquitoes Buzz in People's Ears."

MODEL From my preview, I know that this story begins with a mosquito saying something to an iguana. Then it tells about many other animals. I think something happens to upset the animals. My purpose for reading will be to find out what this is and how this folktale explains why mosquitoes buzz in people's ears.

Reread and Summarize

Have students reread and summarize "Why Mosquitoes Buzz in People's Ears" in sections, as described in the chart below.

Pages 64–65

Let's reread pages 64–65 to recall how the trouble begins.

Summary: The iguana puts sticks in his ears so he doesn't have to hear the mosquito's silly story.

Pages 66–69

Now let's reread pages 66–69 to find out what happens after the iguana puts the sticks in his ears.

Summary: The python is upset when the iguana doesn't answer him. This starts a series of events that results in the death of an owlet. Mother Owl is too sad to wake the sun, so the night cannot end.

Pages 70–77

As we reread pages 70–77, let's see how the animals try to solve their problem.

Summary: King Lion calls a meeting. Mother Owl says she won't wake the sun because the monkey killed her owlet, but each animal says it was another's fault.

Pages 78–82

Let's reread pages 78–82 to recall why mosquitoes buzz in people's ears.

Summary: The iguana explains that the mosquito started the whole thing by annoying him. Mother Owl is satisfied and hoots for the sun to come up. The mosquito hides, but she still buzzes in people's ears because she has a guilty conscience.

FLUENCY BUILDER Use *Intervention Practice Book* page 71.
Point out the sentences on the bottom half of the page. Remind students to pay attention to the slashes and to read each phrase or unit smoothly. Model appropriate pace, expression, and phrasing as you read each sentence, and have students read it after you. Then have students practice by reading the sentences aloud three times to a partner.

INTERVENTION PRACTICE BOOK
page 71

Directed Reading: "Grandpa Tells Why," pp. 142–149

BRIGHT SURPRISES
pp. 142–149

Page 142

Have students read the title of the story aloud. Point out the main characters in the illustration. Then ask students to read page 142 to find out what the characters are talking about. Ask: **Why do the animals need to have a meeting?** (*There was no rain, so there was no food on the plains. The animals were hungry.*) **CAUSE AND EFFECT/ CHARACTERS' MOTIVATIONS**

Page 143

Have students read page 143 to find out where the animals go and what they find. Ask: **What happens in this part of the story?** (*The animals go over the plains. They find a tree with good things to eat, but they cannot reach the branches. Grandpa Turtle says the tree will let them eat when they say its name.*) (Focus Skill) **SUMMARIZE**

Pages 144–145

Have students read pages 144–145 to find out whether the animals learn the tree's name. Ask: **Why do Gray Rabbit and Long-Tail Snake forget the name that the king tells them?** (*Possible response: because they both fall in a hole on the way back*) **DRAW CONCLUSIONS**

Ask: **Who will go next?** Model using the strategy of making and confirming predictions.

> **MODEL** I remember that the animals have three leaders. Two of them have already gone to the king. I predict that now Grandpa Turtle will go. (Focus Strategy) **MAKE AND CONFIRM PREDICTIONS**

Page 146

Have students read page 146 to confirm their prediction. Ask: **Do you think Grandpa Turtle will forget the name?** (*Accept reasonable responses.*) **MAKE PREDICTIONS**

Pages 147–148

Have students read pages 147–148 to confirm their prediction and to learn what happens when Grandpa Turtle returns. Ask: **What happens after the animals say the tree's name?** (*The tree bends down and puts food on the ground.*) **SEQUENCE**

Why do you think the tree's name is Please-May-We? (*Accept reasonable responses.*) **MAKE JUDGMENTS**

Summarize the selection. Ask students to think about what happened first, next, and last in "Grandpa Tells Why" and to summarize the story in four sentences. Then have them complete *Intervention Practice Book* page 73.

INTERVENTION PRACTICE BOOK

page 73

Answers to *Think About It* Questions

1. Gray Rabbit and Long-Tail Snake forget the name of the tree. Grandpa Turtle does not forget its name. The animals say the name three times, and the tree gives them food. **SUMMARY**

2. Possible response: The king is a big, strong animal, and he is angry. They are scared that the king will eat them. **INTERPRETATION**

3. To compare and contrast, students may use a simple chart, with one column for each character. **MAKE A CHART**

AFTER

Skill Review
pages 92–93

USE SKILL CARD 18B

(Focus Skill) **Summarize**

RETEACH the skill. Have students look at **side B of Skill Card 18: Summarize.** Read the skill reminder and the directions at the top of the card with them.

Have a student reread page 142 of "Grandpa Tells Why" aloud as the others follow along in their books. Ask volunteers to read aloud each of the three summaries on the skill card. Then tell students to reread Summary 1 silently, decide whether or not it is a good summary, and explain why or why not. (*Possible response: It is not a good summary because it is too long, includes unimportant details, and uses the same words as the story.*)

Follow the same procedure with Summary 2 and then with Summary 3. Students should note that Summary 2 tells the most important events, while Summary 3 leaves out important information and gives the reader's own opinion. On the basis of their discussion, students should determine that Summary 2 is the best summary.

Read the direction line at the bottom of the card with students. After they have written their summaries, have them share and discuss their work.

FLUENCY BUILDER Use *Intervention Practice Book* page 71. Explain that students will practice the sentences on the bottom half of the page by reading them aloud on tape. Assign new partners. Have students take turns reading the sentences aloud to each other and then reading them on tape. After they listen to the tape, have them tell how they think they have improved their reading of the sentences. Then have them read the sentences aloud on tape a second time, with improved pacing and tone.

> **INTERVENTION PRACTICE BOOK**
> page 71

Expository Writing: Paragraph That Explains

Build on prior knowledge. Remind students that in "Grandpa Tells Why," Grandpa Turtle explains to the other animals how they can get food from the tree and how they can find out the tree's name. Tell students that they are going to write a paragraph that explains something about a real tree.

Have students name parts of a tree and give facts and details about each part. Jot down their ideas in a graphic organizer like the one shown here.

Parts of a Tree	Facts and Details
trunk	main part of tree; covered with bark
branches	grow out of trunk
leaves	fall off in autumn; grow again in spring
roots	under the ground

Construct the text. "Share the pen" with students in a collaborative group writing effort. As you write the words and phrases dictated by students, guide the process by asking questions and offering suggestions as needed. Work with students in using the information in the graphic organizer to write a paragraph that explains.

- Help students develop an opening sentence that introduces the topic and another sentence that explains the main idea.

- Then guide students to compose sentences that add facts, examples, and details to explain the main idea. Remind them that they need to put their ideas in an order that makes sense.

- Work with students to write a concluding sentence that restates the main idea in different words.

Revisit the text. As students revise the paragraph, encourage them to look for ways to make their sentences more effective. If appropriate, point out ways to incorporate adjectives for how many.

- Have students read the completed paragraph aloud.

On Your Own

Choose a fruit or vegetable that you like. Write a paragraph that explains something interesting about the fruit or vegetable, such as where it grows, what it looks like, or different ways it is prepared and served.

Connect Spelling and Phonics

RETEACH **long vowel /ā/ *ai, ay.*** Tell students that you will say some words in which the letters *ai* stand for the long *a* sound. Have volunteers write each word on the board. Work together to proofread their work.

I. rains*	2. plains*	3. grain*	4. tail*
5. laid*	6. snail	7. waited*	8. afraid*

*Word appears in "Grandpa Tells Why."

Tell students that you will dictate a sentence in which the letters *ay* stand for the long *a* vowel sound. Dictate the sentence, and have students write it: *May I stay and play with Ray?*

Build and Read Longer Words

Remind students that they have learned that the letters *ai* and *ay* can stand for the /ā/ sound. Now they will use what they have learned to help them read some longer words.

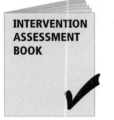

Write the word *haystack* on the board. Remind students that they can read longer words by looking for word parts that they know or by dividing the word into syllables. Cover *hay* and ask a volunteer to identify the shorter word *stack*. Then uncover *hay* and cover *stack*. Remind students that they can use what they have learned about letters and sounds to help them read this shorter word. Uncover the whole word and have students pronounce it. Use appropriate strategies to help students decode the words *raindrop, mayor, strainer, plainly, playmate, trailer, and trailblazer.* Encourage students to build other long words in which the letters *ai* or *ay* stand for the long *a* vowel sound. Suggest that they use a dictionary to look up words they are not sure about.

INTERVENTION
ASSESSMENT
BOOK

FLUENCY BUILDER Have students choose a passage from "Grandpa Tells Why" to read aloud to a partner. You may have students choose passages that they found particularly interesting, or have them choose one of the following options:

- Read page 142. (Total: 101 words)
- Read page 145. (Total: 90 words)

Students read the selected passage aloud to their partners three times. Have students rate each of their own readings on a scale of I to 4. Encourage readers to note their improvement from one reading to the next by completing sentence frames such as *I know my reading improved because* _____ . The partner who listens to the reading should also be encouraged to offer positive comments on the reader's improvement.

Review Vocabulary

To revisit Vocabulary Words with students prior to the weekly assessment, display or read aloud the following sentences. Have students tell whether each statement is true or false and explain why.

1. People are **satisfied** when they lose things that are important to them.
2. One **duty** of a firefighter is to check hoses and other equipment.
3. You might go to a **council** to enjoy the music.
4. Getting into **mischief** will not please your parents.
5. If you want others to understand you, speak **nonsense**.
6. Someone who is not very hungry might eat only a **tidbit**.

You may want to display the Vocabulary Words and definitions on page 179 and have students copy them to use when they study for the vocabulary test.

Review Summarize

To review the focus skill before the weekly assessment, distribute *Intervention Practice Book* page 74. Point out the title, Summarize, and have a student read aloud the directions. Review briefly what students have learned about what to include in a summary. Then have them read the story and identify important information and unimportant details. Tell students to write on the lines a short summary of the story in their own words. Have them share and discuss their summaries.

INTERVENTION PRACTICE BOOK
page 74

Review Test Prep

Ask students to turn to page 93 of the *Pupil Edition*. Call attention to the tips for answering the test questions. Tell students that paying attention to these tips can help them answer not only the test questions on this page but also other test questions like these.

ON YOUR MARK
p. 93

Have a volunteer read the story aloud. Then have students follow along as you read aloud the first test question and the tip that goes with it. Ask volunteers to tell whether each choice is an important idea or an unimportant detail. Have students identify the choice that belongs in a good summary. Then have a student read aloud the second test item and the tip that goes with it. Remind students that they should think about what they have learned about writing a summary before they begin writing their answers to a test question like this one. Encourage students to tell how they might apply the tips on this page in other test situations.

INTERVENTION ASSESSMENT BOOK

Self-Selected Reading

Have students select their own books to read independently. They might choose books from the classroom library shelf, or you may wish to offer a group of appropriate books from which students can choose. Titles might include the following:

- *The World Next Door*. (See page 93M of the *Teacher's Edition* for a lesson plan.)

- *Noisy Nora* by Rosemary Wells. Penguin Putnam, 2000.

- *Handtalk Zoo* by George Ancona and Mary Beth Miller. Aladdin, 1996.

You may also wish to choose additional books that are of the same genre, that are by the same author, or that have the same kind of text structure as the selection.

After students have chosen their books, give each student a copy of My Reading Log, which can be found on page R42 in the back of the *Teacher's Edition*. Have students fill in the information at the top of the form. Then have them use the log to keep track of their reading and to record their responses to the literature.

Conduct student-teacher conferences. Arrange time for each student to confer with you individually about his or her self-selected reading. Have students bring their Reading Logs to share with you at the conference. Students might also like to choose a favorite passage to read aloud to you. Ask questions designed to stimulate discussion about the book. For example, you might ask how the author structured the text or how illustrations or diagrams helped the student understand the topic.

FLUENCY PERFORMANCE Have students read aloud to you the passage from "Grandpa Tells Why" that they selected and practiced earlier with their partners. Keep track of the number of words the student reads correctly. Ask the student to rate his or her own performance on the 1–4 scale. If students are not happy with their oral reading, give them an opportunity to continue practicing and then to reread the passage to you.

See *Oral Reading Fluency Assessment* for monitoring progress.

Use with

"Lon Po Po"

Review Phonics: Long Vowel /ō/oa, oe, ow

Identify the sound. Tell students to listen for the /ō/ sound as you say the words *coat*, *hoe*, and *show*. Then have them repeat three times: *Mom and Joe will row home in the boat*. Ask students to identify the words with the /ō/ sound. (*Joe, row, home, boat*)

Associate letters to sound. Write on the board: *Mom and Joe will row home in the boat*. Point out the CVC pattern and short vowel sound in *Mom*. Then point out the CVCe pattern and long vowel sound in *home*. Underline *oe*, *ow*, and *oa* in *Joe*, *row*, and *boat*. Tell students that the letters *oe*, *ow*, and *oa* can stand for the /ō/ sound they hear in *toad*.

Word blending. Have students repeat after you as you model how to blend the word *boat*. Slide your hand under the letters *boa* as you elongate the sounds /bbōō/. Next, point to the letter *t* and say /t/. Slide your hand again, elongating /bbōōtt/, and then say the word naturally—*boat*.

Apply the skill. *Letter Substitution* Write these words on the board, and have students read each aloud. Make the changes necessary to form the word in parentheses. Have a volunteer read aloud each new word.

**INTERVENTION
PRACTICE
BOOK**

page 76

got (goat)	**tea** (toe)	**gray** (grow)	**cot** (coat)
rod (road)	**hay** (hoe)	**me** (mow)	**flat** (float)

Introduce Vocabulary

PRETEACH **lesson vocabulary.** Tell students that they are going to learn seven new words that they will see again when they read a selection called "Lon Po Po." Teach each Vocabulary Word using the following process.

Use these suggestions or similar ideas to give the meaning or context.

> Write the word.
> Say the word.
> Track the word and have students repeat it.
> Give the meaning or context.

delighted   Have two students role-play, one extending an invitation to the other, who looks delighted.

dusk   Explain that this is the time in the evening just before it gets dark.

embraced   Explain that to embrace is to hug. Point out the *-ed* ending that shows past action.

latch   Close the classroom door and pretend to slide a bar in a latch.

tender	Give examples of tender things, such as cooked vegetables.
brittle	Give examples of things that are brittle, such as a clay pot.
cunning	Give examples of folktale characters who are cunning, such as the wolf in "Little Red Riding Hood."

For vocabulary activities, see Vocabulary Games on pages 2–7.

For vocabulary activities, see Vocabulary Games on pages 2–7.

AFTER

Building Background and Vocabulary

Vocabulary Words

delighted very happy

dusk the time in the evening just before it gets dark

embraced hugged

latch to close a door with a movable bar that fits into a slot

tender easy to chew, soft

brittle easily broken or snapped

cunning able to fool or trick; sly or clever

Apply Vocabulary Strategies

Identify multiple-meaning words. Write on the board: *He locked the door with the latch. Please latch the door after I leave.* Tell students that when a word has more than one meaning, they can often figure out the meaning from the way the word is used. Model using the strategy.

> **MODEL** I notice that the first sentence uses the word *latch* as a noun, but the second one uses it as a verb. This word must have more than one meaning. I know that a latch is a thing—a movable bar of wood or metal that slides into a slot. That meaning makes sense in the first sentence. Since *latch* is an action in the second sentence, it must also mean "to close or lock using a latch."

Guide students in using a similar procedure with the word *embrace*.

RETEACH lesson vocabulary. Provide patterns for a circle and an arrow. Have students make a simple spinner by cutting a circle and arrow from cardboard and joining them with a brad. Tell students to divide the spinner into sections and write a Vocabulary Word in each one. Students take turns spinning the spinner, saying the word the spinner lands on, and using the word in a sentence.

FLUENCY BUILDER Using *Intervention Practice Book* page 75, read each word in the first column aloud and have students repeat it. Then have students work in pairs to read the words in the first column aloud to each other. Follow the same procedure with each of the remaining columns. After partners have practiced reading aloud the words in each column, have them listen to each other as they practice the entire list.

INTERVENTION PRACTICE BOOK

page 75

BEFORE

Reading "Lon Po Po"
pages 96–112

USE SKILL CARD 19A

Focus Skill Compare and Contrast

PRETEACH the skill. Remind students that we compare when we tell how things are alike and that we contrast when we tell how things are different. Have them look at the pictures on **side A of Skill Card 19: Compare and Contrast**. Help students briefly recall details about the characters, setting, and plot of "Little Red Riding Hood" and then of "Goldilocks." Next, read aloud the sentences that tell about the Venn diagram. Read and discuss with students the items in the diagram.

Prepare to Read: "Lon Po Po"

ON YOUR MARK
pages 96–112

Preview. Tell students that they are going to read a folktale called "Lon Po Po." Explain that a folktale is a story that has been passed down through time. No one knows who first told the story, but it is often retold in different forms or versions. Then preview the selection.

- **Pages 96–97:** Under the title I see a smaller title, or subtitle. It says that this is a Red Riding Hood story from China. It was translated and illustrated by Ed Young. In the picture, three girls are waving good-bye to a woman who seems to be leaving on a journey. I think that this story will be different from the "Little Red Riding Hood" story that I know.
- **Pages 98–99:** Here I see the three girls in the dark. One is holding up a candle. I wonder what she is trying to see.
- **Pages 100–101:** In this picture the three girls are in bed. There is also a wolf in the bed. The wolf is wearing a nightcap. I wonder if this wolf is pretending to be the girls' grandmother, the way the wolf does in "Little Red Riding Hood." It will be fun to read this story to see what happens to the three girls.

Set purpose. Model setting a purpose for reading "Lon Po Po."

MODEL **From my preview, I know that this story is a folktale from China. It tells a story that is like "Little Red Riding Hood." One purpose for reading stories is to enjoy them. I will read to enjoy finding out how this story is like "Little Red Riding Hood" and how it is different.**

Reread and Summarize

Have students reread and summarize "Lon Po Po" in sections, as described below.

Pages 97–99

Let's reread pages 97–99 to recall how the wolf gets into the house.

Summary: The children's mother tells them to latch the door, but the wolf tricks them into opening it by pretending to be their grandmother.

Pages 100–103

Now let's reread pages 100–103 to find out how Shang figures out who the wolf is and what she does then.

Summary: Shang feels the wolf's tail and claws, and she sees his hairy face. She tells him that she and her sisters will get him some gingko nuts. They go outside and climb a tall tree.

Pages 104–108

As we reread pages 104–108, let's see what Shang's plan is.

Summary: Shang tells the wolf to sit in a basket and let her pull it up into the gingko tree. She lets go, and the wolf falls to the ground. Shang and Tao pull it higher and let the wolf fall again. Then the three sisters pull the basket all the way up.

Pages 109–112

Let's reread pages 109–112 to recall what happens to the wolf.

Summary: The sisters let the basket fall, and this time the wolf is dead. When their mother comes home, they tell her what happened.

FLUENCY BUILDER Use *Intervention Practice Book* page 75. Point out the sentences on the bottom half of the page. Remind students that their goal is to read each phrase or unit smoothly. Model appropriate pace, expression, and phrasing as you read each sentence, and have students read it after you. Then have students practice by reading the sentences aloud three times to a partner.

INTERVENTION PRACTICE BOOK

page 75

Directed Reading: "The Snow Baby" pp. 150–157

**BRIGHT
SURPRISES**
pp. 150–157

Pages 150-151

Have students read the title of the story aloud. Ask them to read pages 150–151 to find out what the farmer and his wife want. (*a baby of their own*) Ask: **What do you think the farmer will do? Why do you think so?** (*Accept reasonable responses.*) **MAKE PREDICTIONS**

Pages 152–153

Have students read pages 152–153 to find out what the farmer does and confirm their predictions. Remind them that summarizing, or briefly retelling the events of a story, can help readers understand the story. Model the strategy.

> **MODEL** I'll retell the most important events on these pages, using my own words: The farmer goes to climb the mountain. It is a terrible journey, but he keeps going because he does not want to fail his wife. (Focus Strategy) **SUMMARIZE**

Pages 154–155

Tell students to read pages 154–155 to find out what the farmer finds on the mountain. (*a baby girl*) Ask: **Why do the farmer and his wife call the baby Snowflake?** (*because the farmer found her in the snow*) **CAUSE/EFFECT**

What do the hopeful fellows hope? (*Each one hopes that Snowflake will marry him.*) **DRAW CONCLUSIONS**

Page 156

Have students read page 156 to find out what happens to Snowflake. Ask: **How does the snow show Snowflake the way home?** (*The coach and horses leave a trail in the snow that she follows back to her home.*) **STORY EVENTS**

**INTERVENTION
PRACTICE
BOOK**

page 77

How is Snowflake like Shang in "Lon Po Po"? How is she different from Shang? (*Possible responses: Both are clever and save themselves from bad situations. Snowflake is grown up, but Shang is a child. Shang has two sisters, but Snowflake has none.*) (Focus Skill) **COMPARE AND CONTRAST**

Summarize the selection. Ask students to briefly summarize the story. Remind them to tell only the most important events.

Answers to *Think About It* Questions

1. Possible response: Yes, because the baby was found in the snow and when the baby grew up, the snow helped her find her way home. **SUMMARY**

2. Possible responses: No, the journey was too dangerous. Yes, because he believed he had to save the baby. **INTERPRETATION**

3. Ask questions like the following to help students brainstorm ideas for the new ending: *How will Snowflake know that the young man is kind and gentle? Will the snow continue to be an important part of Snowflake's life?* **WRITE A STORY ENDING**

AFTER

Skill Review
pages 116–117

USE SKILL CARD 19B

(Focus Skill) **Compare and Contrast**

RETEACH the skill. Have students look at **side B of Skill Card 19: Compare and Contrast**. Read aloud and discuss the skill reminder with them. Have students read aloud "Little Miss Muffet" and "Meg and the Spider." Discuss how the characters, settings, and events in the two stories are alike and how they are different. Then read aloud the directions, and draw a Venn diagram on the board. Fill in the diagram as students suggest ideas based on their discussion. Have students draw and complete their own diagrams on their papers.

FLUENCY BUILDER Use *Intervention Practice Book* page 75. Explain that students will practice the sentences on the bottom half of the page by reading them aloud on tape. Assign new partners. Have students take turns reading the sentences aloud to each other and then reading them on tape. After they listen to the tape, have them tell how they think they have improved their reading of the sentences. Then have them read the sentences aloud on tape a second time, with improved pacing and tone.

INTERVENTION PRACTICE BOOK

page 75

Expository Writing: Sentences That Compare and Contrast

Have students recall how Snowflake finds her way back home at the end of "The Snow Baby." Then ask whether they recall how the children in the story "Hansel and Gretel" made a trail to follow. If necessary, tell students that Hansel dropped bread crumbs to make a trail so the children could find their way home, but the children got lost because birds ate the crumbs. Explain that students are going to write sentences that compare and contrast the story events at the end of "The Snow Baby" with the events from "Hansel and Gretel."

Display a Venn diagram like the one shown here.

The Snow Baby
The coach and horses leave a trail in the snow.
Snowflake gets home safely.

Both
Characters want to go home.

Hansel and Gretel
Hansel makes a trail of bread crumbs.
Birds eat the crumbs, so the children get lost.

Construct the text. "Share the pen" with students in a collaborative writing effort. Guide them in filling in the Venn diagram to compare and contrast the ending of "The Snow Baby" with similar events in "Hansel and Gretel." Possible responses are shown in the diagram.

- Help students use their responses in the part of the Venn diagram labeled "Both" to compose a sentence that compares the events in the two stories, or tells how they are alike. Write the sentence on the board.

- Similarly, have them use their responses in the rest of the diagram to compose one or more sentences that contrast the events, or tell how they are different.

Revisit the text. With students, go back and read the sentences that compare and contrast.

- Ask: **Have we stated clearly how the story events are alike and how they are different?**

- Ask: **Have we varied our sentences to make our writing more interesting?**

- Have students read the revised sentences aloud.

On Your Own

Think of two stories that have main characters who are alike in some ways and different in other ways. Write sentences that compare and contrast these two characters. Read your sentences to a partner.

Connect Spelling and Phonics

RETEACH **Long vowel /ō/oa, oe, ow.** Tell students that you will say some words in which the letters *oa* stand for the long *o* vowel sound. Have volunteers write each word on the board. Work together to proofread their work.

1. road*   2. coach*   3. groaned*   4. goats*
5. moaned*   6. cloak*   7. coat   8. roam

Word appears in "The Snow Baby."

Tell students that the letters *ow* stand for the long *o* vowel sound in the following sentence. Dictate the sentence, and have students write it: *I make a low throw in the show.*

Build and Read Longer Words

Remind students that they have learned that the letters *oa*, *oe*, and *ow* can stand for the /ō/ sound. Now they will use what they have learned to help them read some longer words.

Write the word *rowboat* on the board. Cover *boat* and ask students to read the smaller word *row*. Then cover *row* and have them read the smaller word *boat*. Uncover the whole word and have students blend the word parts to form the word *rowboat*. Similarly, use appropriate strategies to help students decode the words *tiptoe*, *raincoat*, *floating*, and *bowling*.

**INTERVENTION
ASSESSMENT
BOOK**

Encourage students to build other long words in which the letters *oa* stand for the long *o* vowel sound. Suggest that they use a dictionary to look up words they are not sure about.

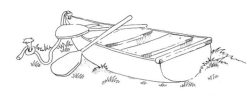

FLUENCY BUILDER Have students choose a passage from "The Snow Baby" to read aloud to a partner. You may have students choose passages that they found particularly interesting, or have them choose one of the following options:

- Read the last paragraph on page 150 and all of page 151. (From *Late one evening . . . .* Total: 116 words)

- Read the last paragraph on page 154 and all of page 155. (From *At last . . . .* Total: 97 words)

Students read the selected passage aloud to their partners three times. Have students rate each of their own readings on a scale of 1 to 4. Encourage readers to note their improvement from one reading to the next by completing sentence frames such as *I know my reading improved because* _____. The partner who listens to the reading should also be encouraged to offer positive comments on the reader's improvement.

Review Vocabulary

To revisit vocabulary words with students prior to the weekly assessment, display a word line like the one shown here.

least surprised _____ **most surprised**

Have students listen to the following questions and take turns indicating on the word line how surprised they would be. Ask them to explain why they would or would not be surprised in each instance. If needed, ask follow-up questions to check students' understanding of the Vocabulary Words.

How surprised would you be if . . .

1. you **latch** the gate and the dog gets out of the yard?
2. the sun rose at **dusk**?
3. a mother **embraced** her child?
4. a baseball fan was **delighted** to get tickets for a home game?
5. a raw carrot was **tender**?
6. a **cunning** character in a story pretends to be something she is not?
7. a baked potato was **brittle**?

Correct responses: Accept responses that reflect an understanding of the Vocabulary Words.

You may want to display the Vocabulary Words and definitions on page 189 and have students copy them to use when they study for the vocabulary test.

⭐ (Focus Skill) Review Compare and Contrast

**INTERVENTION
PRACTICE
BOOK**

page 78

To review the focus skill before the weekly assessment, distribute *Intervention Practice Book* page 78. Point out the title, Compare and Contrast, and read the directions with students. You may choose to guide students through the activity, or have them complete it independently and then share and explain their answers.

Review Test Prep

Ask students to turn to page 121 of the *Pupil Edition*. Call attention to the tips for answering the test questions. Tell students that paying attention to these tips can help them answer not only the test questions on this page but also other test questions like these.

ON YOUR MARK

page 121

**INTERVENTION
ASSESSMENT
BOOK**

✓

Ask volunteers to read the stories aloud. Then have students follow along as you read aloud the directions, the first test item, and the tip that goes with it. Have students identify the correct choice and tell how they figured it out. Follow a similar procedure with the second item. Encourage students to tell how they might apply the tips on this page in other test situations as well.

Self-Selected Reading

Have students select their own books to read independently. They might choose books from the classroom library shelf, or you may wish to offer a group of appropriate books from which students can choose.

- *Ella and Her Mean Cousins.* (See page 117K of the *Teacher's Edition* for a lesson plan.)
- *Busy Bea* by Nancy Poydar. Macmillan, 1994.
- *Jack's Garden* by Henry Cole. Greenwillow, 1995.

After students have chosen their books, give each student a copy of My Reading Log, which can be found on page R42 in the back of the *Teacher's Edition*. Have students fill in the information at the top of the form. Then have them use the log to keep track of their reading and to record their responses to the literature.

Conduct student-teacher conferences. Arrange time for each student to confer with you individually about his or her self-selected reading. Have students bring their Reading Logs to share with you at the conference. Students might also like to choose a favorite passage to read aloud to you. Ask questions about the book to stimulate discussion. For example, you might ask the student to compare and contrast the characters, setting, or plot of a story with others that he or she has read.

FLUENCY PERFORMANCE Have students read aloud to you the passage from "The Snow Baby" that they selected and practiced earlier with their partners. Keep track of the number of words the student reads correctly. Ask the student to rate his or her own performance on the 1–4 scale. If students are not happy with their oral reading, give them an opportunity to continue practicing and then to reread the passage to you again.

See *Oral Reading Fluency Assessment* for monitoring progress.

LESSON 20

BEFORE
Building Background and Vocabulary

Use with

"The Crowded House"

Review Phonics: Long Vowels /ē/*e*, /ī/*i*, /ō/*o*

Identify the sound. Tell students to listen for the long vowel sounds as you say *we*, *mind*, and *fold*. Then have them repeat twice: *She told me to go find that kind of old clock.* Ask students to identify the words with the long *e* sound they hear in *we*. Have students repeat the sentence. Ask them to identify the words with the long *i* sound they hear in *mind*. Follow a similar procedure for words with the long *o* sound.

Associate letters to sounds. Write on the board: *She told me to go find that kind of old clock.* Underline the *e* in *She* and *me*. Tell students that in words like *she* and *me*, *e* stands for the /ē/ sound. Underline the *o* in *told*, *go*, *old*. Point out that in words in which *o* comes at the end of a word or is followed by *ld*, the *o* often stands for the /ō/ sound. Underline the *i* in *find* and *kind*. Tell students that in words in which *i* is followed by *nd*, the *i* often stands for the /ī/ sound.

Word blending. Have students repeat after you as you model how to blend the word *told*. Point to the *t* and say /t/. Point to the *o* and say /ō/. Slide your hand under the *to* as you elongate the sounds /ttōō/. Point to the *l* and say /l/. Slide your hand under *tol*, as you elongate /ttōōll/. Point to *d* and say /d/. Slide your hand under the whole word, elongating /ttōōlld/, and then say the word naturally—*told*. Follow a similar procedure with *me* and *find*.

Apply the skill. *Vowel Substitution* Write the following words on the board, and have students read each aloud. Change as needed to form the word in parentheses. Have a volunteer read aloud each new word.

INTERVENTION PRACTICE BOOK

page 80

say (so)	**show** (she)	**mend** (mind)	**now** (no)
grand (grind)	**held** (hold)	**fund** (find)	**way** (we)

Introduce Vocabulary

PRETEACH **lesson vocabulary.** Tell students that they are going to learn six new words that they will see again when they read a selection called "The Crowded House." Teach each Vocabulary Word using the process shown at the right.

Use these or similar ideas to give the meaning or context.

wits   Give examples of when you need to keep your wits about you, such as in an emergency.

> Write the word.
> Say the word.
> Track the word and have students repeat it.
> Give the meaning or context.

wailing	Give examples of when one might hear wailing, such as at a time of great disappointment.
faring	Explain that asking how you are faring is the same as asking how you are getting along.
advice	Give advice on how to cross the street safely.
dreadful	Give examples of things students might consider dreadful, such as bad weather at a picnic.
farewell	Role-play saying good-bye, waving as you walk away.

For vocabulary activities, see Vocabulary Games on pages 2–7.

Vocabulary Words

wits mind, the ability to think

wailing (*noun*) a loud, long cry expressing unhappiness or pain

faring getting along

advice opinion about how to solve a problem

dreadful very bad

farewell good-bye

AFTER

Building Background and Vocabulary

Apply Vocabulary Strategies

Identify related words. Tell students that when words are related, they can often use the meaning of one word to figure out the meaning of the other. Write *fare*, *faring*, and *farewell* on the board and model using the strategy.

> **MODEL** I know that *fare* means "to get along." Although the *e* was dropped when the *-ing* ending was added, I see that same word in *faring*. This must be another form of *fare*. I've heard people say *farewell* when they leave, so from that experience and knowing what *fare* means, I can figure out that *farewell* means "good-bye and may you get on well."

Guide students in using a similar procedure with the word *wits*. (*witty*, *unwitting*)

RETEACH **lesson vocabulary.** Provide a set of word cards for each student or pair of students. Read aloud or write on the board the meaning of one of the Vocabulary Words and the first letter in that word. Students match the correct word card to the definition. Continue until students have matched all the words.

FLUENCY BUILDER Using *Intervention Practice Book* page 79, read each word in the first column aloud and have students repeat it. Then have students work in pairs to read the words in the first column aloud to each other. Follow the same procedure with each of the remaining columns. After partners have practiced reading aloud the words in each column, have them listen to each other as they practice the entire list.

INTERVENTION PRACTICE BOOK

page 79

(Focus Skill) Author's Purpose

PRETEACH **the skill.** Remind students that an author has a purpose for writing a book or an article. Knowing the author's purpose helps readers know what to expect and what to look for when they read. Have students look at **side A of Skill Card 20: Author's Purpose.** Read aloud the definition of author's purpose, and ask students to explain the small diagram at the top of the page. Then have volunteers read aloud the purposes shown on the large graphic. For each purpose, encourage students to give examples of books, articles, or other pieces of writing they have read. Provide additional examples as necessary.

Prepare to Read: "The Crowded House"

Preview. Tell students that they are going to read a play called "The Crowded House." Explain that a play is a story that can be performed for an audience and that when you read a play, you read a script that gives the names of the characters and the lines that each character speaks. Stage directions tell what the characters do or how they say their lines. The story is divided into parts, called scenes. After discussing the genre, preview the selection.

ON YOUR MARK
pages 120–135

- **Pages 120–121:** I see the title, "The Crowded House," and the names of the author and illustrator. On page 121 I see a list with the names of the characters in the play. There are a lot of characters. Maybe that's why the house is crowded. From the picture, I guess that the setting must be a farm.

- **Pages 122–123:** At the top of page 122, I see the heading Scene 1. I know that the curtain rises at the start of a play, so I think the section *At Rise* describes what the audience sees when the play begins. The names of the characters are in capital letters and dark type. I can see from the illustration why this play is called "The Crowded House."

- **Pages 124–127:** Scene 1 continues on pages 124–126. At the bottom of page 126, I see the word *Curtain* in capital letters. Scene 2 begins on page 127. Now the house looks more crowded than ever because there is a goat in it, too.

- **Pages 128–131:** As I quickly look at the rest of the pages, I notice that even though the people in the illustrations are the same, each set of pages shows them doing different things. I also see that chickens and a donkey are added to the crowd.

Set purpose. Model setting a purpose for reading "The Crowded House."

MODEL From my preview, this play looks like it will be lively and funny. One purpose for reading a play is for enjoyment. I will enjoy reading to find out what happens to the family in the crowded house.

Reread and Summarize

Have students reread and summarize "The Crowded House" in sections, as described below.

Pages 122–126

Let's reread pages 122–126 to recall what happens in Scene 1.

Summary: The large family is crowded in its small house. They ask Bartholomew, the wisest man in the village, for advice. He tells them to bring their goat in the house to live with them.

Pages 127–129

Now let's reread Scene 2 on pages 127–129 to find out what happens when the family brings the goat into the house.

Summary: The house is more crowded than ever. When Bartholomew comes back, he tells the family to bring their chickens inside to live with them.

Pages 130–131

As we reread Scene 3 on pages 130–131, let's see how the family is getting along.

Summary: Things are worse than ever in the crowded house. Bartholomew tells the family to bring their donkey inside, too.

Pages 132–134

Let's reread Scene 4 on pages 132–134 to recall how the problem is solved.

Summary: The family is very unhappy. Bartholomew tells them to put all the animals back in the barnyard. Now the house seems much less crowded, and the family is happy.

FLUENCY BUILDER Use *Intervention Practice Book* page 79.
Point out the sentences on the bottom half of the page. Remind students that their goal is to read each phrase or unit smoothly. Model appropriate pace, expression, and phrasing as you read each sentence, and have students read it after you. Then have students practice by reading the sentences aloud three times to a partner.

INTERVENTION
PRACTICE
BOOK

page 79

Directed Reading: "Good Advice" pp. 158–165

BRIGHT SURPRISES
pp. 158–165

Explain to students that this story is a play. Tell students that understanding the format, or the way a play is written down, helps readers understand what they are reading. Point out that the characters are listed first, and then the stage setting is described. Then point out that each time a character speaks, the character's name will be in dark type followed by a colon and the actual words the person says.

Read page 158 aloud. Ask: **Where and when does this play take place? How do you know?** Model the strategy of using text structure and format.

> **MODEL** This is a play, and all plays begin with a list of the characters and a description of where and when the action takes place. I see the words *Time* and *Stage setting* in dark type, and when I read these sections I see that the play takes place on a Friday morning in the middle of summer, both inside and outside the Gold family's home.
> (Focus Skill) **USE TEXT STRUCTURE AND FORMAT**

Then have students read page 159 to find out how the play begins. Ask: **What problem do the Golds have? How will they try to solve it?** (*They don't have enough space in their house. Mr. Gold will ask Ms. Post, the wisest person in town, for advice.*) **PROBLEM/SOLUTION**

Pages 160–161

Have students read pages 160–161 to find out what advice Ms. Post gives. (*She tells the family to bring the hens indoors.*) Ask: **Is the Golds' problem getting better or worse? Why?** (*worse; because the house is more crowded now*) **STORY EVENTS**

From what you have read so far, what do you think the author's purpose is for writing this play? Why do you think so? (*to entertain; because it is funny and interesting; it does not give information or try to persuade readers*) (Focus Skill) **AUTHOR'S PURPOSE**

Pages 162–163

Have students read pages 162–163 to find out whether the Golds' problem is solved. (*No, the house is more crowded than ever.*) **What advice do you think Ms. Post will give next? Why?** (Accept reasonable responses.) **MAKE PREDICTIONS**

Page 164

Have students read page 164 to find out how the story ends. (*The Golds take the animals outside. The house seems bigger.*) **SUMMARIZE**

Has the house really gotten bigger? (Possible response: *No, it just seems like there's more room now that the animals are outside again.*) **MAIN IDEA**

Summarize the selection. Have students state the problem of the story in one sentence and then summarize the story by telling about Ms. Post's advice.

INTERVENTION
PRACTICE
BOOK

page 81

Answers to *Think About It* Questions

1. Possible response: The Golds lived in a tiny home. They wanted more room, but they couldn't get a bigger home. Ms. Post's advice was to bring their animals in to live in their home. **SUMMARY**

2. Possible responses: I think she gave them good advice, because their house felt bigger when the animals left. **INTERPRETATION**

3. Help students brainstorm "pearls of wisdom" they have learned from parents, grandparents, or teachers. Suggest that they also think of fables and folktales that teach a lesson. **WRITE A STORY**

AFTER

Skill Review
pages 142–143

USE SKILL CARD 20B

(Focus Skill) Author's Purpose

RETEACH **the skill.** Have students look at **side B of Skill Card 20: Author's Purpose.** Read aloud and discuss the skill reminder and directions with them. Explain that the paragraphs are taken from different books and articles. Have students read each paragraph aloud and identify the author's main purpose and second purpose, if any. Students should explain how they determined the author's purpose in each case. [Answers: (1) to inform and to entertain; (2) to entertain; (3) to persuade; (4) to give instructions and to inform]

FLUENCY BUILDER Use *Intervention Practice Book* page 79. Explain that students will practice the sentences on the bottom half of the page by reading them aloud on tape. Assign new partners. Have students take turns reading the sentences aloud to each other and then reading them on tape. After they listen to the tape, have them tell how they think they have improved their reading of the sentences. Then have them read the sentences aloud on tape a second time, with improved pacing and tone.

INTERVENTION PRACTICE BOOK

page 79

Expository Writing: Prewriting

Build on prior knowledge. Ask students to recall what they have learned about expository writing. Tell them that now they are going to learn about doing expository writing when they take a writing test.

Remind students that the first thing they should do when they take a writing test is to read and analyze the prompt. Write this prompt on the board: *Students have jobs or chores to do in the classroom. Before you begin writing, think of another job or chore that students could do to keep the classroom neat and running well. Now write a paragraph to your classmates. Explain what the chore is and how to do it. (45 minutes)*

Have students identify the **writing form** (*expository writing*), the **topic** (*a classroom job or chore*), the **audience** (*classmates*), and any **special instructions**. (*to explain what the chore is and how to do it*)

Point out that students have 45 minutes to write this paragraph. Discuss how they would budget their time. Write numbers on the board to show that 10 minutes for prewriting, 25 minutes for drafting, and 10 minutes for revising and proofreading add up to a total of 45 minutes.

Display a graphic organizer like the one shown here.

Job or chore:
What it is:
How to do it:

Construct the text. "Share the pen" with students in a collaborative group writing effort. As students dictate words and phrases, write them in the graphic organizer, guiding the process by asking questions and offering suggestions as needed.

- Point out that this is the prewriting step of the writing process. To make the point that, on an actual test, students' time will be limited, set a timer and allow 10 minutes for this step.

Revisit the text. Go back and reread the prompt together. Ask: **Can we use the information in our chart to carry out the instructions in this prompt? Have we given enough details so that a reader would know how to do this chore?**

- Have students use the information from the graphic organizer to develop an oral presentation.

On Your Own

Most children enjoy outdoor games and activities. Think of an outdoor game or activity you enjoy. Now write a paragraph explaining what the activity is and why you enjoy it.

Connect Spelling and Phonics

RETEACH long vowels /ē/*e*, /ī/*i*, /ō/*o*. Tell students that you will say some words that have the long vowel sounds for *e*, *i*, and *o*. Have volunteers write each word on the board. Work together to proofread their work.

1. go	2. kind*	3. told*	4. we*
5. she*	6. bind	7. gold*	8. both*

*Word appears in "Good Advice."

Dictate the following sentence, and have students write it: *Can he find the cold dog?*

Build and Read Longer Words

Remind students that they have learned that the letters *e*, *i*, and *o* can stand for long vowel sounds in certain words. Now they will use what they have learned to help them read some longer words.

INTERVENTION ASSESSMENT BOOK

Write the word *program* on the board. Remind students that they can read longer words by dividing a word into syllables. Draw a line after the word part *pro*. Explain that often when you divide a longer word after a vowel and before a consonant, the vowel in the first syllable has the long sound. Cover *gram* and ask students to read the word part *pro*. Then cover *pro* and have students blend the sounds to read the word part *gram*. Uncover the whole word and have students blend the word parts to form the word *program*. Use this and other appropriate strategies to help students decode the words *locust*, *moment*, *recall*, and *librarian*. Encourage students to build other long words in which the letters *e*, *i*, and *o* stand for the long vowel sound. Suggest that they use a dictionary to look up words they are not sure about.

FLUENCY BUILDER Have students choose a passage from "Good Advice" to read aloud to a partner. You may have students choose passages that they found particularly interesting, or have them choose one of the following options:

- Read page 159. (Total: 102 words)
- Read page 162. (Total: 88 words)

Students read the selected passage aloud to their partners three times. Have students rate each of their own readings on a scale of 1 to 4. Encourage readers to note their improvement from one reading to the next by completing sentence frames such as *I know my reading improved because* _____. The partner who listens to the reading should also be encouraged to offer positive comments on the reader's improvement.

Review Vocabulary

To revisit the Vocabulary Words prior to the weekly assessment, have students listen as you read aloud each of the following sentence beginnings. Call on a volunteer to complete each sentence so that it makes sense. Alternatively, you might write the sentence beginnings on the board with the Vocabulary Words underlined, and have volunteers read aloud and complete the sentences.

1. When the weather is **dreadful**, I like to _____.
2. I kept my **wits** about me when _____.
3. You might hear **wailing** if _____.
4. A person might ask for **advice** about _____.
5. You say **farewell** when _____.
6. How you are **faring** might depend on _____.

Correct responses: Accept responses that reflect an understanding of the Vocabulary Words.

You may want to display the Vocabulary Words and definitions on page 199 and have students copy them to use when they study for the vocabulary test.

 ## Review Author's Purpose

To review the focus skill before the weekly assessment, distribute *Intervention Practice Book* page 82. Point out the title, Author's Purpose, and read the directions and purposes with students. You may choose to guide students through the page, or have them work independently and then share and explain their work.

INTERVENTION
PRACTICE
BOOK

page 82

Review Test Prep

Ask students to turn to page 143 of the *Student Edition*. Call attention to the tips for answering the test questions. Tell students that paying attention to these tips can help them answer not only the test questions on this page but also other test questions like these.

ON YOUR MARK

page 143

Have a volunteer read paragraph A aloud. Then have students follow along as you read aloud the first test item and the tip that goes with it. Have students identify the correct answer choice. Then read aloud item 2 and have students explain how they determined the authors' purposes. Encourage students to tell how they might apply the tips on this page in other test situations as well.

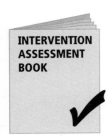

INTERVENTION
ASSESSMENT
BOOK

✔

Self-Selected Reading

Have students select their own books to read independently. They might choose books from the classroom library shelf, or you may wish to offer a group of appropriate books from which students can choose.

- *Paul Bunyan Moves Out.* (See page 143K of the *Teacher's Edition* for a lesson plan.)
- *Potluck* by Anne Shelby. Orchard, 1994.
- *Let's Eat* by Ann Zamorano. Scholastic, 1997.

You may also wish to choose additional books that are the same genre as the selection. After students have chosen their books, give each student a copy of My Reading Log, which can be found on page R42 in the back of the *Teacher's Edition*. Have students fill in the information at the top of the form. Then have them use the log to keep track of their reading and to record their responses to the literature.

Conduct student-teacher conferences. Arrange time for each student to confer with you individually about his or her self-selected reading. Have students bring their Reading Logs to share with you at the conference. Students might also like to choose a favorite passage to read aloud to you. Ask questions designed to stimulate discussion of the book. For example, you might ask how the student determined the author's purpose for writing the book and how well the student feels that the book fulfills the author's purpose.

FLUENCY PERFORMANCE Have students read aloud to you the passage from "Good Advice" that they selected and practiced earlier with their partners. Keep track of the number of words the student reads correctly. Ask the student to rate his or her own performance on the 1–4 scale. If students are not happy with their oral reading, give them an opportunity to continue practicing and then to read the passage to you again.

See *Oral Reading Fluency Assessment* for monitoring progress.

Use with

"Leah's Pony"

BEFORE Review Phonics: Long Vowel /ī/*y*

Identify the sound. Tell students to listen for the /ī/ sound as you say *sky*. Then have them repeat three times: *Why will Ty try to fly my kite?* Ask them to identify the words with the /ī/ sound.

Associate letters to sound. Write on the board: *Why will Ty try to fly my kite?* Underline each *y* and the *i-e* in *kite*. Remind students that *i-e* often stands for the long *i* vowel sound. Explain that *y* can also stand for this sound. Have students listen for the /ī/ sound in *Why*, *Ty*, *try*, *my* and *fly*. Then write the word pairs *try/tries* and *dry/dries* on the board. Remind students that *ie* can also stand for the /ī/ sound. Explain that when a long *i* word ends in *y*, students should change the *y* to *i* before adding *-es*.

Word blending. Have students repeat after you as you model blending and reading *fly*. Point to *f* and say /f/. Point to *l* and say /l/. Slide your hand under *fl* as you slowly blend and elongate the sounds /ffll/. Next, point to *y* and say /ī/. Slide your hand under the whole word, elongating all the sounds /ffllīī/, and then say the word naturally—*fly*.

**INTERVENTION
PRACTICE
BOOK**

page 84

Apply the skill. *Letter Substitution* Write each word on the board for students to read aloud. Make the changes needed to form the word in parentheses. Have a volunteer read aloud each new word.

me (my)	**flow** (fly)	**crow** (cry)	**tree** (try)
be (by)	**show** (shy)	**slow** (sly)	**free** (fry)

Introduce Vocabulary

PRETEACH lesson vocabulary. Tell students that they are going to learn six new words that they will see again when they read a selection called "Leah's Pony." Teach each Vocabulary Word using the following process.

Use these or similar ideas to give the meaning or context.

> Write the word.
> Say the word.
> Track the word and have students repeat it.
> Give the meaning or context.

county	Note that a state is part of the country and a county is part of a state.
auctioneer	Point out the word *auction*. Relate to fundraising auctions or sales. Explain that an auctioneer is a person who runs an auction.
bid	Pretend to have an item that students want, and have them participate in a mock auction, making bids.
clutched	Hold on tightly to a book or other item.

| **glistened** | Mention familiar objects that glisten, such as a diamond or an icicle in the sun. |
| **galloped** | Relate to TV westerns that show horses galloping. |

For vocabulary activities, see Vocabulary Games on pages 2–7.

For vocabulary activities, see Vocabulary Games on pages 2–7.

AFTER

Building Background and Vocabulary

Apply Vocabulary Strategies

Use sentence and word context. Write on the board: *A strong wind tugged at the kite. Emily clutched the kite string.* Tell students that they can sometimes figure out the meaning of a word by looking for a clue in the same sentence or one nearby. Read the sentences aloud and model using the strategy.

> **MODEL** I'm not sure what *clutched* means, but the first sentence says a strong wind tugged at the kite. The kite must have been hard to hold onto. Emily must have held onto the string tightly, so that's what *clutched* must mean—"held on tightly."

RETEACH lesson vocabulary. Have students use word cards and sorting pockets to sort the Vocabulary Words in different ways. For example, have them sort the words into nouns and verbs, and share their results. Then have them sort by the number of syllables in each word and again share their results.

> ## Vocabulary Words
>
> **county** a section of a state
>
> **auctioneer** a person who is hired to run a public sale
>
> **bid** the amount of money that is offered to buy something
>
> **clutched** held tightly
>
> **glistened** shone or sparkled
>
> **galloped** ran at a horse's or pony's top speed

FLUENCY BUILDER Using *Intervention Practice Book* page 83, read each word in the first column aloud and have students repeat it. Then have students work in pairs to read the words in the first column aloud to each other. Follow the same procedure with each of the remaining columns. After partners have practiced reading aloud the words in each column separately, have them listen to each other as they practice the entire list.

INTERVENTION PRACTICE BOOK

page 83

⭐ **Focus Skill** **Fact and Opinion**

PRETEACH **the skill.** Tell students that some statements are facts and others are opinions. Give examples, such as *This marker is red* and *I think blue is prettier than red*. Then have students look at **side A of Skill Card 21: Fact and Opinion.** Read aloud and discuss the definitions. Next, have students read aloud each statement and refer back to the definitions to decide whether the statement is fact or opinion. Point out the clue phrases in sentences 2, 5, and 6. Explain that phrases like *in my opinion*, *I think*, and *I believe* often signal that a statement is an opinion.

Prepare to Read: "Leah's Pony"

Preview. Tell students that they are going to read a selection called "Leah's Pony." Explain that this is a kind of fiction called historical fiction. The story is partly fiction, but it is set in a real time in the past. The author of "Leah's Pony" made up the characters and story events, but the story takes place at a time in history when real people suffered through the same kinds of troubles as Leah's family and their neighbors do. After discussing the genre, preview the selection.

ON YOUR MARK

pages 148–161

- **Pages 148–149:** I see the title "Leah's Pony," and the names of the author and illustrator. The girl in the picture must be Leah, with her pony.

- **Pages 150–151:** Here I see Leah on her pony. She looks happy.

- **Pages 152–155:** The old-fashioned car in the picture on page 153 shows me that this story takes place many years ago. In the picture on page 154, Leah doesn't look happy like she did before. The sign in front of the house says "farm auction." I wonder if this farm belongs to Leah's family and why an auction, or sale, is being held. Maybe this is why Leah does not look happy.

- **Pages 156–157:** In this picture, Leah is clutching some money in her hands. She looks worried and sad.

- **Pages 158–160:** I see a tractor on page 158. Maybe this is being sold at the auction. On page 159 Leah is talking to a man in a suit. I wonder who he is. On page 160 Leah looks surprised to see her pony. I'd like to find out why.

Set Purpose. Model setting a purpose for reading "Leah's Pony."

MODEL From my preview, I know that this story is about a girl named Leah and that the story events take place in the past. I know that one purpose for reading is to enjoy a story and another is to learn. I think I will read this selection both to enjoy it and to find out what life was like during the time in history when this story takes place.

Reread and Summarize

Have students reread and summarize "Leah's Pony" in sections, as described below.

> **Pages 150–153**
>
> **Let's reread pages 150–153 to recall what caused hard times for Leah's family.**
>
> Summary: Leah's papa bought her a pony the year the corn grew tall. Then hard times began because there was no rain and crops could not grow. Papa can't pay back money he has borrowed from the bank. He says they might have to leave the farm.
>
> **Pages 154–157**
>
> **Now let's reread pages 154–157 to find out what Leah decides to do.**
>
> Summary: Leah sells her pony to Mr. B. At the auction she buys her father's tractor for one dollar.
>
> **Pages 158–159**
>
> **As we reread pages 158–159, let's see what Leah's neighbors do.**
>
> Summary: Leah's neighbors buy items at low prices and then give them all back to Leah's family.
>
> **Pages 160–161**
>
> **Let's reread pages 160–161 to recall how the story ends.**
>
> Summary: The next morning Leah discovers that Mr. B. has given her pony back to her.

FLUENCY BUILDER Use *Intervention Practice Book* page 83. Point out the sentences on the bottom half of the page. Remind students that their goal is to read each phrase or unit smoothly. Model appropriate pace, expression, and phrasing as you read each sentence, and have students read it after you. Then have students practice by reading the sentences aloud three times to a partner.

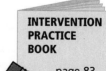

INTERVENTION
PRACTICE
BOOK

page 83

Directed Reading: "Auction Day" pp. 166–172

Pages 166–167

Read aloud the title and ask what an auction is. Have students read pages 166–167 to find out why the boy in the illustration goes to the bank. (*to see how much money he has because he wants to buy a pony*) Ask: **Why does Ty work at the store?** (*to earn more money so he will have enough to buy the pony*) **CHARACTERS' MOTIVATIONS**

> **BRIGHT SURPRISES**
> pp. 166–172

Pages 168–169

Have students read pages 168–169 to find out whether Ty earns enough money for the pony. (*Yes, he has six dollars in the bank and has earned four more dollars.*) Ask: **When Ty's neighbors say that he'll have his hands full if he tries to tame a wild pony, are they stating a fact or an opinion? Explain your answer.** (*They are expressing an opinion because they are telling what they think or believe.*) (Focus Skill) **FACT AND OPINION**

Page 170

Ask students to read page 170. Ask: **What happens at the auction?** Model using the strategy of self-questioning.

> **MODEL** When I read about the auction, I didn't understand at first how Ty was able to buy Blue Sky for only ten dollars. I asked myself why no one else made a bid and why everyone clapped. Asking these questions helped me realize that everyone wanted Ty to have the pony.
> (Focus Strategy) **SELF-QUESTION**

Page 171

Have students read page 171 to find out what happens when Ty gets Blue Sky home. Ask: **Why do you think Ty frees Blue Sky?** (*Possible responses: She is wild and wants to be free. Ty wants her to be happy.*) **CAUSE AND EFFECT**

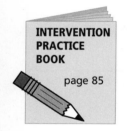

INTERVENTION PRACTICE BOOK

page 85

Do you think Ty was right to let Blue Sky go free? (*Responses will vary.*) **MAKE JUDGMENTS**

Summarize the selection. Ask students to summarize the story by using three sentences to identify Ty's problem, his solution to his problem, and the outcome.

Answers to *Think About It* Questions

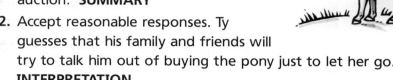

1. He works to save money. He takes all his money out of the bank. He uses all that money to buy Blue Sky at the auction. **SUMMARY**

2. Accept reasonable responses. Ty guesses that his family and friends will try to talk him out of buying the pony just to let her go. **INTERPRETATION**

3. Encourage students to think about the setting and about Ty's feelings about Blue Sky. Their diary entries should describe what happened and explain why Ty let her go. **WRITE A DIARY ENTRY**

AFTER

Skill Review
pages 166–167

USE SKILL CARD 21B

(Focus Skill) Fact and Opinion

RETEACH **the skill.** Have students look at **side B of Skill Card 21: Fact and Opinion**. Read aloud the skill reminder and questions. Call on volunteers to take turns reading the sentences in the speech balloons. Have students identify each statement as a fact or an opinion and explain how they can tell.

FLUENCY BUILDER Use *Intervention Practice Book* page 83. Explain that students will practice the sentences on the bottom half of the page by reading them aloud on tape. Assign new partners. Have students take turns reading the sentences aloud to each other and then reading them on tape. After they listen to the tape, have them tell how they think they have improved their reading of the sentences. Then have them read the sentences aloud on tape a second time, with improved pacing and tone.

INTERVENTION PRACTICE BOOK

page 83

Research Report: Narrowing a Topic

Build on prior knowledge. Ask whether students know what a research report is. If necessary, explain that a research report is a written report on a certain topic. Students first choose a topic and then do research to find information about that topic. Then they use the research results to write a report.

Write this prompt on the board: *Write a short research report about an area of your state. Choose the area where you live or another part of your state that you would like to learn about.*

Point out that students could begin researching this topic by looking up the name of their state in an encyclopedia and finding the name of an area or region that they would like to report on.

California

Display a diagram like this one.

Construct the text. "Share the pen" with students in a collaborative writing effort. Guide them in filling in the graphic organizer to narrow their topic, asking questions and offering suggestions as needed.

- Use an encyclopedia to help students locate the names of specific regions in your state. Work with them to choose a region they would like to use as the topic for a report. Write the name of the region in the middle section of the diagram.

- Point out that the topic is still probably too broad for a short report. Help students use the encyclopedia to choose a specific feature of the region. Write the name of the feature in the bottom section of the diagram.

- Guide students in developing a strong topic sentence that tells the main idea. Write on the board as they dictate.

Revisit the text. With students, review the graphic organizer, pointing out the progression from general to specific. Ask: **Does our topic sentence express the main idea we listed in the bottom section of the organizer?**

- Tell students that they might use the Internet, encyclopedia, nonfiction books, or other sources to find facts about their topic. Explain that they should take careful notes in their own words, rather than copy directly from the source.

On Your Own

Think of a topic that you would like to learn more about. Look up the topic in an encyclopedia or nonfiction book. Practice taking notes by writing down three facts in your own words. Show a partner the notes you took and the source you used.

Connect Spelling and Phonics

RETEACH **long vowel /ī/y.** Tell students that you will say some words in which the letter *y* stands for the /ī/ sound. Have volunteers write each word on the board. Work together to proofread their work.

I. cry	2. fly	3. dry	4. fry
5. Ty*	6. by*	7. sky*	8. my*

*Word appears in "Auction Day."

Dictate the following sentence and have students write it: *Ty will try to spy my shy cat.*

Build and Read Longer Words

Remind students that they have learned that the letter *y* can stand for the /ī/ sound. Now they will use what they have learned to help them read some longer words.

Write the word *myself* on the board. Remind students that they can read longer words by looking for smaller words in a longer word or by looking for familiar spelling patterns. Cover *self* and point out the familiar word *my*. Then cover *my*. Have students blend the sounds to read *self*. Uncover *my* and have students read the word *myself*. Use similar appropriate strategies to help students decode the words *nearby*, *trying*, *hairdryer*, and *skyscraper*. Encourage students to build other long words in which the letter *y* stands for the long *i* vowel sound. Suggest that they use a dictionary to look up words they are not sure about.

INTERVENTION ASSESSMENT BOOK

FLUENCY BUILDER Have students choose a passage from "Auction Day" to read aloud to a partner. You may have students choose passages that they found particularly interesting, or have them choose one of the following options:

- Read page 169. (Total: 107 words)
- Read page 171. (Total: 118 words)

Students read the selected passage aloud to their partners three times. Have students rate each of their own readings on a scale of 1 to 4. Encourage readers to note their improvement from one reading to the next by completing sentence frames such as *I know my reading improved because* _____. The partner who listens to the reading should also be encouraged to offer positive comments on the reader's improvement.

Review Vocabulary

To revisit the Vocabulary Words with students prior to the weekly assessment, display or read aloud the following sentences. Have students tell whether each statement makes sense and explain why.

1. The **auctioneer** asked for bids on each item at the sale.
2. The person who made the lowest **bid** at the auction got the item.
3. The **county** is one of twenty in the state.
4. The tree branch **glistened** after the ice storm.
5. The turtle **galloped** across the yard.
6. My brother **clutched** his teddy bear while I read him a story.

You may want to display the Vocabulary Words and definitions on page 209 and have students copy them to use when they study for the vocabulary test.

**INTERVENTION
PRACTICE
BOOK**

page 86

 (Focus Skill) **Review Fact and Opinion**

To review the focus skill before the weekly assessment, distribute *Intervention Practice Book* page 86. Point out the title, Fact and Opinion, and read the directions aloud. You may choose to guide students through the activity, or have them complete it with a partner and then share and discuss their work with the group.

Review Test Prep

Ask students to turn to page 171 of the *Student Edition*. Call attention to the Tips for answering the test questions. Tell students that paying attention to these tips can help them answer not only the test questions on this page but also other test questions like these.

**ON YOUR
MARK**

page 171

Have students follow along as you read aloud the story and the directions. Ask a volunteer to read aloud the first test question and the tip that goes with it. Have students identify the correct choice and explain how they determined which statement is a fact. Follow a similar procedure with the second question. Encourage students to tell how they might apply the tips on this page in other test situations as well.

**INTERVENTION
ASSESSMENT
BOOK**

✔

Self-Selected Reading

Have students select their own books to read independently. They might choose books from the classroom library shelf, or you may wish to offer a group of appropriate books from which students can choose. Titles might include the following:

- *When the Rains Came.* (See page 167K of the *Teacher's Edition* for a lesson plan.)

- *Mailing May* by Michael Tunnell. Morrow/Avon, 2000.

- *The Carrot Seed* by Ruth Krauss. HarperCollins, 1989

You might also like to choose books that are the same genre or by the same author as the selection. After students have chosen their books, give each student a copy of My Reading Log, which can be found on page R42 in the back of the *Teacher's Edition*. Have students fill in the information at the top of the form. Then have them use the log to keep track of their reading and to record their responses to the literature.

Conduct student-teacher conferences. Arrange time for each student to confer with you individually about his or her self-selected reading. Have students bring their Reading Logs to share with you at the conference. Students might also like to choose a favorite passage to read aloud to you. Ask questions about the book to stimulate discussion. For example, you might ask which character the student liked best, when and where the story takes place, or how the student feels about the story problem and its resolution.

FLUENCY PERFORMANCE Have students read aloud to you the passage from "Auction Day" that they selected and practiced earlier with their partners. Keep track of the number of words the student reads correctly. Ask the student to rate his or her own performance on the 1–4 scale. If students are not happy with their oral reading, give them an opportunity to continue practicing and then to reread the passage to you again.

See *Oral Reading Fluency Assessment* for monitoring progress.

LESSON 22

BEFORE

Building
Background
and Vocabulary

"Yippee-Yay!"

Review Phonics: Consonant /j/*g, dge*

Identify the sound. Tell students to listen for the /j/ sound as you say *gym*. Then have them repeat three times: *Ginger is the giraffe at the gate by the edge of the gym.* Ask them to identify the words that have the /j/ sound. (*Ginger, giraffe, edge, gym*)

Associate letters to sound. Write on the board: *Ginger is the giraffe at the gate by the edge of the gym.* Circle the word *gate*. Remind students that the letter *g* often stands for the /g/ sound at the beginning of *gate*. Then underline each *g* in the words *Ginger, giraffe,* and *gym*. Have students identify the letter that follows each *g*. Explain that when *e, i,* or *y* follows *g*, the *g* usually stands for the /j/ sound. If any other letter follows *g*, the *g* stands for the /g/ sound. Finally, underline the *dge* in *edge*. Point out that these letters can also stand for the /j/ sound.

Word blending. Have students repeat after you as you model blending and reading the word *giraffe*. Point to *g* and say /j/. Slide your hand under the letters *gi* as you slowly elongate the sounds of the first syllable /jjəə/. Next, point to *r* and say /r/. Point to *a* and say /a/. Point to *ffe* and say /f/. Slide your hand under the letters *raffe* as you slowly elongate the sounds for the second syllable /rraaff/. Then elongate the two syllables /jjəə-rraaff/ and say the word naturally—*giraffe*.

INTERVENTION
PRACTICE
BOOK

page 88

Apply the skill. *Letter Substitution* Write these words on the board, and have students read each aloud. Change as needed to form the word in parentheses. Have a volunteer read aloud each new word.

gum (gym)   **hem** (gem)   **bad** (badge)   **term** (germ)
log (lodge)   **cave** (cage)   **gull** (gel)   **dog** (dodge)

Introduce Vocabulary

PRETEACH **lesson vocabulary.** Tell students that they are going to learn six new words that they will see again when they read a selection called "Yippee-Yay!" Teach each Vocabulary Word using the process shown below.

Use the following suggestions or similar ideas to give the meaning or context.

ranchers	Relate to a cattle ranch on a TV western. Point out the suffix *-er* and the *-s* ending.
tending	Relate to a parent or a babysitter taking care of a child.

> Write the word.
> Say the word.
> Track the word and have students repeat it.
> Give the meaning or context.

profit	Hold up a pencil. Tell students that it cost ten cents to make, and you paid twenty-five. Help them figure the profit.
corral	Compare to a fenced-in yard.
stray	Relate to a stray cat or dog.
market	Relate to an open market where people sell a variety of goods.

For vocabulary activities, see Vocabulary Games on pages 2–7.

AFTER

Building
Background
and Vocabulary

Apply Vocabulary Strategies

Identify multiple-meaning words. Write on the board: *We adopted the stray cat. My mother told us not to stray from the yard.* Tell students that when a word has more than one meaning, they can often figure out the meaning from the way the word is used. Model using the strategy.

> **MODEL** I know the word *stray* is used as an adjective in the first sentence to tell about the cat. The cat is lost or wandering. I see that *stray* is used as a verb, an action word, in the second sentence. It must mean "wander." Mother told the children not to wander from the yard.

Guide students in using a similar procedure with *corral*, *profit*, and *market*.

RETEACH **lesson vocabulary.** Provide patterns for a circle and an arrow. Have students make a simple spinner by cutting a circle and arrow from cardboard and putting them together with a brad. Tell students to write the Vocabulary Words on the spinner. Students take turns spinning the spinner, saying the word the spinner lands on, and using the word in a sentence.

FLUENCY BUILDER Using *Intervention Practice Book* page 87, read each word in the first column aloud and have students repeat it. Then have students work in pairs to read the words in the first column aloud to each other. Follow the same procedure with each of the remaining columns. After partners have practiced reading aloud the words in each column, have them listen to each other as they practice the entire list.

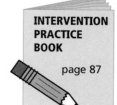

INTERVENTION
PRACTICE
BOOK

page 87

BEFORE

Reading "Yippee-Yay!" *pages 170–185*

USE SKILL CARD 22A

Focus Skill Main Idea and Details

PRETEACH the skill. Tell students that when they read a selection, they should figure out the most important idea it tells about. Knowing the main, or most important, idea helps readers understand the selection. Then have students look at **side A of Skill Card 22: Main Idea and Details**. Read aloud the definitions of main idea and details. Then have volunteers read aloud the information in the diagram. Discuss how each of the details gives more information about the main idea.

Prepare to Read: "Yippee-Yay!"

ON YOUR MARK pages 170–185

Preview. Tell students that they are going to read a selection called "Yippee-Yay!" Explain that this selection is expository nonfiction. It explains information and ideas about a topic. Remind students that nonfiction tells about real people and events. Expository nonfiction may include diagrams with labels to help readers understand information. After discussing the genre, preview the selection.

- **Pages 170–171:** I see that under the title "Yippee-Yay!" there is a smaller title, "A Book About Cowboys and Cowgirls," which tells me the topic of this expository nonfiction selection. I also see the name of the author and illustrator, Gail Gibbons. The picture shows a rider on a bucking horse.
- **Pages 172–173:** The pictures on these pages have labels. The picture on page 173 seems to be a diagram that shows the parts of a cowboy's clothing.
- **Pages 174–177:** On these pages, I see more diagrams that look very interesting. The pictures show things that cowboys and cowgirls do. I think it will be fun to read this selection and find out more about cowboys and cowgirls.

Set purpose. Model setting a purpose for reading "Yippee-Yay."

> MODEL **From my preview, I know that this selection is expository nonfiction that gives ideas and information about the real lives of cowboys and cowgirls. One purpose for reading is to locate information. I think I will read this selection to learn what real cowboys and cowgirls did and what equipment they used.**

Reread and Summarize

Have students reread and summarize "Yippee-Yay!" in sections, as described below.

Pages 172–175

Let's reread pages 172–175 to recall what cowboys did in the Old West.

Summary: Cowboys tended cattle, rounded them up, and moved them on long cattle drives. They spent much of their time on horseback.

Pages 176–179

Now let's reread pages 176–179 to find out more about roundups and trail drives.

Summary: All the cattle were rounded up and brought to one place. They were branded to show who they belonged to. After the roundup, cowboys took the cattle to the railroad, a difficult trip that could take many months.

Pages 180–183

As we reread pages 180–183, let's see what cowboys did on a trail drive and why trail drives were such hard work.

Summary: Each cowboy on a trail drive had special tasks to do. The days were very long, and the work was hard. When cowboys finally got to town, they wanted to get cleaned up and have some fun.

Pages 184–185

Let's reread pages 184–185 to recall what cowhands do today.

Summary: Cowboys and cowgirls today compete in rodeos. They still tend cattle, but now they use modern equipment.

FLUENCY BUILDER Use *Intervention Practice Book* page 87.
Point out the sentences on the bottom half of the page.
Remind students that their goal is to read each phrase or unit smoothly. Model appropriate pace, expression, and phrasing as you read each sentence and have students read it after you. Then have students practice by reading the sentences aloud three times to a partner.

INTERVENTION PRACTICE BOOK

page 87

Directed Reading: "A Cookie for the Cowboys" pp. 174–181

**BRIGHT
SURPRISES**
pp. 174–181

Pages 174–175

Have students read aloud the title and discuss the illustrations. Have them read pages 174–175 to find out what kind of "Cookie" the selection is about. Ask: **What is the "Cookie" in the title?** (*George Gemson, the cook on the cattle drive*) **UNDERSTAND FIGURATIVE LANGUAGE**

Ask: **What is a greenhorn?** (*a new cowhand*) **IMPORTANT DETAILS**

Pages 176–177

Have students read pages 176–177 to find out more about what cowhands do on the trail. Ask: **What sentence tells the main idea on page 176?** (*Tending cattle is hard work.*) **What details support the main idea?** (*You'll ride horses, get dirty, eat dust, move cattle, and keep an eye out for strays.*) (Focus Skill) **MAIN IDEA AND DETAILS**

Why does Cookie get up at three in the morning? (*He has a lot to do to get breakfast ready by sunrise.*) **DRAW CONCLUSIONS**

Pages 178–179

Ask students to read pages 178–179 to find out about the chuck wagon. Ask: **What is a chuck wagon?** (*the wagon with the cook's supplies*) **Why is the chuck wagon important?** (*because all of the supplies needed for the trail are kept there*) (Focus Skill) **MAIN IDEA**

Page 180

Ask: **What else does Cookie do besides cook?** (*doctoring, cutting hair*)

What do you think *jack-of-all-trades* means? Model the strategy of using context to confirm meaning.

> **MODEL** The term *jack-of-all-trades* is new to me. There's nothing else in that sentence that gives me a clue to its meaning, so I'll look at the sentences before it. In addition to being a cook, Cookie says he doctors people and cuts hair. These seem to be examples of the things he does. I think a jack-of-all-trades is a person who does a lot of different things. (Focus Strategy) **USE CONTEXT TO CONFIRM MEANING**

Do you think Cookie likes his job? Why or why not? (*Accept reasonable responses.*) **CHARACTERS' EMOTIONS**

Summarize the selection. Ask students to summarize in a few sentences what they learned about life on a cattle drive.

**INTERVENTION
PRACTICE
BOOK**

page 89

Answers to *Think About It* Questions

1. Possible responses: Cookie's job is not easy. He wakes up early, cooks for the cowboys, treats snakebites, and cuts hair. **SUMMARY**

2. Possible response: The cowhands have to start working early, and it takes a long time to cook breakfast over a campfire. **INTERPRETATION**

3. You may suggest writing new words to a familiar tune, such as "Home on the Range." Encourage students to share their songs or poems with classmates. **WRITE A POEM**

AFTER

Skill Review
pages 192–193

USE SKILL CARD 22B

(Focus Skill) Main Idea and Details

RETEACH the skill. Have students look at **side B of Skill Card 22: Main Idea and Details**. Read aloud the skill reminder. Call on volunteers to read aloud the sentences below the picture. Help them identify details about what is kept in a chuck wagon and the sentence that expresses the main idea. (*A chuck wagon holds many things.*) Read aloud the directions, and draw the diagram on the board. Write in the diagram the main idea sentence and detail sentences that students identified. Have students copy the completed diagram on their papers.

FLUENCY BUILDER Use *Intervention Practice Book* page 87. Explain that students will practice the sentences on the bottom half of the page by reading them aloud on tape. Assign new partners. Have students take turns reading the sentences aloud to each other and then reading them on tape. After they listen to the tape, have them tell how they think they have improved their reading of the sentences. Then have them read the sentences aloud on tape a second time, with improved pacing and tone.

INTERVENTION PRACTICE BOOK

page 87

Research Report: Outline

Build on prior knowledge. Remind students that a research report is a written report on a certain topic. Tell students that after they have done their research and taken notes, they need to organize the information. One way to organize information is by making an outline that shows main ideas and details.

Display the following outline. Explain that it shows some main ideas and details that students may recall from "A Cookie for the Cowboys."

Cookie's Job

I. **Cookie cooks for the cowhands.**
   A. **He gets up early to start breakfast.**
   B. **He makes coffee.**
   C. **He bakes rolls and cooks beans and bacon.**

II. _____
   A. _____
   B. _____
   C. _____

Construct the text. "Share the pen" with students in a collaborative writing effort. Guide them in completing the outline as a group, asking questions and offering suggestions as needed. Fill in the outline with their dictation.

- Point out the way the outline is organized. The main ideas are labeled with Roman numerals, and the details about each main idea are labeled with capital letters.

- Have students reread page 180 of "A Cookie for the Cowboys" to find information to complete the outline. For example, the second main idea might be *Cookie is a jack-of-all-trades.* Supporting details might include *A. He does doctoring. B. He takes care of snakebites. C. He cuts hair.*

Revisit the text. Have students read the entire outline. Ask: **Are the sentences labeled I and II really the main ideas? Do the lettered sentences tell details about each main idea?**

- Have students copy the outline on their papers.

On Your Own

Choose a passage from your social studies textbook. Take notes. Then organize your notes into an outline. Share your outline with a partner.

Connect Spelling and Phonics

RETEACH consonant /j/ **g, dge.** Tell students that you will say four words in which the letter *g* is followed by the letter *e*. Then tell them that you will say two words in which the letters *dge* stand for the /j/ sound. Next, tell them you will say two words in which the letter *g* is followed by the letter *i*. Have volunteers write each word on the board. Work together to proofread their work.

1. gem	2. germ	3. gently*	4. range*
5. judge*	6. nudge*	7. giant	8. ginger

*Word appears in "A Cookie for the Cowboys."

Dictate the following sentence and have students write it: *A giant cat nudged the fudge and did not budge.*

Build and Read Longer Words

Remind students that they have learned that the letter *g* often stands for the /j/ sound when it is followed by *e*, *i*, or *y*. The letter pattern *dge* also stands for the /j/ sound. Now they will use what they have learned to help them read some longer words.

Write the word *gigantic* on the board. Remind students that when they see a longer word in which a single consonant appears between two vowels, they can try saying the first syllable with a long vowel sound. Point out the CVC pattern and its short vowel sound in the second and third syllables. Use this and other appropriate strategies to help students decode the words *meteorology*, *germinate*, *gemstone*, and *hedgehog*. Encourage students to build other long words in which the /j/ sound is spelled *g* or *dge*. Suggest that they use a dictionary to look up words they are not sure about.

INTERVENTION ASSESSMENT BOOK

FLUENCY BUILDER Have students choose a passage from "A Cookie for the Cowboys" to read aloud to a partner. You may have students choose passages that they found particularly interesting, or have them choose one of the following options:

- Read the paragraphs on pages 174 and 175. (Total: 102 words)
- Read pages 178 and 179. (Total: 114 words)

Students read the selected passage aloud to their partners three times. Have students rate each of their own readings on a scale of 1 to 4. Encourage readers to note their improvement from one reading to the next by completing sentence frames such as *I know my reading has improved because _____.* The partner who listens to the reading should also be encouraged to offer positive comments on the reader's improvement.

Review Vocabulary

To revisit the Vocabulary Words with students prior to the weekly assessment, display a word line like the one shown here.

least surprised ——————————————————— most surprised

Have students listen to the following questions and take turns indicating on the word line how surprised they would be. Ask them to explain why they would or would not be surprised in each instance. If needed, ask follow-up questions to check students' understanding of the Vocabulary Words.

How surprised would you be if. . .

1. **ranchers** moved to the city with their cattle?
2. Little Bo Peep was **tending** her cows?
3. no business ever made a **profit**?
4. a **market** had nothing for you to buy?
5. cows were standing in the **corral**?
6. an organization took in **stray** cats and dogs and offered them for adoption?

Correct responses: Accept responses that reflect an understanding of the Vocabulary Words.

You may want to display the Vocabulary Words and definitions on page 219 and have students copy them to use when they study for the vocabulary test.

⭐(Focus Skill) **Review Main Idea and Details**

**INTERVENTION
PRACTICE
BOOK**

page 90

To review the focus skill before the weekly assessment, distribute *Intervention Practice Book* page 90. Point out the title, Main Idea and Details, and read the directions aloud. You may choose to guide students through the activity, or have them complete it with a partner and then share and discuss their work with the group.

Review Test Prep

Ask students to turn to page 193 of the *Pupil Edition*. Call attention to the tips for answering the test questions. Tell students that paying attention to these tips can help them answer not only the test questions on this page but also other test questions like these.

**ON YOUR
MARK**

page 193

**INTERVENTION
ASSESSMENT
BOOK**

✓

Read the directions to students, and have a volunteer read the paragraph and list aloud. Read aloud the first test question and the tip that goes with it. Have students identify the main idea and explain how they figured it out. Then read aloud the second question and tip. Have students identify the detail that does not support the main idea and explain why it does not. Encourage students to tell how they might apply the tips on this page in other test situations as well.

Self-Selected Reading

Have students select their own books to read independently. They might choose books from the classroom library shelf, or you may wish to offer a group of appropriate books from which students can choose. Titles might include these:

- *Pony Express to the Rescue.* (See page 197S of the *Teacher's Edition* for a lesson plan.)
- *The Zebra-Riding Cowboy* by Angela Shelf Medearis. Henry Holt, 1997.
- *Rain Song* by Lezlie Evans. Houghton Mifflin, 1997.

You may also wish to suggest books that are the same genre or are by the same author as the selection. After students have chosen their books, give each student a copy of My Reading Log, which can be found on page R42 in the back of the *Teacher's Edition*. Have students fill in the information at the top of the form. Then have them use the log to keep track of their reading and to record their responses to the literature.

Conduct student-teacher conferences. Arrange time for students to confer with you individually about their self-selected reading. Have students bring their Reading Logs to share with you at the conference. Students might also like to choose a favorite passage to read aloud to you. Ask questions designed to stimulate discussion of the book. For example, you might ask students to tell you the main idea of a nonfiction book and give examples of supporting details from the book.

FLUENCY PERFORMANCE Have students read aloud to you the passage from "A Cookie for the Cowboys" that they selected and practiced earlier with their partners. Keep track of the number of words the student reads correctly. Ask the student to rate his or her own performance on the 1–4 scale. If students are not happy with their oral reading, give them an opportunity to continue practicing and then to read the passage to you again.

See *Oral Reading Fluency Assessment* for monitoring progress.

Use with

"Boom Town"

Review Phonics: Long Vowel /ī/*igh*

Identify the sound. Tell students to listen for the /ī/ sound as you say the word *sigh*. Then have them repeat three times: *She tries to find bright lights that shine high up in the sky at night.* Ask them to identify the words that have the /ī/ sound.

Associate letters to sound. Write on the board *She tries to find bright lights that shine high up in the sky at night.* Circle *tries, find, shine,* and *sky.* Underline the letters that stand for the /ī/ sound (*ie, i, i-e, y*). Then underline the *igh* in the words *bright, lights, high,* and *night.* Tell students that the letters *igh* also stand for the long *i* vowel sound.

Word blending. Have students repeat after you as you model blending and reading the word *night*. Point to *n* and say /n/. Point to *igh* and say /ī/. Slide your hand under the letters *nigh* as you slowly elongate the sounds /nnīī/. Point to *t and say* /t/. Slide your hand under the whole word, elongating all the sounds /nnīītt/, and then say the word naturally—*night*.

Apply the skill. *Letter Substitution* Write the following words on the board, and have students read each aloud. Change as needed to form the words in parentheses. Have a volunteer read aloud each new word.

mitt (might)	**fret** (fright)	**net** (night)	**lit** (light)
hay (high)	**flit** (flight)	**sit** (sight)	**say** (sigh)

Introduce Vocabulary

PRETEACH **lesson vocabulary.** Tell students that they are going to learn seven new words that they will see again in a selection called "Boom Town." Teach each Vocabulary Word using the following process.

Use these or similar ideas to give the meaning or context.

stagecoach	Explain that a stagecoach was a coach, pulled by horses, used to carry passengers and mail.
nuggets	Relate to small chunks of chocolate in cookies or chunks of gold.
skillet	Relate to a frying pan.
miners	Relate to a mine—a large hole or deep tunnel made for taking minerals from the earth. Point out the suffix *-er* meaning "one who."

> Write the word.
> Say the word.
> Track the word and have students repeat it.
> Give the meaning or context.

INTERVENTION
PRACTICE
BOOK

page 92

settle	Relate to the pioneers who made their homes in new parts of the country.
boom town	Point out that this is a compound word meaning "a town that grows rapidly in size."
landmark	Give examples of famous landmarks, such as the Statue of Liberty.

For vocabulary activities, see Vocabulary Games on pages 2–7.

For vocabulary activities, see Vocabulary Games on pages 2–7.

Vocabulary Words

stagecoach horsedrawn vehicle with four wheels and a covered top

nuggets small chunks

skillet heavy iron pan used for cooking and frying

miners people whose job it is to work in a mine and extract minerals or ores from the earth

settle to make a home in a new place

boom town a community that experiences sudden and rapid growth

landmark an object or feature that marks a boundary or identifies a place

---

AFTER

Building Background and Vocabulary

Apply Vocabulary Strategies

Use familiar word parts. Write the word *landmark* on the board. Remind students that they can sometimes figure out the meaning of a word by looking for shorter words or syllables that they recognize. Model using the strategy.

> **MODEL** When I look at this long word, I see the familiar word *land* in it. When I cover up *land* I see another familiar word—*mark*. I know that putting a mark on something helps people identify it. I can figure out that a landmark is something that marks the land or identifies a place.

Guide students in following a similar procedure to figure out the meanings of *stagecoach* (a coach that goes in stages or steps) and *boom town* (a town that booms or grows quickly).

RETEACH **lesson vocabulary.** Have students take turns pantomiming scenes that illustrate the meaning of a Vocabulary Word. The other students guess the word and hold up the correct word card.

FLUENCY BUILDER Using *Intervention Practice Book* page 91, read each word in the first column aloud and have students repeat it. Then have students work in pairs to read the words in the first column aloud to each other. Follow the same procedure with each of the remaining columns. After partners have practiced reading aloud the words in each column, have them listen to each other as they practice the entire list.

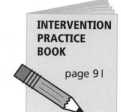

INTERVENTION PRACTICE BOOK

page 91

⭐ (Focus Skill) **Fact and Opinion**

PRETEACH the skill. Ask what students recall about fact and opinion. Then have them look at **side A of Skill Card 23: Fact and Opinion** and read aloud the explanations in the boxes at the top. Have students take turns reading aloud the sentences in the other boxes, identifying each sentence as a fact or an opinion. Point out that if students aren't sure, they can match the colors with the colors of the boxes at the top. Discuss why each sentence is a fact or an opinion, emphasizing the difference between statements that can be proved in some way and those that cannot.

Prepare to Read "Boom Town"

Preview. Tell students that they are going to read a historical fiction selection called "Boom Town." Have them recall what they know about historical fiction. Emphasize that although the story is partly made-up, the setting is a real time and place in the past. After discussing the genre, preview the selection.

ON YOUR MARK

pages
196–213

- **Pages 196–197:** I see the title and the names of the author and illustrator. The picture shows a little town. I can tell from the way people are dressed and from other picture clues that this story must take place long ago. The girl with the pie on page 197 may be an important character. I wonder who she is.

- **Pages 198–205:** On page 198 I see a large building and many tents. I will read the first paragraph to find out what kind of place this is. (*Read aloud.*) I think the girl in the pictures must be telling this story. In the pictures I see her with her family at their cabin, and I see her carrying what looks like a heavy pail of berries. I can guess from the pictures on pages 202–205 that the girl is baking pies. On page 205 a boy has a sign that says "Amanda's Fine Pies." I wonder if Amanda is opening a store to sell her pies.

- **Pages 206–213:** As I look through the rest of the story, I see pictures of people working at different jobs. It also looks like the town is growing. Maybe Amanda and her pies have something to do with this.

Set purpose. Model setting a purpose for reading "Boom Town."

MODEL From my preview I know that this selection is a historical fiction story about a family that moves to the California gold fields. One purpose for reading is to understand the important ideas in a story. I'll read this selection to understand what life was like in California at the time that people came here to look for gold.

Reread and Summarize

Have students reread and summarize "Boom Town" in sections, as described below.

Pages 198–201

Let's reread pages 198–201 to recall what the town was like when the family came to California.

Summary: There was hardly a town at all when Amanda's family came to live there. Amanda was so bored that she decided to try baking a pie in a skillet.

Pages 202–205

Now let's reread pages 202–205 to find out how Amanda's pie turned out.

Summary: After a few tries Amanda figured out how to bake a good pie. Pretty soon miners were coming to buy her pies. She got her brothers to help her start a bakery.

Pages 206–209

As we reread pages 206–209, let's see how the town began to grow.

Summary: Amanda told Peddler Pete that he should open a store. Soon more and more people came to live in the town, and more businesses opened.

Pages 210–213

Let's reread pages 210–213 to recall why the story is called "Boom Town."

Summary: The town grows so quickly that soon Amanda's bakery is right in the middle of a busy town filled with people. Amanda is happy that it all began with her pies.

FLUENCY BUILDER Use *Intervention Practice Book* page 91. Point out the sentences on the bottom half of the page. Remind students that their goal is to read each phrase or unit smoothly. Model appropriate pace, expression, and phrasing as you read each sentence, and have students read it after you. Then have students practice by reading the sentences aloud three times to a partner.

INTERVENTION
PRACTICE
BOOK

page 91

Directed Reading: "How Grandmama Tamed the West" pp. 182–189

Pages 182–183

Have students read the title aloud. Then have them read pages 182–183 to find out what Grandmama did when she went out West. (*started a stagecoach business, busted broncos*) Ask: **Why does the author say that the horses got to Dry Gulch the day before they left Mud Flats?** (*to make the story funny; to make readers laugh*) **AUTHOR'S PURPOSE**

BRIGHT
SURPRISES
pp. 182–189

Pages 184–185

Have students look at the illustration and then read pages 184–185 to find out what Grandmama is doing. (*digging for gold*) Ask: **Is this sentence fact or opinion: *All that gear was not light, and Rube was a sorrowful sight?* Explain your answer.** (*opinion; could prove how much the gear weighed but not that it was "light;" some might disagree with that opinion and also that Rube was a sorrowful sight*)
(Focus Skill) **FACT AND OPINION**

How did Pike become a boom town? (*People came to see Grandmama's pile of dirt and stayed in Pike, so the town grew quickly.*) **CAUSE AND EFFECT**

Pages 186–187

Ask students to read pages 186–187 to find out what else Grandmama did. Ask: **What happens in this part of the story?** (*Grandmama finds two nuggets. She gets bored with mining and becomes a sheriff.*) **SUMMARIZE**

What does the author mean when she says that the bank robbers ran like lightning? (*They ran very fast, as fast as a flash of lightning.*) **UNDERSTAND FIGURATIVE LANGUAGE**

Page 188

Have students read page 188 to see how the towns thanked Grandmama. (*by naming streets Main Street after her, Emma Lee Main*) Ask: **Do you think this is the real reason that many towns have streets called Main Street?** (*No, the author is making a joke.*) **AUTHOR'S PURPOSE/MAKE JUDGMENTS**

Ask: **How did Grandmama tame the West?** Model using the strategy of self-questioning.

> **MODEL** When I read this story, I wasn't sure why it is called "How Grandmama Tamed the West." I asked myself how someone could tame a part of the country and what Grandmama did that made the West a tamer place. Asking myself these questions helped me understand that she tamed the West by stopping fights and putting bank robbers in jail.
> (Focus Strategy) **SELF-QUESTION**

INTERVENTION
PRACTICE
BOOK

page 93

Summarize the selection. Have students work with partners to summarize the selection by drawing a set of three pictures and writing a one-sentence caption for each picture.

Answers to *Think About It* Questions

1. Grandmama started a stagecoach business. Then, she busted broncos. Next, she became a miner. Finally, she became a sheriff. **SUMMARY**

2. Accept reasonable responses. The storyteller gives Grandmama many compliments and claims that Main Streets around the country have been named after Emma Lee Main, the author's grandmother. **INTERPRETATION**

3. Tell students to decide which of Grandmama's adventures is their favorite and to think about how Grandmama would tell about it. Remind them that when they write about what happened, they should be sure to use the first person—I. **WRITE A POSTCARD**

AFTER

Skill Review
pages 220–221

USE SKILL CARD 23B

(Focus Skill) Fact and Opinion

RETEACH **the skill.** Have students look at side B of Skill Card 23: Fact and Opinion. Read aloud the skill reminder. Then have students take turns reading aloud the statements made by people in the picture. Ask whether each statement is a fact or an opinion, and have students explain their reasoning.

FLUENCY BUILDER Use *Intervention Practice Book* page 91. Explain that students will practice the sentences on the bottom half of the page by reading them aloud on tape. Assign new partners. Have students take turns reading the sentences aloud to each other and then reading them on tape. After they listen to the tape, have them tell how they think they have improved their reading of the sentences. Then have them read the sentences aloud on tape a second time, with improved pacing and tone.

INTERVENTION PRACTICE BOOK

page 91

Research Report: Introduction

Build on prior knowledge. Have students recall the steps they have learned for writing a research report. (*choose a topic, research and take notes, make an outline*) Tell them that the next step is to write a draft.

Display the following outline and graphic organizer. Explain that the graphic organizer shows the parts of a research report.

Boom Towns

I. What is a boom town?
  A. Boom towns grew very fast.
  B. They were often out West.
  C. Many were started by gold miners.
II. What made boom towns grow?
  A. Miners needed supplies.
  B. People started businesses.
  C. More people came.

Title: Boom Towns

Introduction:

Middle:

Conclusion:

Point out that the introduction introduces the topic. The introduction should also grab the reader's interest. Tell students that they will follow their outlines when they actually write their reports, using the main ideas identified by the roman numerals as topic sentences for each paragraph. The other sentences add facts and examples. The conclusion sums up the main idea of the report and draws a conclusion from the information.

Construct the text. "Share the pen" with students in a collaborative group writing effort to draft an introduction to a research report on boom towns. Use the outline above if you wish.

- Discuss the main idea your introduction will express about the topic and how to grab the reader's interest.

- Work with students to write the draft of the introduction.

Revisit the text. Have students reread the introduction. Ask: **Does this introduction give the reader a clear understanding of our topic?**

Keep a copy of this introduction to use in Lessons 24 and 26.

> **On Your Own**
>
> Write a paragraph about how boom towns grew.
> Begin with a topic sentence that tells the main idea.
> Write two more sentences that give facts or
> examples to support your main idea.

Connect Spelling and Phonics

RETEACH **long vowel /ī/ igh.** Tell students that you will say some words in which the letters *igh* stand for the /ī/ sound. Have volunteers write each word on the board. Work together to proofread their work.

I. night*	2. right*	3. fights*	4. high*
5. thigh	6. plight*	7. might*	8. light*

*Word appears in "How Grandmama Tamed the West."

Dictate the following sentence and have students write it: *That sight gave me a big fright.*

Build and Read Longer Words

Remind students that they have learned that the letters *igh* can stand for the /ī/ sound. Now they will use what they have learned to help them read some longer words.

INTERVENTION ASSESSMENT BOOK

Write the word *brightness* on the board. Remind students that they can read longer words by looking for prefixes or suffixes and for root words. Cover the suffix *-ness* and have students blend the sounds to read *bright*. Then uncover *-ness*. Tell students that you know that the suffix *-ness* means "the state or condition of." You can figure out that *brightness* means "the state, quality, or condition of being bright." Use appropriate strategies to help students decode the words *brightly, frighten, lighting, slightly, highlight.* Encourage students to build other long words in which the letters *igh* stand for the long *i* vowel sound. Suggest that they use a dictionary to look up words they are not sure about.

FLUENCY BUILDER Have students choose a passage from "How Grandmama Tamed the West" to read aloud to a partner. You may have students choose passages that they found particularly interesting, or have them choose one of the following options:

- Read page 183. (Total: 112 words)

- Read the last paragraph on page 186 and all of page 187. (From *Grandmama had . . .* to *. . . for her.* Total: 106 words)

Students read the selected passage aloud to their partners three times. Have the student rate each reading on a scale from 1 to 4. Encourage readers to note their improvement from one reading to the next by completing sentence frames such as *I know my reading improved because* _____. The partner who listens to the reading should also be encouraged to offer positive comments on the reader's improvement.

Review Vocabulary

To revisit the Vocabulary Words with students prior to the weekly assessment, have students show their understanding by answering questions such as the following.

1. Would you have wanted to **settle** in the West? Why or why not?
2. If you owned a **skillet**, what would you use it for?
3. What would you do if you found gold **nuggets**?
4. What do you think it was like to be a **miner** during the Gold Rush?
5. Would riding in a **stagecoach** be more or less interesting than riding in a car or a bus? Why?
6. Amanda made pies to sell. What skills or talents might you have liked to contribute to a **boom town**?
7. Name a **landmark** that you would include in directions to your home or school.

Correct responses: Accept responses that reflect an understanding of the Vocabulary Words.

You may want to display the Vocabulary Words and definitions on page 229 and have students copy them to use when they study for the vocabulary test.

INTERVENTION
PRACTICE
BOOK

page 94

(Focus Skill) Review Fact and Opinion

To review the focus skill before the weekly assessment, distribute *Intervention Practice Book* page 94. Point out the title, Fact and Opinion, and read the directions aloud. You may choose to guide students through the activity, or have them complete it with a partner and then share and discuss their work with the group.

Review Test Prep

Ask students to turn to page 221 of the *Pupil Edition*. Call attention to the tips for answering the test questions. Tell students that paying attention to these tips can help them answer not only the test questions on this page but also other test questions like these.

**ON YOUR
MARK**

page 221

INTERVENTION
ASSESSMENT
BOOK

✔

Have a volunteer read the passage aloud. Then read aloud the directions, the first test question, and the tip that goes with it. Have students identify the correct answer choice. Ask them to explain why this choice is correct and the others are incorrect. Follow a similar procedure with the second question. Encourage students to tell how they might apply the tips on this page in other test situations as well.

Self-Selected Reading

Have students select their own books to read independently. They might choose books from the classroom library shelf, or you may wish to offer a group of appropriate books from which students can choose.

- *A Gold Rush Diary.* (See page 22 IM of the *Teacher's Edition* for a lesson plan.)

- *The Tortilla Factory* by Gary Paulsen. Harcourt Brace, 1995.

- *Zora Hurston and the Chinaberry Tree* by William Miller. Lee & Low, 1996.

After students have chosen their books, give each student a copy of My Reading Log, which can be found on page R42 in the back of the *Teacher's Edition*. Have students fill in the information at the top of the form. Then have them use the log to keep track of their reading and to record their responses to the literature.

Conduct student-teacher conferences. Arrange time for each student to confer with you individually about his or her self-selected reading. Have students bring their Reading Logs to share with you at the conference. Students might also like to choose a favorite passage to read aloud to you. Ask questions about the book to stimulate discussion. For example, for a nonfiction book, you might ask a student to give examples of important facts, and ask whether the author states any opinions, what those opinions might be, and how the student recognized them.

FLUENCY PERFORMANCE Have students read aloud to you the passage from "How Grandmama Tamed the West" that they selected and practiced earlier with their partners. Keep track of the number of words the student reads correctly. Ask the student to rate his or her own performance on the 1–4 scale. If students are not happy with their oral reading, give them an opportunity to continue practicing and then to reread the passage to you again.

See *Oral Reading Fluency Assessment* for monitoring progress.

Use with

"Cocoa Ice"

Review Phonics: Long Vowel /ē/ *y, ie*

Identify the sound. Tell students to listen for the /ē/ sound as you say the word *piece*. Then have them repeat three times: *Our dog, Chief, is a sneaky candy thief.* Ask them to identify the words with the /ē/ sound. (*Chief, sneaky, candy, thief*)

Associate letters to sound. Write on the board: *Our dog, Chief, is a sneaky candy thief.* Point out the *ea* in *sneaky* and remind students that the letters *ea* can stand for the /ē/ sound. Then underline the *y* in *sneaky*. Explain that *y* can also stand for /ē/. Follow a similar procedure for the *ie* in *Chief* and *thief*.

Word blending. Have students repeat after you as you model how to blend and read the word *Chief*. Point to *Ch* and say /ch/. Point to *ie* and say /ē/. Slide your hand under the letters *Chie* as you slowly elongate the sounds /chēē/. Next, point to *f* and say /f/. Slide your hand under the whole word, elongating all the sounds /chēēff/, and then say the word naturally.

**INTERVENTION
PRACTICE
BOOK**

page 96

Apply the skill. Write the following words on the board, and have students read each aloud. Then ask students to add *-es* to each word, changing the spelling as needed. Have them identify the letter or letters that stand for the /ē/ sound in both the original and the new words.

puppy (puppies)   **study** (studies)   **story** (stories)   **kitty** (kitties)
bunny (bunnies)   **jelly** (jellies)   **family** (families)   **copy** (copies)

Introduce Vocabulary

PRETEACH lesson vocabulary. Tell students that they are going to learn seven new words that they will see again when they read a selection called "Cocoa Ice." Teach each Vocabulary Word using the process shown at the right.

Use the following suggestions or similar ideas to give the meaning or context.

harvest	Give examples of crops that farmers gather or harvest.
pulp	Give examples of pulp from familiar fruits and vegetables, such as oranges and tomatoes.
machete	Explain that a machete has a sharp blade that is used to cut through tough stalks when harvesting crops.

> Write the word.
> Say the word.
> Track the word and have students repeat it.
> Give the meaning or context.

trading	In the past, trading posts were used to sell or exchange goods. Identify the root word *trade*.
schooner	Relate to sailboats that students may have seen.
support	Give examples of structural elements, such as pillars, and columns that support buildings and bridges.
bargain	Relate to the idea of discussing price with a seller at a flea market.

For vocabulary activities, see Vocabulary Games on pages 2–7.

For vocabulary activities, see Vocabulary Games on pages 2–7.

Vocabulary Words

harvest to gather a crop

pulp the soft part of certain fruits and vegetables

machete a heavy knife used as a tool for cutting plants

trading used for the purpose of exchanging one thing for another

schooner a ship that has two or more masts with sails in the front and back

support to hold the weight of

bargain to talk about a trade in order to get a better deal

AFTER

Building Background and Vocabulary

Apply Vocabulary Strategies

Identify multiple-meaning words. Write on the board: *This year's harvest was plentiful. The farmer will harvest the corn.* Tell students that when a word has more than one meaning, they can often figure out the meaning from the way the word is used. Model using the strategy.

> **MODEL** I know that the word *harvest* is used as a noun in the first sentence. A harvest is the result of one season's planting of any product or crop. In the second sentence I see that *harvest* is used as a verb; here it must mean "gather or bring in" a crop.

Guide students in using a similar procedure with the words *support* and *bargain*.

RETEACH **lesson vocabulary.** Provide patterns for a circle and an arrow. Have students make a simple spinner by cutting a circle and arrow from cardboard and joining them with a brad. Tell students to write the Vocabulary Words on the spinner. Students take turns spinning the pointer, saying the word it lands on, and using the word in a sentence.

FLUENCY BUILDER Using *Intervention Practice Book* page 95, read each word in the first column aloud and have students repeat it. Then have students work in pairs to read the words in the first column aloud to each other. Follow the same procedure with each of the remaining columns. After partners have practiced reading aloud the words in each column, have them listen to each other as they practice the entire list.

INTERVENTION PRACTICE BOOK

page 95

BEFORE

Reading
"Cocoa Ice"
pages 224–253

USE SKILL CARD 24A

(Focus Skill) Compare and Contrast

PRETEACH **the skill.** Have students recall what it means to compare and contrast. Then have them look at **side A of Skill Card 24: Compare and Contrast** and tell what they see in the pictures. Have students read aloud and discuss the likenesses and differences listed below the pictures. Ask whether students would make any additions or changes to this list. Then draw a Venn diagram on the board, and have students tell how to complete it.

Prepare to Read: "Cocoa Ice"

Preview. Tell students that they are going to read a selection called "Cocoa Ice." Explain that this selection is informational fiction, which means that the story uses fictional characters and events to give information about a topic. After discussing the genre, preview the selection with students.

ON YOUR MARK
pages 224–253

- **Pages 224–225:** First, I read the title and the names of the author and illustrator. Then I see that the girl in the picture on page 224 is dressed for very cold weather. The picture at the top of page 225 shows another girl, who is dressed for warm weather. Maybe these girls are the main characters, but it looks as if they live in different places.

- **Pages 226–239:** On page 226, I see the heading "Cocoa." As I look through the pages, I see more pictures of the second girl and other people. It looks like they are doing different kinds of jobs, and they seem to live in a warm place. I wonder what they are doing.

- **Pages 240–252:** On page 240, I see the heading "Ice." I guess this must be the second part of the story "Cocoa Ice." Looking at the pictures, I can see why this part is called "Ice." It shows people living and working in a cold place. Their clothes look old-fashioned. On page 249, workers seem to be cutting ice into blocks. I am curious to find out more about what they are doing,

Set purpose. Model setting a purpose for reading "Cocoa Ice."

MODEL From my preview, I know that this selection is a story that has two parts and gives information about a topic. One purpose for reading is to enjoy the story, and another is to learn new information. I think I will read this selection to find out what kind of work the people in both parts of the story are doing and why.

Reread and Summarize

Have students reread and summarize "Cocoa Ice" in sections, as described below.

Pages 226–231

Let's reread pages 226–231 to recall what Santo Domingo is like.

Summary: In Santo Domingo the weather is hot. Many trees grow there, including the cacao tree. To make chocolate, the girl and her family spread cacao beans and pulp to dry in the sun.

Pages 232–239

Now let's reread pages 232–239 to find out what happens to the chocolate.

Summary: While the cocoa beans are drying, the girl goes hunting for conchs. When a schooner comes, the sailor named Jacob gives her a sweet-smelling little bag. The girl and her father take home a block of ice. Her mother uses cacao pulp and ice to make cocoa ice.

Pages 240–245

As we reread pages 240–245, let's see what Maine is like.

Summary: Winter in Maine is very cold. The girl who lives there tells how her father and Uncle Jacob hope the ice on the river will freeze thick and clear so they can sell it in hot countries far away.

Pages 246–252

Let's reread pages 246–252 to recall what happens to the ice.

Summary: The men cut the ice into blocks. Uncle Jacob sails away on the schooner to take ice to Santo Domingo and bring back chocolate. The girl gives him the balsam pillow she made. The girl helps her mother make chocolate ice cream.

FLUENCY BUILDER Use *Intervention Practice Book* page 95. Point out the sentences on the bottom half of the page. Remind students that their goal is to read each phrase or unit smoothly. Model appropriate pace, expression, and phrasing as you read each sentence and have students read it after you. Then have students practice by reading the sentences aloud three times to a partner.

INTERVENTION
PRACTICE
BOOK

page 95

Making Connections
pages 258–259

Pages 190–191

Pages 192–193

Pages 194–195

INTERVENTION PRACTICE BOOK

page 97

Directed Reading: "Harvest Time," pp. 190–196

BRIGHT SURPRISES
pp. 190–196

Have students read the title and describe the illustrations. Then have them read pages 190–191 to find out what Lizzie and her family do at harvest time. (*have a harvest party*) Ask: **How are Galveston Island and the tropics alike? How are they different?** (*Alike: Bananas grow in both places. Different: Sometimes the winters on Galveston Island are too cold for banana plants.*)
(Focus Skill) **COMPARE AND CONTRAST**

Have students read pages 192–193 to find out about the memory-makers. Ask: **Why does Lizzie choose a ship for her memory-maker?** (*It represents the ship that brought her dad's grandparents to Galveston Island.*) **CHARACTERS' MOTIVATIONS**

Ask: **Why does Lizzie say the glitter looks like swirly snow when she shakes her memory-maker?** Model the strategy of creating mental images.

> **MODEL** When I read this part of the story, I didn't understand at first what Lizzie meant. Then I tried to imagine what would happen if I filled a jar with water and glitter and then shook it. I can picture in my mind the little flashes of glitter swirling around and this reminds me of a snowstorm. (Focus Strategy) **CREATE MENTAL IMAGES**

Ask students to predict what will happen next. Have them read pages 194–195 to confirm their predictions. Ask: **Why do you think Lizzie's family has a party at harvest time?** (*to enjoy the special treats they make from the bananas*) **DRAW CONCLUSIONS**

What memories do you think Lizzie made? (*Accept reasonable responses.*) **IDENTIFY WITH CHARACTERS**

Summarize the selection. Ask students to think about what happened first, next, and last in the story. Then have students summarize it in three sentences.

Answers to *Think About It* Questions

1. Possible response: They are thankful that Grandma and Grandpa Jakoby had studied hard to speak English, had planted bananas, and had left their cold and snowy home to come to Galveston Island. **SUMMARY**

2. Possible response: They have a harvest party only in years the banana trees make fruit. In some years, there are no bananas because the winter is too cold or a storm blows the flowers off the plants. **INTERPRETATION**

3. Remind students to include the reason for the party in their invitations. They should choose a date and time and explain the memory-maker tradition. **WRITE AN INVITATION**

AFTER

Skill Review
pages 260–261

USE SKILL CARD 24B

Compare and Contrast

RETEACH the skill. Have students look at **side B of Skill Card 24: Compare and Contrast**, and read aloud the skill reminder. Call on volunteers to read aloud the directions for making cocoa ice and ice cream. Then draw a Venn diagram on the board, and fill it in as students decide how the two processes are alike and different. Students can copy the completed diagram on their papers.

FLUENCY BUILDER Use *Intervention Practice Book* page 95. Explain that students will practice the sentences on the bottom half of the page by reading them aloud on tape. Assign new partners. Have students take turns reading the sentences aloud to each other and then reading them on tape. After they listen to the tape, have them tell how they think they have improved their reading of the sentences. Then have them read the sentences aloud on tape a second time, with improved pacing and tone.

INTERVENTION
PRACTICE
BOOK

page 95

Expository Writing: Edit a Paragraph

Build on prior knowledge. Have students take out their copies of the introductory paragraph about boom towns that they drafted as a group in the previous lesson or duplicate the copy you saved. Tell them that the next step in the process of writing a research report is to edit their draft by revising it and then proofreading to correct errors.

Display the following chart, and explain how students can use these marks when they revise their work. Give simple examples.

Editor's Marks	
Mark	**Meaning**
$\land$	Add something
$\mathcal{l}$	Cut something
$\sim$	Transpose

Construct the text. "Share the pen" with students in a collaborative group writing effort to revise their introductory paragraph.

- Ask: **Are there any facts or details we should add? Is there anything we should cut? Can we move a phrase to a better place in the sentence?**

- Show revisions on the board, and have students copy them on their papers.

Revisit the text. Have students reread the introduction. Explain that after revising, they need to proofread their work.

- Ask: **Did we indent our paragraph? Are our sentences complete? Have we spelled all the words correctly?**

- Guide students through proofreading the paragraph.

On Your Own

Draft a short paragraph about harvesting bananas. Look back at "Harvest Time" for information. Then revise your paragraph, using editor's marks if you need them. Proofread your paragraph and make any corrections. Share your work with a partner.

Connect Spelling and Phonics

RETEACH **long vowel /ē/y, ie.** Tell students that you will say six words in which the letter *y* stands for the /ē/ sound and two in which *ie* stands for the /ē/ sound. Identify the type for each group of words before you read it. Have volunteers write each word on the board. Work together to proofread their work.

1. party*	2. sunny*	3. tasty*	4. happy
5. tidy	6. funny	7. chief	8. grief

*Word appears in "Harvest Time."

Dictate the following sentences for students to write, explaining that in the first one, *y* will stand for the /ē/ sound and that in the second one, *ie* will stand for that sound. *Andy has a hungry bunny. The thief had the bag for a brief time.*

Build and Read Longer Words

Remind students that they have learned that the letter *y* and the letter pattern *ie* can stand for the /ē/ sound. Now they will use what they have learned to help them read some longer words.

Write the word *floppy* on the board. Remind students that often they can read longer words by dividing the word into syllables. Draw a line between the two consonants in the middle of *floppy*. Point out the CVC pattern in the first syllable. Have students blend the sounds to read *flop*. Then have students use what they know about the /ē/ sound that the letter *y* can stand for to read the second syllable. Help students blend the syllables to read *floppy*. Use appropriate strategies to help students decode the words *belief, worrying, worries*. Encourage students to build other long words in which the /ē/ sound is represented by *y* or *ie*. Suggest that they use a dictionary to look up words they are not sure about.

INTERVENTION ASSESSMENT BOOK

FLUENCY BUILDER Have students choose a passage from "Harvest Time" to read aloud to a partner. You may have students choose a passage that they found particularly interesting, or have them choose one of the following options:

- Read pages 192 and the first paragraph on page 193. (Total: 124 words)
- Read page 195. (Total: 116 words)

Students read the selected passage aloud to their partners three times. Have students rate each of their own readings on a scale of 1 to 4. Encourage readers to note their improvement from one reading to the next by completing sentence frames such as *I know my reading improved because _____*. The partner who listens to the reading should also be encouraged to offer positive comments on the reader's improvement.

Weekly Review

Review vocabulary. To revisit the Vocabulary Words with students prior to the weekly assessment, display a word line like the one shown here.

not strange at all —————————————————— **very strange**

Have students listen to the following questions and take turns indicating on the word line how strange each event would be. Have them explain their reasons. If needed, ask follow-up questions to check students' understanding of the Vocabulary Words.

How strange would it be if . . .

  1. you could **harvest** bubble gum?
  2. **pulp** from an orange was in your orange juice?
  3. a **machete** was used to cut hair?
  4. there were many goods to exchange at a **trading** post?
  5. a **schooner** had no sails?
  6. you could **bargain** at a yard sale or open market?

Correct responses: Accept responses that reflect an understanding of the Vocabulary Words.

You may want to display the Vocabulary Words and definitions on page 239 and have students copy them to use when they study for the vocabulary test.

 ## ⭐ Review Compare and Contrast

To review the focus skill before the weekly assessment, distribute *Intervention Practice Book* page 98. Point out the title, Compare and Contrast, and read the directions aloud. You may choose to guide students through the activity, or have them complete it with a partner and then share and discuss their work with the group.

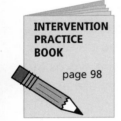

**INTERVENTION
PRACTICE
BOOK**

page 98

Review Test Prep

Ask students to turn to page 261 of the *Pupil Edition*. Call attention to the tips for answering the test questions. Tell students that paying attention to these tips can help them answer not only the test questions on this page but also other test questions like these.

**ON YOUR
MARK**

page 261

Have volunteers read aloud the stories "Henry" and "Albert." Then read aloud question 1 and the tip that goes with it. Have students identify the correct choice and explain their thinking. Follow the same procedure with question 2. Encourage students to tell how they might apply the tips on this page in other test situations as well.

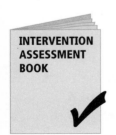

**INTERVENTION
ASSESSMENT
BOOK**

Self-Selected Reading

Have students select their own books to read independently. They might choose books from the classroom library shelf, or you may wish to offer a group of appropriate books from which students can choose. Titles might include the following:

- *The Chocolate Journey.* (See page 26 IM of the *Teacher's Edition* for a lesson plan.)

- *Across the Big Blue Sea* by Jakki Wood. National Geographic Society, 1998.

- *How a Seed Grows* by Helene J. Jordan. HarperCollins, 2000.

After students have chosen their books, give each student a copy of My Reading Log, which can be found on page R42 in the back of the *Teacher's Edition*. Have students fill in the information at the top of the form. Then have them use the log to keep track of their reading and to record their responses to the literature.

Conduct student-teacher conferences. Arrange time for each student to meet with you individually to discuss his or her self-selected reading. Have students bring their Reading Logs to share with you at the conference. Students might also like to choose a favorite passage to read aloud to you. Ask questions about the book designed to stimulate discussion. For example, you might ask the student to compare and contrast this book with another he or she has read.

FLUENCY PERFORMANCE Have students read aloud to you the passage from "Harvest Time" that they selected and practiced earlier with their partners. Keep track of the number of words the student reads correctly. Ask the student to rate his or her own performance on the 1–4 scale. If students are not happy with their oral reading, give them an opportunity to continue practicing and then to read the passage to you again.

See *Oral Reading Fluency Assessment* for monitoring progress.

Use with

"If You Made a Million"

Review Phonics: Vowel Diphthong /oi/ *oi, oy*

Identify the sound. Tell students to listen for the /oi/ sound as you say *joy* and *boil*. Then have them repeat three times: *Boys with toys enjoy making noise.* Ask which words have the /oi/ sound.

Associate letters to sound. Write on the board: *Boys with toys enjoy making noise.* Underline *oy* and *oi* each time they appear. Explain that when the letters *oy* and *oi* come together, they usually stand for the /oi/ sound heard in *Boys, toys, enjoy,* and *noise.*

Word blending. Have students repeat after you as you model how to blend and read *Boys.* Point to *B* and say /b/. Point to *oy* and say /oi/. Slide your hand under *Boy* as you slowly elongate the sounds /bbooii/. Next, point to *s* and say /z/. Slide your hand under the whole word, elongating all the sounds /bbooiizz/, and then say the word naturally.

INTERVENTION
PRACTICE
BOOK

page 100

Apply the skill. *Letter Substitution* Write the following words on the board, and have students read each aloud. Change as needed to form the word in parentheses. Have a volunteer read aloud each new word.

owl (oil)	**bee** (boy)	**nose** (noise)	**coal** (coil)
jay (joy)	**pose** (poise)	**too** (toy)	**can** (coin)

Introduce Vocabulary

PRETEACH **lesson vocabulary.** Tell students that they are going to learn six new words that they will see again when they read a selection called "If You Made a Million." Teach each vocabulary word using the process below.

Use these suggestions or similar ideas to give the meaning or context.

> Write the word.
> Say the word.
> Track the word and have students repeat it.
> Give the meaning or context.

congratulations	Role-play giving an award; say, "Congratulations!"
receive	Have a student help you role-play receiving a note.
amount	Display the same amount of money, using five pennies and a nickel.
choices	Relate to the idea that students have choices about how to use their free time. Point out the -*s* ending.
combinations	Show combinations of coins. Point out the -*s* ending for the plural.

value   Explain that money has value or worth. One $5 bill and five $1 bills have the same value.

For vocabulary activities, see Vocabulary Games on pages 2–7.

For vocabulary activities, see Vocabulary Games on pages 2–7.

AFTER
Building Background and Vocabulary

Apply Vocabulary Strategies

Use syllabication. Write the word *value* on the board. Remind students that they can sometimes figure out how to pronounce a new word by dividing the word into syllables. Model using the strategy.

> **MODEL** I know that some syllables end with a consonant, so I'll start by breaking this word after the *l*. Now I see the CVC pattern in the first syllable and I know this indicates a short vowel sound—/val/. I also recognize the letter pattern *ue* in the second syllable; these letters appear in the word *fuel* and make the /yo͞o/ sound. I'll try combining the sounds /val/ and /yo͞o/.

Guide students in using a similar procedure to decode *combinations*.

RETEACH lesson vocabulary. Provide a set of word cards for each student or pair of students. Read aloud or write on the board the meaning of one of the Vocabulary Words and the first letter, digraph, or syllable in that word. Students match the correct word card to the definition. Continue until students have matched all the words.

Vocabulary Words

congratulations an expression said to someone who has won or earned something

receive get

amount the total number of things

choices decisions about what to choose

combinations sets of things grouped together

value worth

FLUENCY BUILDER Using *Intervention Practice Book* page 99, read each word in the first column aloud and have students repeat it. Then have students work in pairs to read the words in the first column aloud to each other. Follow the same procedure with each of the remaining columns. After partners have practiced reading aloud the words in each column, have them listen to each other as they practice the entire list.

INTERVENTION PRACTICE BOOK

page 99

(Focus Skill) Main Idea and Details

PRETEACH the skill. Have students recall briefly what they have learned about main idea and details. Then have them look at **side A of Skill Card 25: Main Idea and Details**. Read aloud the definitions, and ask a student to read aloud the paragraph. Point out that the main idea of this paragraph is stated in the first sentence. Then call attention to the cartoon strip, and have two volunteers take turns reading aloud the words of the two characters. Call on students to tell in their own words how to figure out an unstated main idea.

Prepare to Read: "If You Made a Million"

Preview. Tell students that they are going to read a selection called "If You Made a Million." Explain that this selection is expository nonfiction. Have students recall that the purpose of expository nonfiction is to give information about a topic. Tell students to look for facts about money as they read the selection. Then preview the selection together.

ON YOUR MARK

pages
264–289

- **Pages 264–265:** On page 264, I see the title and the names of the author and illustrator. I can tell by looking at the illustration on page 264 and the real penny on page 265 that this story probably uses fantasy to give information about money.

- **Pages 266–271:** In these illustrations I see a character that looks like a mathematical magician, some funny signs, and funny things happening. I also see real coins and a dollar bill. There seem to be more coins on each page. The title is "If You Made a Million." I wonder if the story will tell about making a million dollars.

- **Pages 272–273:** I can see that pages 272–273 must give information about a bank. I know that people keep money in banks. I think I can learn more about banks by reading this story.

Set purpose. Model setting a purpose for reading "If You Made a Million."

MODEL From my preview, I know that this selection combines an amusing fantasy story with information about an important real-life topic, money. One purpose for reading is to gain information. I think I will read this selection to find out more about banks and other information related to money.

Reread and Summarize

Have students reread and summarize "If You Made a Million" in sections, as described below.

Pages 264–271

Let's reread pages 268–275 to recall facts about earning money.

Summary: You can do jobs to earn money. Different combinations of coins can have the same value. You can use the money you earned to buy things.

Pages 272–278

Now let's reread pages 272–278 to find out what else you can do with money and other interesting facts about it.

Summary: You can save your money in a bank and earn interest. The longer you leave your money in the bank, the more money you will have. Different combinations of coins and bills can have the same value.

Pages 279–284

As we reread pages 279–284, let's see what else banks do.

Summary: Instead of paying with coins or bills, you can use a check. Checks go to a clearinghouse that tells the banks to take money from the person who is buying something and give it to the person who is selling. You can also borrow money from the bank, but you must pay back more than you borrow.

Pages 285–289

Let's reread pages 285–289 to recall what you could do if you made a million dollars.

Summary: If you made a million dollars, you could spend it or put it in the bank to earn interest. You would have to make choices.

FLUENCY BUILDER Use *Intervention Practice Book*, page 99. Point out the sentences on the bottom half of the page. Remind students that their goal is to read each phrase or unit smoothly. Model appropriate pace, expression, and phrasing as you read each sentence, and have students read it after you. Then have students practice by reading the sentences aloud three times to a partner.

INTERVENTION
PRACTICE
BOOK

page 99

Making Connections
pages 294–295

Directed Reading: "Penny Savers," pp. 198–205

Read aloud the title, and have students use the title and illustration on page 198 to predict what the story is about. (*saving money*) Have them read pages 198–199 to confirm their predictions. **MAKE PREDICTIONS**

Bright Surprises
pp. 198–205

Pages 198–199

Ask: **Why does Roy want to save his money?** (*so he will have enough to buy things he really wants*) **CHARACTERS' MOTIVATIONS**

Pages 200–201

Have students read page 200 to find the main idea. Ask: **Which sentence on this page expresses the main idea?** (*The last sentence: Joy has discovered how it helps to save.*) **How do you know this is the main idea?** (*All of the other sentences give details that tell about this main idea.*) (Focus Strategy) **MAIN IDEA AND DETAILS**

Have students read page 201 to find out why Mrs. Boyd saves coins. (*so she'll have the right coins she needs to ride the bus*) **CHARACTERS' MOTIVATIONS**

Pages 202–203

Ask students to read pages 202–203 to find out more about how the Boyds save money. Model the strategy of adjusting reading rate.

> **MODEL** The second and third paragraphs on page 202 have information about banks. This is new information to me and may be more difficult than what I have read so far. I'll slow down my reading rate to make sure I understand it. (Focus Strategy) **ADJUST READING RATE**

Ask: **What are two meanings for the expression** *It pays to save?* (*It makes sense to save your money. You can earn money, or get paid, for saving money.*) **UNDERSTAND FIGURATIVE LANGUAGE**

Why else is it important to save? (*so you have money in an emergency*) **GENERALIZE**

INTERVENTION PRACTICE BOOK

page 101

Summarize the selection. Ask students to think about what they learned from reading "Penny Savers." Have them summarize why the Boyd family saves money by writing one sentence about each member of the family.

Answers to *Think About It* Questions

1. Possible response: You can buy after you know all your choices; you can save up money to buy something expensive; you can put money in the bank to make more money. **SUMMARY**

2. Possible response: When you save for a rainy day, you put money aside. That way, you'll have money to help with a problem you haven't planned for. **INTERPRETATION**

3. It may be helpful to write the discussion in the form of a play in which each family member is a character. Add stage directions as needed. **WRITE A CONVERSATION**

Skill Review
pages 296–297

USE SKILL CARD 25B

(Focus Skill) Main Idea and Details

RETEACH the skill. Have students look at **side B of Skill Card 25: Main Idea and Details**. Call on volunteers to read aloud the skill reminder and directions and to take turns reading aloud the details in the diagram. Have students discuss the details and determine the main idea. Guide them to formulate a main-idea sentence, and write it on the board. *(Possible response: Many different kinds of items have been used as money.)* Review the details to confirm that each of them gives more information about this main idea.

FLUENCY BUILDER Use *Intervention Practice Book*, page 99. Explain that students will practice reading the sentences on the bottom half of the page by reading them aloud on tape. Assign new partners. Have students take turns reading the sentences aloud to each other and then reading them on tape. After they listen to the tape, have them tell how they think they have improved their reading of the sentences. Then have them read the sentences aloud on tape a second time, with improved pacing and tone.

INTERVENTION PRACTICE BOOK

page 99

Expository Writing: Publishing

Build on prior knowledge. Have students take out their copies of the introductory paragraph about boom towns that they drafted and edited in previous lessons. Tell them that the next step in the process of writing a research report is to publish their work. Explain that they need to decide on the form they wish to use to share what they have written.

Display the following chart, and explain that these are some ways that students might publish a research report.

Publishing a Report	
By yourself	Write a report. Add drawings or graphics. Give an oral report. Make a tape recording.
With a partner or small group	Combine reports to create a book. Present your report as a role-play.
As a class	Create a bulletin board. Read aloud reports for invited guests.

Create a graphic. Have students tell how they might use each of the methods listed in the chart to publish a report with the introduction they wrote.

- Have students create a simple drawing or graphic that they might use to illustrate a written report or to serve as a visual aid for an oral report.

- "Share the pen" with students by working with them to write a caption, labels, or heading for their graphic, as appropriate.

Revisit the text. Have students reread the introduction they wrote. Discuss how they might present it as part of an oral report.

- Give students an opportunity to practice presenting the introduction orally.

On Your Own

Draft and edit a short paragraph about saving money. Look back at "Penny Savers" for ideas and information. Decide how you want to publish your paragraph. Have a partner read your published paragraph or listen to your oral presentation.

Connect Spelling and Phonics

RETEACH vowel diphthong /oi/*oi, oy.* Tell students that you will say some words in which the letters *oi* stand for the /oi/ sound. Have volunteers write each word on the board. Work together to proofread.

l. oil   2. coins*   3. spoiled*   4. point*
5. soil   6. hoist   7. join   8. broil

***Word appears in "Penny Savers."**

Tell students that you will read a sentence in which the /oi/ sound is spelled *oy.* Dictate this sentence and have students write it: *The boy had a toy that gave him joy.*

Build and Read Longer Words

Remind students that they have learned that the letters *oi* and *oy* can stand for the /oi/ sound. Now they will use what they have learned to help them read some longer words.

Write the word *enjoyment* on the board. Remind students that they can sometimes read a longer word by dividing it into syllables. Tell students that when they see longer words with *oi* or *oy,* they should break the word before or after the letters but not between them. Frame each syllable in *enjoyment* and help students read it. Then help them blend the syllables to read the word. Follow a similar procedure with the word *ointment,* pointing out that in this word, the /oi/ sound does not end a syllable; the break occurs between the *t* and the *m.* Use appropriate strategies to help students decode the words *boiling, soybean, appointment, oily.* Encourage students to build other long words in which the letters *oi* or *oy* stand for the /oi/ sound. Suggest that they use a dictionary to look up words they are not sure about.

INTERVENTION
ASSESSMENT
BOOK

FLUENCY BUILDER Have students choose a passage from "Penny Savers" to read aloud to a partner. You may have students choose a passage that they found particularly interesting, or have them choose one of the following options:

- Read page 202. (Total: 129 words)
- Read page 204. (Total: 107 words)

Students read the selected passage aloud to their partners three times. Have students rate each of their own readings on a scale of 1 to 4. Encourage readers to note their improvement from one reading to the next by completing sentence frames such as *I know my reading improved because* _____. The partner who listens to the reading should also be encouraged to offer positive comments on the reader's improvement.

Review Vocabulary

To revisit the Vocabulary Words with students prior to the weekly assessment, display or read aloud the following sentences. Have students tell whether each statement is true or false, and explain why.

1. People never **receive** gifts on their birthdays.
2. People say "**Congratulations!**" to a runner who loses a race.
3. If something has great **value**, you should throw it in the trash.
4. These are different **combinations** of numbers: 4, 3, 2 and 6, 2, 8.
5. Scientists measure the **amount** of rain that falls.
6. A menu offers **choices** about what to eat.

You may want to display the Vocabulary Words and definitions on page 249 and have students copy them to use when they study for the vocabulary test.

INTERVENTION
PRACTICE
BOOK

page 102

(Focus Skill) Review Main Idea and Details

To review the focus skill before the weekly assessment, distribute Intervention Practice Book page 102. Point out the title, Main Idea and Details, and read the directions aloud. You may choose to guide students through the activity, or have them complete it with a partner and then share and discuss their work in a small group.

Review Test Prep

Ask students to turn to page 297 of the *Pupil Edition*. Call attention to the tips for answering the test questions. Tell students that paying attention to these tips can help them answer not only the test questions on this page but also other test questions like these.

ON YOUR
MARK

page
297

Call on volunteers to read aloud the paragraphs "Spending Money" and "Earning Money." Then read aloud the directions for number 1, and ask students to read aloud the item, choices, and tip. Have students identify the correct choice and explain how they figured it out. Read aloud the directions for number 2, and have students formulate a main-idea sentence. Write the sentence on the board. Encourage students to tell how they might apply the tips on this page in other test situations as well.

INTERVENTION
ASSESSMENT
BOOK

Self-Selected Reading

Have students select their own books to read independently. They might choose books from the classroom library shelf, or you may wish to offer a group of appropriate books from which students can choose.

- *What Is Money?* (See page 297M of the *Teacher's Edition* for a lesson plan.)
- *Just Enough Carrots* by Stuart J. Murphy. HarperCollins, 1997.
- *If You Give a Mouse a Cookie* by Laura Joffe Numeroff. HarperCollins, 2000.

After students have chosen their books, give each student a copy of My Reading Log, which can be found on page R42 in the back of the *Teacher's Edition*. Have students fill in the information at the top of the form. Then have them use the log to keep track of their reading and to record their responses to the literature.

Conduct student-teacher conferences. Arrange time for each student to confer with you individually about his or her self-selected reading. Have students bring their Reading Logs to share with you at the conference. Students might also like to choose a favorite passage to read aloud to you. Ask questions designed to stimulate discussion of the book. For example, you might ask students to identify the main idea or ideas in a nonfiction book and to give examples of supporting details.

FLUENCY PERFORMANCE Have students read aloud to you the passage from "Penny Savers" that they selected and practiced earlier with their partners. Keep track of the number of words the student reads correctly. Ask the student to rate his or her own performance on the 1–4 scale. If students are not happy with their oral reading, give them an opportunity to continue practicing and then to read the passage to you again.

See *Oral Reading Fluency Assessment* for monitoring progress.

LESSON 26

BEFORE

Building
Background
and Vocabulary

"I'm in Charge of Celebrations"

Review Phonics: Vowel Variants /o͞o/oo, /o͝o/oo

Identify the sound. Tell students to listen for the /o͞o/ sound as you say the word *tooth*. Then have them repeat the following three times: *The man by the pool has a blue suit and new boots.* Ask them to identify the words with the /o͞o/ sound. (*pool, blue, suit, new, boots*) Then ask students to repeat the following three times: *The cook read a good book.* Have students identify the words with the /o͝o/ sound. (*cook, good, book*)

Associate letters to sounds. Write this on the board: *The man by the pool has a blue suit and new boots.* Underline *ue* in *blue*, *ui* in *suit*, and *ew* in *new*. Remind students that these letters often stand for the /o͞o/ sound. Underline the *oo* in *pool* and *boots*. Explain that *oo* can also stand for the /o͞o/ sound. Then write this on the board: *The cook read a good book.* Underline the *oo* in *cook*, *good*, and *book*. Tell students that *oo* can also stand for the /o͝o/ sound they hear in *cook*, *good,* and *book*.

Word blending. Have students repeat after you as you model blending and reading *look*. Point to *l* and say /l/. Point to *oo* and say /o͝o/. Slide your hand under *loo* as you slowly elongate the sounds /llo͝o/. Next point to *k* and say /k/. Slide your hand under the whole word, elongating all the sounds /llo͝okk/, and then say the word naturally—*look*.

Apply the skill. *Vowel Substitution* Write the words below on the board, and have students read each aloud. Change each word as needed to form the word in parentheses. Have a volunteer read aloud each new word, trying each sound for the letters *oo*, if necessary.

INTERVENTION
PRACTICE
BOOK

page 104

boat (boot)	**sun** (soon)	**shake** (shook)	**broke** (brook)
moan (moon)	**lake** (look)	**hike** (hook)	**grim** (groom)

Introduce Vocabulary

PRETEACH **lesson vocabulary.** Tell students that they are going to learn six new words that they will see again when they read a selection called "I'm in Charge of Celebrations." Teach each Vocabulary Word by using the process shown at the right.

> Write the word.
> Say the word.
> Track the word and have students repeat it.
> Give the meaning or context.

Use the following suggestions or similar ideas to give the meaning or context.

admiring   Admire something in the classroom.

choosy   Role-play a scene in which a student is a store clerk and
             you are the picky customer.

average	Recount the events of an ordinary school day.
signal	Give a familiar example—buds on trees signal the coming of spring in some places.
tracks	Relate to making footprints or tracks in sand or snow.
celebrations	Give examples of familiar celebrations.

For vocabulary activities, see Vocabulary Games on pages 2–7.

For vocabulary activities, see Vocabulary Games on pages 2–7.

Vocabulary Words

admiring looking at with wonder or respect

choosy picky, hard to please

average ordinary, not special

signal to make known, to announce

tracks prints left in the ground by an animal or person

celebrations joyous events that honor holidays, achievements, or happy occasions

Apply Vocabulary Strategies

Identify multiple-meaning words. Write the following on the board: *We saw the <u>track</u> of a bear in the soft dirt near our campsite. The train moved swiftly along the <u>track</u>.* Tell students that when a word has more than one meaning, they can often figure out the appropriate meaning from the way the word is used. Model using the strategy.

> **MODEL** **I know that the word *track* in the first sentence means "the print left by a bear's foot." In the second sentence, however, the word *train* lets me know that here, *track* is a specialized word meaning "the rails on which a train runs."**

Guide students in using a similar procedure with the word *signal*.

RETEACH lesson vocabulary. Have students print the Vocabulary Words neatly on cards. Tell them to cut the words apart to make letter cards and then mix up the letters in a box. Using the word cards on page T93 as a reference, students should pick out the letters to reconstruct each word. Have them tell the meaning of each word after they have completed it.

FLUENCY BUILDER Using *Intervention Practice Book* page 103, read each word in the first column aloud and have students repeat it. Then have students work in pairs to read the words in the first column aloud to each other. Follow the same procedure with each of the remaining columns. After partners have practiced reading aloud the words in each column, have them listen to each other as they practice the entire list.

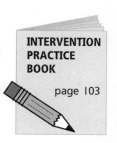

INTERVENTION
PRACTICE
BOOK

page 103

BEFORE

Reading "I'm in
Charge of
Celebrations"
pages 302–317

USE SKILL CARD 26A

★
(Focus Skill) **Summarize**

PRETEACH **the skill.** Have students recall what they have learned about summarizing. Then have them look at **side A of Skill Card 26: Summarize.** Read aloud the question at the top, and call on volunteers to read aloud and explain in their own words the sentences on the stick-on notes. Read aloud the second question, and have students read aloud and discuss the answers.

Prepare to Read: "I'm in Charge of Celebrations"

Preview. Tell students that they are going to read a long poem called "I'm in Charge of Celebrations." Explain that a poem uses imagery, or vivid descriptions, to help readers create pictures in their minds. Poems also use figurative language, which may compare two things or express an idea in an unusual way. Poems may use rhythm and sometimes rhyme to create an effect. After discussing the genre, do a preview of the selection.

ON YOUR
MARK

pages
302–317

- **Pages 302–303:** On page 303 I see the title and the names of the author and the illustrator. The picture shows a large bird and a girl standing with her arms raised. I see sand and a cactus, so I think this poem may be about the desert.

- **Pages 304–309:** The text on these pages is in two columns. It does not look like the text of a story or nonfiction selection. The pictures show the girl writing in a notebook, running or dancing, and watching a rainbow. I see plants and animals, too.

- **Pages 310–315:** On these pages, I see more pictures of the girl and things in nature. I think this poem might tell about special things she sees in the desert.

Set purpose. Model setting a purpose for reading "I'm in Charge of Celebrations."

(MODEL) From my preview, I know that this poem tells about the wonders of nature in the desert. One purpose for reading is to learn about something, and another is to enjoy the selection. I think I will read this selection to enjoy the poem and to learn more about the desert.

Reread and Summarize

Have students reread and summarize "I'm in Charge of Celebrations" in sections, as described below.

Pages 302–307

Let's reread pages 302–307 to recall how the girl chooses her celebrations.

Summary: The girl who narrates the poem lives in the desert. When something happens that she wants to celebrate, she writes the date in her notebook. One celebration is Dust Devil Day, when she saw dust devils and danced with them.

Pages 308–312

Now let's reread pages 308–312 to find out what else the girl celebrates.

Summary: Other days the girl celebrates are the days she saw a triple rainbow, a green cloud that looked like a parrot, and a coyote that stopped and looked at her.

Pages 313–314

As we reread pages 313–314, let's see what The Time of Falling Stars is.

Summary: The girl celebrates The Time of Falling Stars to remember the night she was watching a meteor shower and saw a fireball in the sky.

Pages 315–317

Let's reread pages 315–317 to recall when and how the girl celebrates the New Year.

Summary: The girl chooses a spring day around the end of April to celebrate the New Year. She walks through the desert beating her drum, admiring the plants and animals.

FLUENCY BUILDER Use *Intervention Practice Book* page 103. Point out the sentences on the bottom half of the page. Remind students that their goal is to read each phrase or unit smoothly. Model appropriate pace, expression, and phrasing as you read each sentence, and have students read it after you. Then have students practice by reading the sentences aloud three times to a partner.

INTERVENTION PRACTICE BOOK

page 103

Directed Reading: "Book of Days," pp. 206–212

Have a volunteer read the title. Explain that this story is in the form of a journal, so each page has a different date.

BRIGHT SURPRISES
pp. 206–212

Pages 206–207

Have students read pages 206–207 to find out who is writing the journal and why. (*Sue's little sister; because she misses Sue*) **CHARACTERS' MOTIVATIONS**

Ask: **Were you able to picture what the girl describes in the last sentence on page 207?** Model the strategy of creating mental images.

> **MODEL** When I read this sentence, I closed my eyes and imagined seeing the little green sweet pea sprouts. I could see their soft, curly stems that will grab onto things to help the plant climb toward the light as it grows.
> (Focus Strategy) **CREATE MENTAL IMAGES**

Pages 208–209

Have students read pages 208–209 to find out what else the girl writes about. Ask: **Why does the girl say that the fruit trees look like they are holding secrets?** (*Their buds are closed up tight, as if something secret is inside.*) **INTERPRET IMAGERY**

How does the girl know that the fox is back and that it has baby foxes? (*She sees the tracks of a fox and baby foxes in the sand.*) **DRAW CONCLUSIONS**

Page 210

Have students read page 210 to find out what happens on April 21. Ask: **How can you summarize the story so far?** (*A girl writes a journal to tell what she does while her big sister is away. She takes care of flowers, helps plant a garden, looks at fruit trees, and goes to the river. On April 21, she sees a rainbow and makes a wish.*) (Focus Skill) **SUMMARIZE**

What do you think the girl wishes for? (*Accept reasonable responses.*) **SPECULATE**

Page 211

Have students look at the illustration on page 211 and predict what will happen. (*Sue will come home.*) **MAKE PREDICTIONS**

How does the girl feel at the end of the story? How do you know? (*Happy, excited; she writes about the best news and the biggest celebration of all, and uses many exclamation marks that show excitement.*) **CHARACTERS' EMOTIONS**

INTERVENTION PRACTICE BOOK

page 105

Summarize the selection. Ask students to think about what happened first, next, and last in "Book of Days." Then have them summarize the story in three sentences.

Answers to *Think About It* Questions

1. Possible response: She writes so that she will feel less lonely while Sue is away. She writes about things she does on her own and about things she remembers doing with Sue. **SUMMARY**

2. Possible response: She will stop writing in her book of days because her sister Sue will be home again. She can talk to Sue instead of writing to her. **INTERPRETATION**

3. Encourage students to prepare for writing by jotting down ideas and words related to their chosen topic. They may want to share their writing with a classmate. **WRITE A JOURNAL ENTRY**

AFTER

Skill Review
pages 322–323

USE SKILL CARD 26B

⭐(Focus Skill) Summarize

RETEACH **the skill.** Have students look at **side B of Skill Card 26: Summarize** and read aloud the skill reminder. Call attention to the illustration, and ask a volunteer to read aloud the paragraph. Have another student read aloud the summary that Tess wrote. Then read aloud the question and discuss the summary with students, encouraging them to apply what they have learned about writing a good summary.

FLUENCY BUILDER Use *Intervention Practice Book* page 103. Explain that students will practice the sentences on the bottom half of the page by reading them aloud on tape. Assign new partners. Have partners take turns reading the sentences aloud to each other and then reading them on tape. After they listen to the tape, have them tell how they think they have improved their reading of the sentences. Then have them read the sentences aloud on tape a second time, with improved pacing and tone.

INTERVENTION PRACTICE BOOK

page 103

Expressive Writing: Poetic Images

Build on prior knowledge. Remind students that in "Book of Days" the girl writes about sweet pea sprouts reaching for the sun with soft, curly fingers. Point out that this description uses vivid words like *soft* and *curly* and compares the plant stems to fingers. Tell students that the girl might have used this same image in a poem.

Display a graphic organizer like the one shown here. Tell students that they are going to write sentences using colorful words and figurative language, or comparisons, to describe other things from "Book of Days" in a poetic way.

Object to Describe	Colorful Words	Comparisons
an apple		
a beautiful rock		

Construct the text. "Share the pen" with students in a collaborative group writing effort to complete the graphic organizer. Guide students in choosing two or three vivid words and an interesting comparison for each object. Offer suggestions and ask questions as needed.

- Help students use ideas from the graphic organizer to compose poetic sentences. Write the sentences on the board.

Revisit the text. Go back and read each poetic sentence. Ask: **Does this sentence have images that show how we feel about what we are describing?**

- Ask: **How can we make our sentences more interesting and more poetic? Are there colorful adjectives that we can add?**

- Have students copy the revised sentences on their papers.

On Your Own

Choose something in nature that you enjoy watching or looking at. Write a short unrhymed poem that describes what you chose. Use colorful words and perhaps an interesting comparison.

Connect Spelling and Phonics

RETEACH vowel variants /o͞o/*oo*, /o͝o/*oo*. Tell students that you will say some words in which the letters *oo* stand for the /o͞o/ sound. Have volunteers write each word on the board. Work together to proofread their work.

l. soon*	2. pools*	3. choosy*	4. broom
5. too*	6. blooms*	7. room	8. spoon

*Word appears in "Book of Days."

Tell students that you will say a sentence in which the letters *oo* stand for the /o͝o/ sound. Dictate the following sentence and have students write it: *Take a good look at this book.*

Build and Read Longer Words

Remind students that they have learned that the letters *oo* can stand for the /o͞o/ sound and the /o͝o/ sound. Now they will use what they have learned to help them read some longer words.

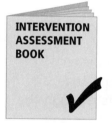

INTERVENTION ASSESSMENT BOOK

Write the word *afternoon* on the board. Remind students that sometimes they can read longer words by looking for smaller words in the longer word. Cover *noon* and have students read *after*. Cover *after* and have them read *noon*. Then have them read the whole word. Follow a similar procedure with the word *cookbook*. Use appropriate strategies to help students decode the words *unhook, cooking, crooked,* and *outlook.* Encourage students to build other long words in which the letters *oo* stand for either the /o͞o/ or /o͝o/ sound. Suggest that they use a dictionary to look up words they are not sure about.

FLUENCY BUILDER Have students choose a passage from "Book of Days" to read aloud to a partner. You may have students choose passages that they found particularly interesting, or have them choose one of the following options:

- Read page 206. (Total: 93 words)
- Read page 208. (Total: 94 words)

Students should read the selected passage aloud to their partners three times. Have students rate each of their own readings on a scale of l to 4. Encourage readers to note their improvement from one reading to the next by completing sentence frames such as *I know my reading improved because* _____. The partner who listens to the reading should also be encouraged to offer positive comments on the reader's improvement.

Review Vocabulary

To revisit the Vocabulary Words prior to the weekly assessment, have students listen as you read aloud each of the following sentence beginnings. Call on a volunteer to complete each sentence so that it makes sense. Alternatively, you might write the sentence beginnings on the board with the Vocabulary Words underlined, and have volunteers read aloud and complete the sentences.

1. My favorite **celebrations** are _____.
2. I remember **admiring** _____.
3. On an **average** day, I _____.
4. I would recognize **tracks** left by _____.
5. You might want to be **choosy** when _____.
6. If I were a king or queen, I would like someone to **signal** my arrival by _____.

Correct responses: Accept responses that reflect an understanding of the Vocabulary Words.

You may want to display the Vocabulary Words and definitions on page 259 and have students copy them to use when they study for the vocabulary test.

Review Summarize

To review the focus skill before the weekly assessment, distribute *Intervention Practice Book* page 106. Point out the title, Summarize, and read the directions aloud. You may choose to guide students through the activity, or have them complete it with a partner and then share and discuss their work with the group.

Review Test Prep

Ask students to turn to page 323 of the *Pupil Edition*. Call attention to the tips for answering the test questions. Tell students that paying attention to these tips can help them answer not only the test questions on this page but also test questions like these.

ON YOUR MARK
page 323

Have a student read the paragraph and directions aloud. Ask another student to read aloud question 1, the answer choices, and the tip. Have students identify the correct choice and tell why this idea belongs in a summary and the other choices do not. Then read aloud question 2 and the tip that goes with it, and have students formulate a summary sentence. Write the sentence on the board. Encourage students to tell how they might apply the tips on this page in other test situations as well.

**INTERVENTION
PRACTICE
BOOK**

page 106

**INTERVENTION
ASSESSMENT
BOOK**

Self-Selected Reading

Have students select books to read independently. They might choose books from the classroom library shelf, or you may wish to offer a group of appropriate books from which students can choose. Titles might include these:

- *Music Makes Joy.* (See page 323K of the *Teacher's Edition* for a lesson plan.)

- *Listen to the Rain* by Bill Martin, Jr., and John Archambault. Henry Holt, 1988.

- *Happy Birthday, Danny and the Dinosaur!* by Syd Hoff. HarperCollins, 1999

After students have chosen their books, give each student a copy of My Reading Log, which can be found on page R42 in the back of the *Teacher's Edition*. Have students fill in the information at the top of the form. Then have them use the log to keep track of their reading and to record their responses to the literature.

Conduct student-teacher conferences. Arrange time for each student to meet with you individually to discuss his or her self-selected reading. Have students bring their Reading Logs to share with you at the conference. Students might also like to choose a favorite passage to read aloud to you. Ask questions about the book to stimulate discussion. For nonfiction, you might ask what information the student learned from the text, how the author structured the text, or how illustrations or diagrams helped the student understand the topic. Encourage students to summarize what they read.

FLUENCY PERFORMANCE Have students read aloud to you the passages from "Book of Days" that they selected and practiced earlier with their partners. Keep track of the number of words each student reads correctly. Ask the student to rate his or her own performance on the 1–4 scale. If students are not happy with their oral reading, give them an opportunity to continue practicing and then to read the passage to you again.

See *Oral Reading Fluency Assessment* for monitoring progress.

BEFORE
Building Background and Vocabulary

Use with

"Alejandro's Gift"

Review Phonics: Consonant /s/c

Identify the sound. Tell students to listen for the /s/ sound as you say the words *cent* and *trace*. Then have them repeat three times: *He can race through the city on his cycle to get celery.* Ask them to identify the words with the /s/ sound. (*race, city, cycle, celery*)

Associate letters to sound. Write on the board: *He can race through the city on his cycle to get celery.* Circle the word *can*. Remind students that the letter *c* often stands for the /k/ sound at the beginning of *can*. Then underline the *ce, ci* or *cy* in the words *race, city, cycle,* and *celery*. Explain that when the letter *c* is followed by *e, i,* or *y*, the *c* usually stands for the /s/ sound.

Word blending. Have students repeat after you as you model how to blend and read the word *race*. Point to *r* and say /r/. Point out the *a-e* pattern in the word, and remind students that this usually indicates a long vowel sound. Point to *a* and say /ā/. Slide your hand under the letters *ra* as you slowly elongate the sounds /rrāā/. Next, point to the letters *ce* and say /s/. Slide your hand under the whole word, elongating all the sounds — /rrāāss/, and then say the word naturally—*race*.

Apply the skill. *Letter Substitution* Write the following words on the board, and have students read each aloud. Change as needed to form the word in parentheses. Have a volunteer read aloud each new word.

nine (nice)	**case** (cease)	**kitty** (city)	**plate** (place)
ape (ace)	**canter** (center)	**empress** (cypress)	**fading** (facing)

Introduce Vocabulary

PRETEACH **lesson vocabulary.** Tell students that they are going to learn six new words that they will see again when they read a selection called "Alejandro's Gift." Teach each Vocabulary Word using the process shown below at the right.

Use the following suggestions or similar ideas to give the meaning or context.

shunned   Explain that campers might stay away from, or shun, animals such as bears or skunks. Point out the *-ed* ending that shows action in the past.

INTERVENTION PRACTICE BOOK

page 108

> Write the word.
> Say the word.
> Track the word and have students repeat it.
> Give the meaning or context.

cherished	Give examples of people or items that students cherish. Point out the *-ed* ending that shows action in the past.
growth	Give examples of familiar plants particular to deserts or forests.
windmill	Sketch or show a picture of a windmill; explain that it uses the wind to make power.
ample	Give examples of places that offer ample, or more than enough, room to run and play, such as a gym.
furrows	Relate to grooves in planted fields students may have seen.

> ## Vocabulary Words
> **shunned** stayed away from
>
> **cherished** cared about deeply
>
> **growth** plant life growing in a certain area
>
> **windmill** a machine that uses the wind to make power
>
> **ample** more than enough
>
> **furrows** long, deep grooves dug into soil

For vocabulary activities, see Vocabulary Games on pages 2–7.

AFTER
Building Background and Vocabulary

Apply Vocabulary Strategies

Use syllabication. Write the word *ample* on the board. Remind students that they can sometimes figure out how to pronounce a new word by dividing it into syllables. Model using the strategy.

> **MODEL** When I look at this word I notice that it has the C*le* pattern at the end, so I know I should divide it into syllables before the *ple*. Now I see the familiar word part *am* and I know the *a* has the /a/ sound. The letter pattern *ple* is also familiar from words like *apple* and *simple*. I can blend these sounds to read *ample*.

Guide students in decoding *furrows* by dividing between the double consonants, identifying familiar words *fur* and *rows*, and using sounds for letter patterns /ûr/*ur* and /ō/*ow*.

RETEACH lesson vocabulary. Have students use word cards and sorting pockets to sort the Vocabulary Words in different ways. They might sort the words into nouns, verbs, and adjectives or by the number of syllables in each word. Each time have students share their results.

FLUENCY BUILDER Using *Intervention Practice Book* page 107, read each word in the first column aloud, and have students repeat it. Then have students work in pairs to read the words in the first column aloud to each other. Follow the same procedure with each of the remaining columns. After partners have practiced reading aloud the words in each column, have them listen to each other as they practice the entire list.

INTERVENTION PRACTICE BOOK

page 107

(Focus Skill) Cause and Effect

PRETEACH **the skill.** Have students watch as you drop a piece of scrap paper. Ask why the paper is on the floor. (*because you dropped it*) Tell students that this is an example of a cause and its effect. Then have them look at **side A of Skill Card 27: Cause and Effect** and read aloud the definitions. Call on volunteers to read aloud the sentences in the first pair of boxes. Discuss the cause-and-effect relationship, and then have a student read aloud the sentence below the boxes. Point out the word *because*, and explain that this word is often used to signal causes and effects. Follow a similar procedure with the second set of boxes and the sentence below them, pointing out the signal word *so*. Encourage students to think of other examples of causes and effects. Write the examples on the board with arrows pointing from causes to effects.

Prepare to Read: "Alejandro's Gift"

Preview. Tell students that they are going to read a selection called "Alejandro's Gift." Explain that this selection is realistic fiction. Have students recall that realistic fiction tells about characters, settings, and events that are like people, places, and events in real life. After discussing the genre, preview the selection with students.

ON YOUR MARK

pages
326–340

- **Pages 326–327:** On these pages I see the title and the names of the author and illustrator. The picture shows a man sitting near a small pond or water hole with a shovel beside him. The setting looks like a desert. I also see many different animals and birds. I think the man may be Alejandro. He looks as if he enjoys the peaceful setting and the animals around him.

- **Pages 328–331:** The first paragraph of the story is very short. (*Read the first paragraph aloud.*) I can see the house in the picture on page 328 and Alejandro patting his pet mule or burro. The other pictures on these pages show Alejandro working in his garden. He seems to be very fond of animals.

- **Pages 332–336:** The pictures on pages 332–333 and 334–335 show many different kinds of animals coming to Alejandro's garden and in the desert. On page 336 Alejandro is holding some kind of tool. I wonder what he is doing and whether it has something to do with the desert animals.

Set purpose. Model setting a purpose for reading "Alejandro's Gift."

MODEL From my preview I know that this selection tells about a man named Alejandro who lives in the desert. One purpose for reading is for enjoyment. I think I'll enjoy reading this selection to find out why so many animals come to Alejandro's garden and how he feels about it.

Reread and Summarize

Have students reread and summarize "Alejandro's Gift" in sections, as described below.

Pages 328–330

Let's reread pages 328–330 to recall what Alejandro's life was like.

Summary: Alejandro lived all alone in the desert and had few visitors. He spent a lot of time tending his garden. One day a ground squirrel came to drink water from a garden furrow, and Alejandro felt less lonely.

Pages 331–333

Now let's reread pages 331–333 to find out how Alejandro's life changed.

Summary: The squirrel came again, and so did other animals and birds. Now Alejandro was rarely lonely.

Pages 334–337

As we reread pages 334–337, let's see what Alejandro did for his desert friends.

Summary: Alejandro realized that larger desert animals needed water, too, so he dug a water hole as a gift to them. Days passed, and no animals came to the water hole. When Alejandro saw a skunk dart into the underbrush, he realized what was wrong.

Pages 338–340

Let's reread pages 338–340 to recall how Alejandro solved the problem.

Summary: Alejandro dug a new water hole far from the house and out of sight, and this time the animals came to drink. He could not see them, but he could hear them. He had given the animals a gift, but he felt as if he had received a gift himself.

FLUENCY BUILDER Use *Intervention Practice Book* page 107. Point out the sentences on the bottom half of the page. Remind students that their goal is to read each phrase or unit smoothly. Model appropriate pace, expression, and phrasing as you read each sentence, and have students read it after you. Then have students practice by reading the sentences aloud three times to a partner.

**INTERVENTION
PRACTICE
BOOK**

page 107

Directed Reading: "The Hummingbird Garden," pp. 214–221

BRIGHT SURPRISES pp. 214–221

Have students read the title of the story. Tell them that the boy in the picture on page 215 is named Cyrus. His nickname is Cy. The man is Cy's dad. Have students read pages 214–215 to find out what Cy and his dad are talking about. (*Cy wants a pet. Dad suggests planting a garden for birds.*) **SUMMARIZE**

Pages 214–215

Have students read the first three paragraphs on page 215. Ask: **How do you think Cyrus can have a garden on cement?** Model the strategy of reading ahead.

> **MODEL** I wonder what Cy's dad is thinking of when he says Cy can plant a garden in a backyard covered with cement. I'll read ahead to find out. When I do, I see that Cy's dad explains his idea in the next paragraph. (Focus Strategy) **READ AHEAD**

Pages 216–217

Have students look at the illustrations on pages 216 and 217 and think about the title of the story. Ask: **What do you think Cy decides to do?** (*plant a garden for hummingbirds*) **MAKE PREDICTIONS**

Now have students read pages 216–217 to confirm their predictions. Ask: **Why does Cy poke holes in the bottoms of old boxes and pails?** (*so water will drain out when he plants flowers in them*) **Why does he plant seeds for red flowers?** (*because he read that hummingbirds like red and pink flowers best*) (Focus Skill) **CAUSE AND EFFECT**

Pages 218–219

Ask students to read pages 218–219 to find out whether hummingbirds come. Ask: **How and why do Cy's feelings change?** (*At first he is sad because he doesn't see any hummingbirds, but then he is happy because the hummingbirds come to his garden.*) (Focus Skill) **CAUSE AND EFFECT/ CHARACTERS' EMOTIONS**

Page 220

Have students read page 220 to find out what happens in the fall. (*The birds fly south for the winter.*) **Do you think Cy is happy with his garden? How do you know?** (*Yes, he liked the hummingbirds; he is planning another garden next spring.*) **CHARACTERS' EMOTIONS**

INTERVENTION PRACTICE BOOK

page 109

Summarize the selection. Ask students to think about what happened in the three seasons of the year mentioned in "The Hummingbird Garden." Have them summarize the story in three sentences—one sentence for each season.

Answers to *Think About It* Questions

1. Cy plants a garden. He fills a hummingbird feeder with sweet water. Then he waits for his pets to come. They stay while it is hot, but they go south when winter comes. **SUMMARY**

2. Possible response: Cy's dad feels proud and happy about the changes. Having a garden for birds was his idea, and Cy makes the garden look nice. **INTERPRETATION**

3. You may want to discuss the format of a newspaper story. Remind students that their stories should present facts and not opinions. **WRITE A NEWSPAPER STORY**

AFTER

Skill Review
pages 346–347

USE SKILL CARD 27B

(Focus Skill) Cause and Effect

RETEACH the skill. Have students look at **side B of Skill Card 27: Cause and Effect** and read aloud the skill reminder. Call on volunteers to take turns reading the sentences and identifying causes, effects, and signal words. Have students refer to the definitions in the skill reminder if needed. Encourage students to write their own cause-and-effect sentences on chart paper, indicating cause with an underline, effect with a double underline, and signal words by drawing a circle around them.

FLUENCY BUILDER Use *Intervention Practice Book* page 107. Explain that students will practice the sentences on the bottom half of the page by reading them aloud on tape. Assign new partners. Have students take turns reading the sentences aloud to each other and then reading them on tape. After they listen to the tape, have them tell how they think they have improved their reading of the sentences. Then have them read the sentences aloud on tape a second time, with improved pacing and tone.

INTERVENTION PRACTICE BOOK

page 107

Expressive Writing: Word Choice

Build on prior knowledge. Remind students that the author of "The Hummingbird Garden" uses the exact noun *hummingbirds* rather than the more general noun *birds*. He uses vivid verbs like *raced* and *circled* to show readers exactly how the hummingbirds moved. Then ask students to imagine that Cy writes a letter to Mrs. Cecil to thank her for giving him the pots from her cellar. Explain that Cy's letter will be more interesting if he uses exact nouns and colorful, vivid language.

Display a letter frame like the one shown here.

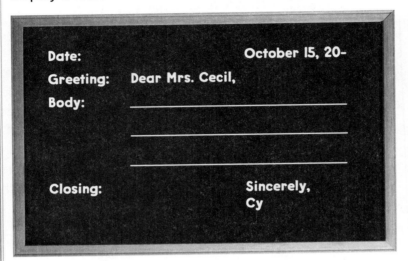

```
Date:                      October 15, 20-
Greeting:  Dear Mrs. Cecil,
Body:      _____
           _____
           _____
Closing:                   Sincerely,
                           Cy
```

Construct the text. "Share the pen" with students in a collaborative group effort to write sentences for the body of Cy's thank-you letter. Suggest that students think about why Cy is thanking Mrs. Cecil and what he might tell her about how his garden turned out.

- Remind students to express Cy's feelings and to describe his garden by using colorful, vivid words.

Revisit the text. Go back and read the sentences. Ask: **Have we used any general nouns that we can replace with more exact nouns? Can we add any vivid verbs?**

- Revise the sentences as necessary, and have students copy them on their papers.

On Your Own

Imagine that a hummingbird could write a letter. Write three sentences that a hummingbird might write in a letter to Cy to thank him for making the garden. Use specific nouns and vivid verbs.

Connect Spelling and Phonics

RETEACH consonant /s/c. Tell students that you will say eight words in which the /s/ sound is spelled *c*. In four of the words the *c* is followed by *e*, in three it is followed by *i*, and in the last it is followed by *y*. Identify which spelling is used before you read each group. Work together to proofread students' spelling.

I. nice*	2. place*	3. ice*	4. cement*
5. city*	6. cinder	7. civic	8. cypress

*Word appears in "Hummingbird Garden."

Tell students that in the following sentences, the /s/ sound spelled *c* is followed by *e* or *i*. Then dictate the sentences and have students write them: *Grace races to the center of the city. She gets rice, ice, celery, and a slice of pie.* Tell students that in the next sentence you will dictate, the *c* is followed by *y*. Dictate and have students write: *The cyclone took away the cycle.*

Build and Read Longer Words

Remind students that they have learned that the letter *c* can stand for the /s/ sound when it comes before *e*, *i*, or *y*. Now they will use what they have learned to help them read some longer words.

INTERVENTION
ASSESSMENT
BOOK

Write the word *misplace* on the board. Remind students that they can read longer words by looking for prefixes, suffixes, and root words. Underline the root word *place*. Have students use what they've learned about the CVCe pattern and the sound that the letters *ce* can stand for to read the word *place*. Point out the prefix *mis-* and remind students that it means "wrongly." Then have them read the whole word and tell what it means. Use appropriate strategies to help students decode the words *celebrate*, *replace*, *recycle*, *cinder*, and *citizen*.

FLUENCY BUILDER Have students choose a passage from "The Hummingbird Garden" to read aloud to a partner. You may have students choose passages that they found particularly interesting, or have them choose one of the following options:

- Read page 215. (Total: 127 words)
- Read page 219. (Total: 107 words)

Students read the selected passage aloud to their partners three times. Have students rate each of their own readings on a scale of I to 4. Encourage readers to note their improvement from one reading to the next by completing sentence frames such as *I know my reading improved because* _____. The partner who listens to the reading should also be encouraged to offer positive comments on the reader's improvement.

Review Vocabulary

To revisit the Vocabulary Words with students prior to the weekly assessment, display a word line like the one shown here.

least surprised ———————————————— most surprised

Have students listen to the following questions and take turns indicating on the word line how surprised they would be. Ask them to explain why they would or would not be surprised in each instance. If needed, ask follow-up questions to check students' understanding of the Vocabulary Words.

How surprised would you be if . . .

1. a **windmill** never moved?
2. your sister threw away a toy she **cherished**?
3. a cat **shunned** a dog?
4. you saw **furrows** filled with water?
5. desert **growth** was found under the ocean?
6. your school cafeteria never had an **ample** supply of food?

Correct responses: Accept responses that reflect an understanding of the Vocabulary Words.

You may want to display the Vocabulary Words and definitions on page 269 and have students copy them to use when they study for the vocabulary test.

INTERVENTION
PRACTICE
BOOK

page 110

(Focus Skill) Review Cause and Effect

To review the focus skill before the weekly assessment, distribute *Intervention Practice Book* page 110. Point out the title, Cause and Effect, and read the directions aloud. You may choose to guide students through the activity, or have them complete it with a partner and then share and discuss their work with the group.

Review Test Prep

Ask students to turn to page 347 of the *Pupil Edition*. Call attention to the tips for answering the test questions. Tell students that paying attention to these tips can help them answer not only the test questions on this page but also other test questions like these.

ON YOUR MARK

page 347

INTERVENTION
ASSESSMENT
BOOK

✔

Have students follow along as you read aloud the directions and the paragraphs. Ask a volunteer to read aloud the first test question, answer choices, and tip. Have students identify the cause and explain how they figured it out. Follow a similar procedure with the second question, having students identify the correct effect. Encourage students to tell how they might apply the tips on this page in other test situations.

Self-Selected Reading

Have students select their own books to read independently. They might choose books from the classroom library shelf, or you may wish to offer a group of appropriate books from which students can choose. Titles might include the following:

- *The Burro's Land*. (See page 347K of the *Teacher's Edition* for a lesson plan.)

- *What's Under the Ocean?* by Janet Craig. Troll, 1996.

- *Zoo Animals* by Dorling Kindersley Staff. Aladdin, 1991.

After students have chosen their books, give each student a copy of My Reading Log, which can be found on page R42 in the back of the *Teacher's Edition*. Have students fill in the information at the top of the form. Then have them use the log to keep track of their reading and to record their responses to the literature.

Conduct student-teacher conferences. Arrange time for each student to meet with you individually to discuss his or her self-selected reading. Have students bring their Reading Logs to share with you at the conference. Students might also like to choose a favorite passage to read aloud to you. Ask questions designed to stimulate discussion of the book. For example, you might ask where the story took place, who the main character was, and what happened at the beginning, middle, and end of the story. Encourage students to talk about the causes and effects of important events in the plot.

FLUENCY PERFORMANCE Have students read aloud to you the passage from "The Hummingbird Garden" that they selected and practiced earlier with their partners. Keep track of the number of words the student reads correctly. Ask the student to rate his or her own performance on the 1–4 scale. If students are not happy with their oral reading, give them an opportunity to continue practicing and then to read the passage to you again.

See *Oral Reading Fluency Assessment* for monitoring progress.

LESSON 28

Building Background and Vocabulary

Use with

"Rocking and Rolling"

Review Phonics: Vowel Variants /ô/ *aw, au(gh)*

Identify the sound. Tell students to listen for the /ô/ sound as you say *draw* and *taught*. Then have them repeat the following three times: *Paul saw a hawk that had caught its food.* Ask which words have the /ô/ sound.

Associate letters to sound. Write this on the board: *Paul saw a hawk that had caught its food.* Underline the *au, aw,* and *augh* in *Paul, saw, hawk,* and *caught.* Tell students that in these words the underlined letters stand for the /ô/ sound. Then have students read the sentence aloud.

Word blending. Have students repeat after you as you model how to blend and read *hawk.* Slide your hand under *haw* as you slowly elongate the sounds /hhôô/. Then point to *k* and say /k/. Slide your hand under the whole word, and say the word naturally—*hawk.* Repeat the procedure, using *caught, saw,* and *Paul.*

INTERVENTION PRACTICE BOOK

page 112

Apply the skill. *Letter Substitution* Write the words below on the board, and have students read each aloud. Change each word as needed to form the word in parentheses. Have a volunteer read aloud each new word.

say (saw)	**clay** (claw)	**drain** (drawn)	**tight** (taught)
hail (haul)	**cat** (caught)	**Dan** (dawn)	**lunch** (launch)

Introduce Vocabulary

PRETEACH **lesson vocabulary.** Tell students that they are going to learn six new words that they will see again when they read a selection called "Rocking and Rolling." Teach each Vocabulary Word by using the process shown at the right.

Use these suggestions or similar ideas to give the meaning or context.

edges	Point to the edges of a desk.
range	Sketch several mountains to show a range. Give an example of a familiar mountain range.
peak	Point to the very top of one mountain in your sketch.
epicenter	Draw a circle on a sheet of paper to represent the center of an earthquake. Then hold another sheet of paper over the circle to represent Earth's surface.

> Write the word.
> Say the word.
> Track the word and have students repeat it.
> Give the meaning or context.

| magma | Relate to the idea of a solid getting hot enough to melt, as with the wax of a candle. |
| coast | Relate to students' visits to the shore or to a beach seen on TV or in a picture. |

For vocabulary activities, see Vocabulary Games on pages 2–7.

For vocabulary activities, see Vocabulary Games on pages 2–7.

AFTER

Building Background and Vocabulary

Apply Vocabulary Strategies

Use reference sources. Write the word *epicenter* on the board. Tell students that this is a word you do not recognize. Explain that sometimes readers can figure out new words by looking for word parts they know. Cover *epi-* and read the word *center*. Explain that you are not familiar with the prefix *epi-*, so the best strategy is to look it up in a dictionary. Model using the strategy.

MODEL The words in a dictionary are arranged in alphabetical order, so I turn to the *e* section. Next, I look at the guide words in dark type at the top of each page. I know that *epi-* will come after *eo* but before *er.* When I find *epi-,* I see its pronunciation, the part of speech it is, its meaning, which is "on" or "over," and example sentences showing it used correctly. I now know that *epicenter* means "on or over the center."

Guide students in using the dictionary to look up *magma*.

RETEACH **lesson vocabulary.** Write the letters of the Vocabulary Words on small squares of construction paper. If possible, use a different color for each word. Place the letters for each word in a separate envelope, and write a clue sentence on the front. Have students figure out the correct word from the clue and combine the letters to form it. Have them refer to the word cards on page T94 to help with spelling.

FLUENCY BUILDER Using *Intervention Practice Book* page 111, read each word in the first column aloud and have students repeat it. Then have students work in pairs to read the words in the first column aloud to each other. Follow the same procedure with each of the remaining columns. After partners have practiced reading aloud the words in each column, have them listen to each other as they practice the entire list.

INTERVENTION PRACTICE BOOK

page 111

(Focus Skill) **Locate Information**

PRETEACH the skill. Tell students that they are going to learn how they can locate information in a book. Have them look at **side A of Skill Card 28: Locate Information**. Read aloud the sentence at the top. Then have volunteers take turns reading aloud the information about the various book parts. You may want to have examples of textbooks or other nonfiction books available for students to look at as well.

Prepare to Read: "Rocking and Rolling"

Preview. Tell students that they are going to read an expository nonfiction selection called "Rocking and Rolling." Help students recall that expository nonfiction explains information and ideas. Explain that an expository nonfiction selection may be divided into sections with headings and may include diagrams and other graphics. After discussing the genre, preview the selection.

ON YOUR MARK
pages 350–364

- **Pages 350–351:** I see what looks like a volcano erupting. The title of the selection and the name of the author and illustrator look like they are written in the cloud of steam coming from the volcano. I wonder if this selection will give information about how volcanoes erupt.

- **Pages 352–353:** At the top of page 352, I see the heading "Down Under." I also see on these pages a large diagram with labels and some other information in a box on page 353. I will read the text in the box to find out more about the topic. (Read aloud the text in the box on page 353.)

- **Pages 354–357:** These pages have the headings "Cracking Up" and "Quake and Shake." I think "Quake and Shake" must tell about earthquakes. From the title, headings, and illustrations, I can guess that the topic of this selection has something to do with how Earth "rocks and rolls," or moves and changes.

Set purpose. Model setting a purpose for reading "Rocking and Rolling."

MODEL From my preview, I know that this selection gives information about Earth and events that make it move and change. One purpose for reading is to learn about a topic. I think I will read this selection to learn about volcanoes, earthquakes, and other events that cause Earth to rock and roll.

Reread and Summarize

Have students reread and summarize "Rocking and Rolling" in sections, as described below.

Pages 352–353

Let's reread pages 352–353 to recall what is below the surface of Earth.

Summary: Earth has four layers—the crust, the mantle, the outer core, and the inner core. The center of Earth is incredibly hot.

Pages 354–357

Now let's reread pages 354–357 to find out what plates are and how they cause earthquakes.

Summary: Earth's solid surface is made up of pieces called plates, which are usually jammed tight against each other. When a plate breaks away, it causes an earthquake.

Pages 358–361

As we reread pages 358–361, let's see how else the earth rocks and rolls.

Summary: A big earthquake may cause a huge wave called a tsunami. There are three different kinds of mountains—fold mountains, dome mountains, and block mountains. Each is formed in a different way. Mount Everest in the Himalayas is the tallest mountain on Earth.

Pages 362–364

Let's reread pages 362–364 to recall how water and wind shape Earth.

Summary: Water and wind both cause erosion, or wearing away, that changes rock into new and different shapes.

FLUENCY BUILDER Use *Intervention Practice Book* page 111. Point out the sentences on the bottom half of the page. Remind students that their goal is to read each phrase or unit smoothly. Model appropriate pace, expression, and phrasing as you read each sentence, and have students read it after you. Then have students practice by reading the sentences aloud three times to a partner.

INTERVENTION PRACTICE BOOK

page 111

Directed Reading: "A Mountain Blows Its Top," pp. 222–228

BRIGHT SURPRISES
pp. 222–228

Before students read the selection, distribute copies of *Practice Book* page 113. Tell students that they will be reading about a volcano called Mount St. Helens. Help them begin filling in their K-W-L charts by having them share what they know and would like to know about volcanoes. Then have them read pages 222–223 to find out about the mountain in the photograph. Ask: **What does the diagram on page 223 show?** (*how the magma pushed up to form a bulge on the north side of Mount St. Helens*) **GRAPHIC AIDS**

Pages 222–223

Ask: **What happened after the plates under the Cascade Range started to shift?** Model using the strategy of adjusting reading rate.

> **MODEL** There is a lot of scientific information on page 223, so this material is more complicated than the descriptive text on page 222, which I read quickly. I'm going to adjust my reading rate, slowing down to make sure I understand this information. I can now answer the question. After the plates started to shift, their edges pushed up magma, causing one side of Mount St. Helens to bulge.
> (Focus Strategy) **ADJUST READING RATE**

Pages 224–225

Have students read pages 224–225 to find out what is happening in the photographs. Ask: **What happened when Mount St. Helens erupted? What happened in the town of Yakima?** (*Dirt, rocks, ice, steam, dust, and hot ash flew out of the mountain. Many tons of ash fell on Yakima.*) **SUMMARIZE**

Pages 226–227

Have students read pages 226–227 to find out what has happened since the big blasts stopped. Ask: **Why does the author say that the land around Mount St. Helens looked like the surface of the moon?** (*because everything was still and covered with ash*) **INTERPRET FIGURATIVE LANGUAGE**

What have people learned from Mount St. Helens? (*The planet is always changing. The changes can cause great damage, but the land also heals.*) **SUMMARIZE**

Now have students close their books. Ask them to open their books again, find the table of contents, and use it to find the page number on which "A Mountain Blows Its Top" begins. (Focus Skill) **LOCATE INFORMATION**

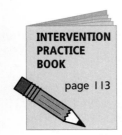

INTERVENTION PRACTICE BOOK

page 113

Summarize the selection. Have students complete their K-W-L charts by writing in the third column what they learned about volcanoes. Then have them use their charts to help them summarize the selection.

Answers to *Think About It* Questions

1. First the earth shook. The magma and hot ash came blasting out of the mountains. Trees and animals were killed. Now new plants and animals live on the mountain. **SUMMARY**

2. Possible responses: It may, because sometimes ash and steam still come from a bulge in the crater. The planet is still changing. **INTERPRETATION**

3. Have students brainstorm words that would describe the day and the feelings of the local residents. Encourage them to use sensory words. **WRITE A DIARY ENTRY**

(Focus Skill) Locate Information

RETEACH the skill. Have students look at **side B of Skill Card 28: Locate Information** and read aloud the skill reminder. Provide a textbook or other book with a table of contents, chapter headings, a glossary, and an index. Have students read aloud and carry out each step in the flowchart, using the book you have provided. You may want to repeat the process with one or more additional books.

FLUENCY BUILDER Use *Intervention Practice Book* page 111. Explain that students will practice the sentences on the bottom half of the page by reading them aloud on tape. Assign new partners. Have students take turns reading the sentences aloud to each other and then reading them on tape. After they listen to the tape, have them tell how they think they have improved their reading of the sentences. Then have them read the sentences aloud on tape a second time, with improved pacing and tone.

INTERVENTION PRACTICE BOOK

page 111

Expressive Writing: Dialogue and Stage Directions

Build on prior knowledge. Have students recall briefly a play or plays that they have read or seen. Explain that when an author writes a play, he or she has to tell who the characters are and what they say. The author also has to provide stage directions that tell actors what their characters should do or how to say their lines.

Display a graphic like the one below. Explain what it shows, and have students read aloud the title, setting, characters' names, dialogue, and stage directions in parentheses. Explain that students are going to add several more lines to this scene of the play.

Ashes

Setting: The town of Yakima, Washington, at about 9:30 A.M. on Sunday, May 18, 1980. Two boys and a girl, age 9, are playing ball in a backyard.

Sam: Look at how dark the sky is getting. It looks like we're going to have a storm.

Gina: (pointing into the distance) I think I see lightning over that way.

Rob: The storm seems to be getting closer. We'd better go in.

(The children head toward the house.)

Construct the text. "Share the pen" with students in a collaborative group effort to write several additional lines of dialogue and stage directions. Suggest that they recall information from "A Mountain Blows Its Top" to decide what should happen next. As students dictate, guide the process by asking questions and offering other suggestions as needed.

- Remind students to use vivid verbs and exact nouns to keep their writing interesting.

Revisit the text. Go back and read the dialogue and stage directions. Ask: **Does our dialogue sound like real people speaking? Are our stage directions clear? Do they make sense?**

- Revise the dialogue and stage directions as necessary.
- Have students act out the entire scene from the beginning.

On Your Own

Write a short scene for a play about two people who come back to Mount St. Helens a few years after it erupted. Remember to tell the names of the characters and what they say and to include stage directions.

Connect Spelling and Phonics

RETEACH **vowel variants /ô/aw, au(gh).** Tell students that you will say some words in which the letters *aw* stand for the /ô/ sound as in *jaw* and one word in which the letters *augh* will stand for that sound. (Identify that word before you say it.) Have volunteers write each word on the board. Work together to proofread.

I. saw*	2. straw	3. fawn	4. flaw
5. claw	6. thaw	7. sprawl	8. caught

*Word appears in "A Mountain Blows Its Top."

Dictate the following sentences, telling students that the words with the /ô/ sound are spelled with *aw*. *My cat was sleeping on the lawn. I crawled up to her. She gave me her paw.* Then dictate this sentence, telling students to use *augh* to spell the word that has the /ô/ sound: *I had taught her to do this trick.*

Build and Read Longer Words

Remind students that they have learned that the letters *aw* and *au(gh)* can stand for the /ô/ sound. Now they will use what they have learned to help them read some longer words.

**INTERVENTION
ASSESSMENT
BOOK**

Write the word *lawmaker* on the board. Remind students that they can sometimes read longer words by looking for smaller words in the longer word. Cover *maker* and have students read the word *law*. Then cover *law*. Have students use what they have learned about the CVCe pattern in *make* and the familiar letter pattern *er* to read the word *maker*. Finally, have students read the compound word and tell what it means. Use appropriate strategies to help students decode the words *sawdust, drawing, lawful, laundry, daughter, caution*. Encourage students to build other long words in which the letters *aw* or *augh* stand for the /ô/ sound. Suggest that they use a dictionary to look up words they are not sure about.

FLUENCY BUILDER Have students choose a passage from "A Mountain Blows Its Top" to read aloud to a partner. You may have students choose a passage that they found particularly interesting, or have them choose one of the following options:

- Read page 224. (Total: 10I words)

- Read page 227. (Total: III words)

Students read the selected passage aloud to their partners three times. Have students rate each of their own readings on a scale of I to 4. Encourage readers to note their improvement from one reading to the next by completing sentence frames such as *I know my reading improved because* _____. The partner who listens to the reading should also be encouraged to offer positive comments on the reader's improvement.

Review Vocabulary

To revisit the Vocabulary Words with students prior to the weekly assessment, display or read aloud the following sentences. Have students tell whether each statement is true or false, and ask them to explain why.

1. One mountain is called a **range**.
2. **Magma** is hot melted rock from inside Earth.
3. If you were to travel to a **coast**, you would find a sea.
4. You might see snow on the **peak** of a mountain.
5. The **edges** of an old book cover might be worn and torn.
6. An **epicenter** is found at the center of a hurricane.

Correct responses: 1. False, 2. True, 3. True, 4. True, 5. True, 6. False

You may want to display the Vocabulary Words and definitions on page 279 and have students copy them to use when they study for the vocabulary test.

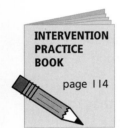

**INTERVENTION
PRACTICE
BOOK**

page 114

Review Locate Information

To review the focus skill before the weekly assessment, distribute *Intervention Practice Book* page 114. Point out the title, Locate Information, and read the introductory material and directions aloud. You may choose to guide students through the activity, or have them complete it with a partner and then share and discuss their work with the group.

Review Test Prep

Ask students to turn to page 369 of the *Pupil Edition*. Call attention to the tips for answering the test questions. Tell students that paying attention to these tips can help them answer not only the test questions on this page but also other test questions like these.

**ON YOUR
MARK**

page
369

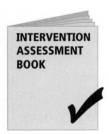

**INTERVENTION
ASSESSMENT
BOOK**

Have a student read aloud the sentence at the top of the page. Call on volunteers to read aloud each test question, set of answer choices, and tip. Have students identify the correct answer for each question and demonstrate how they used the table of contents. Encourage students to tell how they might apply the tips on this page in other test situations as well.

Self-Selected Reading

Have students select books to read independently. They might choose books from the classroom library shelf, or you may wish to offer a group of appropriate books from which students can choose. Titles might include the following:

- *Ring of Fire.* (See page 369M of the *Teacher's Edition* for a lesson plan.)

- *Feel the Wind* by Arthur Dorros. HarperCollins, 2000.

- *What Happens When Volcanoes Erupt* by Daphne Butler. Raintree/Steck-Vaughn, 1995.

After students have chosen their books, give each student a copy of My Reading Log, which can be found on page R42 in the back of the *Teacher's Edition*. Have students fill in the information at the top of the form. Then have them use the log to keep track of their reading and to record their responses to the literature.

Conduct student-teacher conferences. Arrange time for each student to meet with you individually to discuss his or her self-selected reading. Have students bring their Reading Logs to share with you at the conference. Students might also like to choose a favorite passage to read aloud to you. Ask questions designed to stimulate discussion of the book. For nonfiction, you might ask what information the student learned from the text, how the author structured the text, how illustrations or diagrams helped the student understand the topic, and how the student may have used book parts to locate information.

FLUENCY PERFORMANCE Have students read aloud to you the passages from "A Mountain Blows Its Top" that they selected and practiced earlier with their partners. Keep track of the number of words each student reads correctly. Ask the student to rate his or her own performance on the 1–4 scale. If students are not happy with their oral reading, give them an opportunity to continue practicing and then to read the passage to you again.

See *Oral Reading Fluency Assessment* for monitoring progress.

BEFORE

Building
Background
and Vocabulary

Use with

"The Armadillo from Amarillo"

Review Phonics: Digraphs /r/wr, /n/kn

Identify the sound. Tell students to listen for the /r/ sound as you say the word *wrong*. Then have them repeat the following sentence three times: *I wrapped my right wrist*. Ask them to identify the words that begin with the /r/ sound. (*wrapped, right, wrist*) Then ask students to repeat the following sentence three times: *The knight will kneel now*. Have students identify the words that begin with the /n/ sound. (*knight, kneel, now*)

Associate letters to sound. Write this sentence on the board: *I wrapped my right wrist*. Underline the *r* in *right*. Then underline the digraph *wr* in *wrapped* and *wrist*. Explain that the letters *wr* can also stand for the /r/ sound. Then follow a similar procedure for the letters *n* and *kn* in this sentence: *The knight will kneel now*.

Word blending. Have students repeat after you as you model how to blend and read the word *wrist*. Slide your hand under the letters *wri* as you slowly elongate the sounds /rrii/. Then point to *st* and elongate the sounds /sst/. Slide your hand under the whole word, and say the word naturally—*wrist*. Repeat the procedure, using the word *kneel*.

INTERVENTION PRACTICE BOOK

page 116

Apply the skill. *Consonant Substitution* Write the following words on the board, and have students read each aloud. Make the changes necessary to form the word in parentheses. Have a volunteer read aloud each new word.

kit (knit)	**white** (write)	**tree** (knee)	**block** (knock)
trap (wrap)	**lot** (knot)	**twist** (wrist)	**song** (wrong)

Introduce Vocabulary

PRETEACH **lesson vocabulary.** Tell students that they are going to learn six new words that they will see again when they read a selection called "The Armadillo from Amarillo." Teach each Vocabulary Word using the process shown at the right.

Use the following suggestions or similar ideas to give the meaning or context.

eventually	Relate to the idea of practicing a skill and eventually getting better at it.
converse	Demonstrate by having a conversation with a student.
continent	Use a map or globe to locate the United States on the continent of North America.

Write the word.

Say the word.

Track the word and have students repeat it.

Give the meaning or context.

sphere	Use a globe or a ball as an example of a sphere.
universe	Explain that our galaxy, the Milky Way, is just a part of the universe.
homeward	Relate to the idea of heading toward home after a day at the park or after a trip.

For vocabulary activities, see Vocabulary Games on pages 2–7.

For vocabulary activities, see Vocabulary Games on pages 2–7.

Vocabulary Words

eventually sometime in the future, finally

converse talk to one another

continent one of the seven large land areas on Earth

sphere a round object like a ball; a planet

universe everything that exists, including the sun, stars, all the planets, and outer space

homeward toward home

AFTER
Building Background and Vocabulary

Apply Vocabulary Strategies

Use prefixes and suffixes. Write the word *homeward* on the board. Remind students that they can sometimes figure out the meaning of a new word by looking for a familiar root word and a prefix or suffix. Model using the strategy.

MODEL I see the familiar word *home* in this long word. However, I'm not sure of the meaning of the word part -*ward* so I'll check a dictionary. When I do, I see that it is a suffix meaning toward or 'in the direction of." When I put these word parts together, I can figure out that *homeward* means "toward home."

RETEACH **lesson vocabulary.** Provide patterns for a circle and an arrow. Have students make a simple spinner by cutting a circle and arrow from cardboard and putting them together with a brad. Tell students to divide the circle into six sections and write a Vocabulary Word in each. Students take turns spinning the pointer, saying the word it lands on, and using the word in a sentence.

FLUENCY BUILDER Using *Intervention Practice Book* page 115, read each word in the first column aloud and have students repeat it. Then have students work in pairs to read the words in the first column aloud to each other. Follow the same procedure with each of the remaining columns. After partners have practiced reading aloud the words in each column, have them listen to each other as they practice the entire list.

INTERVENTION PRACTICE BOOK

page 115

BEFORE

Reading "The
Armadillo from
Amarillo"
pages 372–391

USE SKILL CARD 29A

(Focus Skill) Cause and Effect

PRETEACH **the skill.** Ask students to give an example of a cause and its effect. Tell them that they are going to learn something more about causes and effects. Have them look at **side A of Skill Card 29: Cause and Effect** and read aloud the definitions. Read aloud the statement above the first diagram and ask students what they think it means. Ask students to examine the diagram, read aloud the cause and effects, and discuss how the events are related. Follow a similar procedure with the second diagram.

Prepare to Read: "The Armadillo from Amarillo"

Preview. Tell students that they are going to read a selection called "The Armadillo from Amarillo." Explain that this selection is an informational narrative, a story that presents facts about a topic. Some elements, such as characters and story events, may be fiction, but the main purpose of the narrative is to give information that helps readers understand the topic. After discussing the genre, preview the selection with students.

ON YOUR
MARK

pages
372–391

- **Pages 372–373:** Along with the title and the name of the author and illustrator, I see the beginning of the story on page 373. The text is in sets of four lines, like a poem. I also see two postcards, and an armadillo with a bundle, as if he is setting off on a journey. He must be the armadillo from Amarillo. I know that this armadillo is a fictional character because real armadillos do not walk on their hind legs and carry things. The postcards make me think that this selection may give information about places the armadillo visits.

- **Pages 374–377:** The pictures on these pages show a city scene and a country scene. I see more postcards. Some of them say *Texas* on them, so I think the armadillo must be traveling through Texas.

- **Pages 378–385:** I can see from these pictures that the armadillo takes a ride on the back of a large bird and travels far. It looks like he is having an exciting journey.

Set purpose. Model setting a purpose for reading "The Armadillo from Amarillo."

MODEL From my preview, I know that this selection tells a story about an armadillo who takes a journey. I also know that it tells information about places he sees. One purpose for reading is for enjoyment and another is for information. I think I will read this selection to enjoy the story and to learn more about the world we live in.

Reread and Summarize

Have students reread and summarize "The Armadillo from Amarillo" in sections, as described below.

Pages 373–377

Let's reread pages 373–377 to recall how Armadillo's journey begins.

Summary: An armadillo from Texas sets out to find out about the world. He travels through the cities, towns, woodlands, and plains of Texas.

Pages 378–381

Now let's reread pages 378–381 to find out what happens when Armadillo meets the eagle.

Summary: The eagle gives Armadillo a ride on her back. He sees the city of Amarillo from the air. The eagle explains to him where Amarillo is located on the earth.

Pages 382–385

As we reread pages 382–385, let's see how Armadillo and the eagle continue their trip.

Summary: Armadillo and the eagle see a space shuttle take off from Cape Canaveral. They get aboard the shuttle.

Pages 386–390

Let's reread pages 386–390 to recall what they see from the space shuttle.

Summary: From out in space, the earth looks like a round ball. When they get home again, Armadillo understands where in the world he is.

FLUENCY BUILDER Use *Intervention Practice Book* page 115. Point out the sentences on the bottom half of the page. Remind students that their goal is to read each phrase or unit smoothly. Model appropriate pace, expression, and phrasing as you read each sentence, and have students read it after you. Then have students practice by reading the sentences aloud three times to a partner.

INTERVENTION
PRACTICE
BOOK

page 115

Directed Reading: "The Place in Space," pp. 230–237

Pages 230–231

Have students read the title of the story and tell what they see in the illustration. Then have them read page 231 to find out what the boy and his mother are talking about. Ask: **What do you think Will will dream about?** (*Possible response: exploring the universe; exploring the entire world in one night*) **MAKE PREDICTIONS**

Pages 232–233

Have students read page 232 and look at the illustration on page 233 to confirm their predictions about Will's dream. Ask: **Where do you think Will and the wren will go? Why?** (*Accept reasonable responses, but they should include seeing the whole world from the sky.*) **MAKE PREDICTIONS**

Why do you think things look smaller as Will goes higher? (*The farther you get from something, the smaller it looks.*) (Focus Skill) **CAUSE AND EFFECT**

Pages 234–235

Ask students to read page 235 to confirm their predictions. **CONFIRM PREDICTIONS**

Ask: **Why does Will say the earth is even prettier than his night-light?** Model using the strategy of rereading to clarify.

> **MODEL** At first I didn't understand why Will would compare the earth to his night-light, so I went back and reread page 231. There he described the night-light as "a blue-and-green sphere that glows as it twirls." That sounds a lot like the earth. Now I see why Will compared the two things. (Focus Strategy) **REREAD TO CLARIFY**

Ask: **Why does Will need to begin his flight homeward?** (*It is almost morning and time to wake up.*) (Focus Skill) **CAUSE AND EFFECT**

Page 236

**INTERVENTION
PRACTICE
BOOK**

page 117

Have students read page 236 to see how the story ends. Ask: **Why does Will smile at the end of the story?** (*He hears a bird and thinks it's the wren from his dream.*) (Focus Skill) **CAUSE AND EFFECT**

Summarize the selection. Ask students to think about what happened first, next, and last in the story. Then have them work in pairs to summarize the story. They can draw a picture showing Will's journey and then write sentences about the trip.

Answers to *Think About It* Questions

1. Possible response: In his dreams, Will goes to the top of a mountain. From there, he and his friend the wren fly so high that they can see his state, then the country, and even two oceans. Then they go into space, and they can see our planet. **SUMMARY**

2. Possible response: She knows because Will tells her about his dreams. **INTERPRETATION**

3. You may wish to discuss seeing an object from another perspective. This is also a good opportunity to discuss maps, what they represent, and how they are used. **DRAW A PICTURE**

AFTER

Skill Review
pages 398–399

USE SKILL CARD 29B

(Focus Skill) Cause and Effect

RETEACH **the skill.** Have students look at **side B of Skill Card 29: Cause and Effect**. Read aloud the skill reminder and directions. Draw the diagram on the board, and guide students to identify three effects. (*Possible responses: We learn about our world. We understand why things happen. We want to learn more.*) Then follow a similar procedure with the second diagram. (*Possible responses: People want to see new places. People want to learn new things. Traveling is fun.*) After the diagrams are complete, help students construct sentences that use signal words to show the causes and effects. For example: *Because we read about our planet, we learn about our world, understand why things happen and want to learn more.*

FLUENCY BUILDER Use *Intervention Practice Book* page 115. Explain that students will practice the sentences on the bottom half of the page by reading them aloud on tape. Assign new partners. Have students take turns reading the sentences aloud to each other and then reading them on tape. After they listen to the tape, have them tell how they think they have improved their reading of the sentences. Then have them read the sentences aloud on tape a second time, with improved pacing and tone.

INTERVENTION PRACTICE BOOK

page 115

Expository Writing: Invitation

Build on prior knowledge. Have students name some events to which people are invited, such as birthday parties, weddings, and holiday celebrations. Explain that writing a letter is a way to invite a friend for a visit or to attend a special event. Ask students to imagine that Will from the story "The Place in Space" wants to invite his friend Jeff to go to a show about planet Earth at a planetarium in his city.

Display a letter frame like the one shown here. Point out the parts of a friendly letter. Then tell students they are going to complete the body of the letter by writing sentences to tell Jeff about the special show.

Heading (address and date)	220 Mountain Street Carson, California 90000 May 3, 20——
Greeting	Dear Jeff,
Body	_____ _____ _____
Time and Place	The special show will take place on Saturday, May 18, at 1 p.m. I hope you can come!
Closing Signature	Your friend, Will

Construct the text. "Share the pen" with students in a collaborative group effort to write two or three sentences telling Jeff about the show. Point out that Will will need to tell Jeff what the event is and why Jeff might enjoy it. As students dictate words and phrases, write them on the board or on chart paper, guiding the process by asking questions and offering suggestions as necessary.

- Encourage students to include details that make the event sound fun and interesting.

Revisit the text. Go back and read the invitation letter. Ask: **Does this letter include all of the important information about the event?**

- Guide students to revise the body of the letter as necessary.
- Have students copy the invitation on their papers.

> **On Your Own**
>
> Suppose your class was planning to visit a museum with great hands-on displays about Earth, and you wanted to invite Will to go with you. Write two or three sentences for the body of an invitation letter. Tell Will about the museum and why you think he would enjoy visiting it with your class.

Connect Spelling and Phonics

RETEACH digraphs **/r/wr, /n/kn.** Tell students that you will say some words in which the letters *wr* stand for the /r/ sound and the letters *kn* stand for the /n/ sound. Have volunteers write each word on the board. Work together to proofread their work.

I. wrist*	2. knew*	3. knife	4. knit*
5. wren*	6. knock*	7. wrap*	8. knelt

*Word appears in "The Place in Space."

Dictate the following sentences and have students write them: *The string had a knot in it. The knight got a knife to cut the string. Then he wrapped the box and gave it to the wren.*

Build and Read Longer Words

Remind students that they have learned that the letters *wr* can stand for the /r/ sound and the letters *kn* can stand for the /n/ sound. Now they will use what they have learned to help them read some longer words.

Write the word *written* on the board. Remind students that they can read longer words by dividing words into syllables and looking for familiar letter patterns. Draw a line between the two consonants in the middle of the word. Have students read the first syllable /rit/. Tell students that the second syllable has the same *en* letter pattern they have seen at the end of the word *happen*. Have students read the whole word. Follow a similar procedure with the word *knitting*. Use appropriate strategies to help students decode the words *wrongly, wrangler, wrenches, knapsack, knotty, knowledge*. Encourage students to build other long words in which the letters *wr* stand for the /r/ sound and the letters *kn* stand for the /n/ sound. Suggest that they use a dictionary to look up words they are unsure of.

INTERVENTION ASSESSMENT BOOK

FLUENCY BUILDER Have students choose a passage from "The Place in Space" to read aloud to a partner. You may have students choose a passage that they found particularly interesting, or have them choose one of the following options:

- Read the first three paragraphs on page 231. (Total: 110 words)

- Read the first three paragraphs on page 232. (Total: 131 words)

Students read the selected passage aloud to their partners three times. Have students rate each of their own readings on a scale of 1 to 4. Encourage readers to note their improvement from one reading to the next by completing sentence frames such as *I know my reading improved because* _____. The partner who listens to the reading should also be encouraged to offer positive comments on the reader's improvement.

Review Vocabulary

To revisit the Vocabulary Words prior to the weekly assessment, have students listen as you read aloud each of the following sentence beginnings. Call on a volunteer to complete each sentence so that it makes sense. Alternatively, you might write the sentence beginnings on the board with the Vocabulary Words underlined, and have volunteers read aloud and complete the sentences.

1. You might **converse** with your friends about _____.
2. The United States is on the **continent** of _____.
3. An example of a **sphere** is a _____.
4. **Eventually**, I would like to _____.
5. You might make the trip **homeward** after _____.
6. The **universe** includes _____.

Correct responses: Accept responses that reflect an understanding of the Vocabulary Words.

You may want to display the Vocabulary Words and definitions on page 289 and have students copy them to use when they study for the vocabulary test.

⭐ Focus Skill — Review Cause and Effect

**INTERVENTION
PRACTICE
BOOK**

page 118

To review the focus skill before the weekly assessment, distribute *Intervention Practice Book* page 118. Point out the title, Cause and Effect, and read the directions for items 1 and 2 aloud. Point out that there is a second set of directions for items 3 and 4. You may choose to guide students through the activity, or have them complete it with a partner and then share and discuss their work with the group.

Review Test Prep

Ask students to turn to page 397 of the *Pupil Edition*. Call attention to the tips for answering the test questions. Tell students that paying attention to these tips can help them answer not only the test questions on this page but also other test questions like these.

**ON YOUR
MARK**

page 397

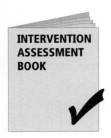

**INTERVENTION
ASSESSMENT
BOOK**

✔

Ask a volunteer to read aloud the paragraphs. Then read aloud the first test item, answer choices, and tip. Have students identify the correct event and the three reasons for it. Read aloud the second question, answer choices, and tip. Have students identify the correct choice and explain how they determined which effects resulted from having no rain. Encourage students to tell how they might apply the tips on this page in other test situations.

Self-Selected Reading

Have students select their own books to read independently. They might choose books from the classroom library shelf, or you may wish to offer a group of appropriate books from which students can choose. Titles might include the following:

- *From Here to There*. (See page 399M of the *Teacher's Edition* for a lesson plan.)

- *Alligator Shoes* by Arthur Dorros. NAL, 1992.

- *Landscapes* by Claude Delafosse. Scholastic, 1996.

After students have chosen their books, give each student a copy of "My Reading Log," which can be found on page R42 in the back of the *Teacher's Edition*. Have students fill in the information at the top of the form. Then have them use the log to keep track of their reading and to record their responses to the literature.

Conduct student-teacher conferences. Arrange time for each student to confer with you individually about his or her self-selected reading. Have students bring their Reading Logs to share with you at the conference. Students might also like to choose a favorite passage to read aloud to you. Ask questions about the book to stimulate discussion. For example, you might ask where the story took place, who the main character was, and what happened at the beginning, middle, and end of the story. Encourage students to talk about how an event or a character's actions may have had more than one cause or effect.

FLUENCY PERFORMANCE Have students read aloud to you the passage from "The Place in Space" that they selected and practiced with their partners. Keep track of the number of words the students read correctly. Ask the student to rate his or her own performance on the 1–4 scale. If students are not happy with their oral reading, give them an opportunity to continue practicing and then to read the passage to you again.

See *Oral Reading Fluency Assessment* for monitoring progress.

Use with

"Visitors from Space"

Review Phonics: Digraphs /f/gh, ph

Identify the sound. Tell students to listen for the /f/ sound as you say *rough* and *phase*. Then have them repeat three times: *Phil phoned the photo store*. Ask them to identify the words with the /f/ sound. (*Phil, phoned, photo*) Then have students repeat aloud three times: *The road was rough and tough*. Have students identify the words with the /f/ sound. (*rough, tough*)

Associate letters to sound. Write on the board: *Phil phoned the photo store*. Underline the letters *ph* each time they appear. Explain that the letters *ph* in these words stand for the /f/ sound. Then write on the board: *The road was rough and tough*. Underline the letters *ough*. Tell students that when the letters *gh* follow the letters *ou*, the *gh* often stands for the /f/ sound.

Word blending. Have students repeat after you as you model how to blend and read *photo*. Slide your hand under the letters *pho* as you slowly elongate the sounds /ffōō/. Then point to the letters *to* as you pronounce the second syllable /ttōō/. Slide your hand under the whole word, and say it naturally—*photo*. Repeat the procedure, using the word *rough*.

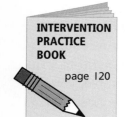

INTERVENTION
PRACTICE
BOOK

page 120

Apply the skill. *Consonant Substitution* Write the following words on the board, and have students read each aloud. Make the changes necessary to form the words in parentheses. Have a volunteer read aloud each new word.

touch (tough)	**pony** (phony)	**bone** (phone)
grab (graph)	**pleasant** (pheasant)	**telegram** (telegraph)

Introduce Vocabulary

PRETEACH **lesson vocabulary.** Tell students that they are going to learn six new words that they will see again when they read a selection called "Visitors from Space." Teach each Vocabulary Word using the process shown at the right.

Use the following suggestions or similar ideas to give the meaning or context.

fluorescent	Give examples of places where fluorescent lights are usually found, such as schools.
force	Push and pull a chair.
loops	Relate to a kite caught by the wind and moving in circles.

> Write the word.
> Say the word.
> Track the word and have students repeat it.
> Give the meaning or context.

nucleus Draw a large circle; then draw a small circle in its center.

particles Give an example, such as dust particles that students may have seen floating in the air or settled on tabletops.

solar wind Relate to the movement of air that students know as wind.

For vocabulary activities, see Vocabulary Games on pages 2–7.

Vocabulary Words

fluorescent bright and glowing

force power that causes motion or change

loops moves in a circling way

nucleus center of a comet

particles tiny pieces

solar wind continuous flow of gases from the Sun

AFTER

Building Background and Vocabulary

Apply Vocabulary Strategies

Use reference sources. Write the word *fluorescent* on the board. Tell students that this is a word you do not recognize. Explain that sometimes readers can figure out the pronunciation and meaning of a new word by looking for word parts they know or by breaking a word into syllables. Sometimes, though, the best strategy is to look up the meaning in a dictionary. Model using the strategy.

> MODEL **A dictionary lists words in alphabetical order, so I'll find the *f* section. On each page, the guide words in dark type at the top tell me what the first and last words are on that page. I'll find *fluorescent* after words that begin with *flo* and before words that begin with *fo*. Its entry includes the pronunciation, part of speech, meaning, and a sentence showing it used correctly.**

Guide students in using the dictionary to look up the word *nucleus*.

RETEACH **lesson vocabulary.** Provide a set of word cards for each student or pair of students. Read aloud or write on the board the meaning of one of the Vocabulary Words and the first letter or two of the word. Students match the correct word card to the definition. Continue until students have matched all the words.

FLUENCY BUILDER Using *Intervention Practice Book* page 119, read each word in the first column aloud and have students repeat it. Then have students work in pairs to read the words in the first column aloud to each other. Follow the same procedure with each of the remaining columns. After partners have practiced reading aloud the words in each column, have them listen to each other as they practice the entire list.

BEFORE

Reading "Visitors from Space"
pages 402–411

USE SKILL CARD 30A

Focus Skill Locate Information

PRETEACH the skill. Remind students that they have learned about using parts of a book to locate information. Have them look at **side A of Skill Card 30: Locate Information.** Call on volunteers to read the information in the chart, repeating the headings To Find, Look Here, and You Will See as they read across each line. Provide an appropriate nonfiction book, and have students demonstrate what they have learned from the chart.

Prepare to Read: "Visitors from Space"

ON YOUR MARK
pages 402–411

Preview. Tell students that they are going to read a selection called "Visitors from Space." Explain that this selection is expository nonfiction, and remind students that expository nonfiction explains information and ideas. Tell them that the selection may be divided into sections with headings that tell what the sections are about and may include illustrations and diagrams with captions and labels. After discussing the genre, preview the selection with students.

- **Pages 402–403:** I see the title, "Visitors from Space," and the names of the author and illustrator. The picture shows a nighttime scene with a bright light in the sky. I wonder what kind of visitors from space I will learn about in this selection.
- **Pages 404–405:** The text on page 404 is divided into two sections with the headings "Look! A Comet" and "Where Do Comets Come From?" There are illustrations on page 405. I think that the "Visitors from Space" that the title tells about must be comets.
- **Pages 406–407:** From the headings on page 406, I know that these pages give information about how a comet starts its travels and how comets change. I see illustrations with captions and labels that will help me understand this information. I think that I can learn a lot about comets by reading this selection.

Set purpose. Model setting a purpose for reading "Visitors from Space."

MODEL From my preview, I know that this selection explains what comets are and how they travel and change. One purpose for reading is to find answers to questions. I think I will read this selection to answer questions about what comets are made of, where they come from, and where they go.

Reread and Summarize

Have students reread and summarize "Visitors from Space" in sections, as described below.

Pages 404–405

Let's reread pages 404–405 to recall what comets are and where they come from.

Summary: Comets look like balls of flame in the sky, but they are made of bits of rock, dust, ice, and gas. Scientists think there is a cloud of comets, called the Oort cloud, wrapped around our Solar System.

Pages 406–407

Now let's reread pages 406–407 to find out how comets travel and change.

Summary: A comet starts to travel when it gets pushed or pulled out of the comet cloud. It starts as a ball of frozen gases that begin to melt as gravity pulls it closer to the sun. The gases form a cloud called a coma. The solar wind blows part of the coma to form a long tail of gas and shorter tails of dust.

Pages 408–409

As we reread pages 408–409, let's see what other information the selection gives about comets.

Summary: Comets glow because the icy particles reflect sunlight, and the gas soaks up sunlight that makes it glow. Comets move around the sun in orbits. They move fast but almost seem to stand still because they are so far away.

Page 410

Let's reread page 410 to recall the name of the most famous comet.

Summary: Halley's Comet is the most famous comet. It comes close to Earth every 76 years.

FLUENCY BUILDER Use *Intervention Practice Book* page 119. Point out the sentences on the bottom half of the page. Remind students that their goal is to read each phrase or unit smoothly. Model appropriate pace, expression, and phrasing as you read each sentence and have students read it after you. Then have students practice by reading the sentences aloud three times to a partner.

INTERVENTION
PRACTICE
BOOK

page 119

Directed Reading: "A Meteor Stopped Here," pp. 238–245

BRIGHT SURPRISES
pp. 238–245

Pages 238–239

Have students read aloud the title of the selection and discuss the photograph on page 238. Help them identify the comet, and tell them that they will read about comets and meteors. Then have them read page 239 to find out what kind of visitors from space it tells about. (*comets*) Ask: **What visitors from space do you think the next part of this selection will tell about?** (*meteors*) **MAKE PREDICTIONS**

Pages 240–241

Have students read pages 240–241 to confirm their predictions. Ask: **How are comets and meteors alike?** (*Both orbit the sun and are part of the solar system; both glow.*) **COMPARE AND CONTRAST**

What is a shooting star? (*a little meteor that glows as it hits the air and looks like a falling star*) **SYNTHESIZE**

Do you think the big meteor the author tells about hit Earth 50,000 years ago? (*Accept reasonable responses.*) **MAKE PREDICTIONS**

Pages 242–243

Ask students to read pages 242–243 to confirm their predictions about whether the meteor hit Earth. Ask: **Why is there a huge crater in Arizona?** (*because that is where the meteor hit Earth*) **What does the author mean by the word** *autograph*? (*An autograph is an individual's signature. The crater is like a signature because it is distinctive and unique.*) **UNDERSTAND FIGURATIVE LANGUAGE**

Ask: **How could you find the main idea on page 242?** Model the strategy of using text structure and format.

> **MODEL** I know that an author may structure a text according to main ideas and details, sequence, or in other ways. I can see that the first sentence on page 242 contains the main idea and that the rest of the sentences are details that give more information about it. I see that the author has organized the whole selection this way.
> (Focus Strategy) **USE TEXT STRUCTURE AND FORMAT**

Page 244

Ask students to read page 244 to find out more about the crater. Ask: **If you have a nonfiction book about meteors and want to know whether it gives information about this crater, how can you find out?** (*Possible responses: look up craters or Arizona in the index; look at chapter titles in the table of contents to see whether any of them might have something to do with famous craters or Arizona*) (Focus Skill) **LOCATE INFORMATION**

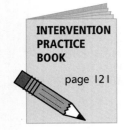

INTERVENTION PRACTICE BOOK

page 121

Summarize the selection. Ask students to think about what they learned in this selection about comets, meteors, and Arizona's meteor crater. Then have students take turns role-playing a visiting scientist. Allow students to come to the board and draw pictures of comets, meteors, and craters and to give facts about them to summarize the selection.

Answers to *Think About It* Questions

1. Possible response: Meteors are a part of our solar system. They are solid, like rock, and they orbit the sun. If a meteor comes close to Earth's atmosphere, it glows brightly. **SUMMARY**

2. Possible response: Comets are made of frozen gases and clouds. Meteors are hard, like rock. We can predict when comets will approach Earth, but most meteors show up without warning. Comets glow because they reflect the sun's light. Meteors glow because they get hot. **INTERPRETATION**

3. For students who may not be familiar with postcards, you may choose to display a few in the classroom. Explain that the note on a postcard is usually very short. **WRITE A POSTCARD**

AFTER

Skill Review
pages 416–417

USE SKILL CARD 30B

⭐(Focus Skill) Locate Information

RETEACH **the skill.** Provide an appropriate nonfiction text if none is available in your classroom library. Have students look at **side B of Skill Card 30: Locate Information.** Read aloud the skill reminder and directions. Then have students take turns reading aloud and answering the questions.

FLUENCY BUILDER Use *Intervention Practice Book* page 119. Explain that students will practice the sentences on the bottom half of the page by reading them aloud on tape. Assign new partners. Have students take turns reading the sentences aloud to each other and then reading them on tape. After they listen to the tape, have them tell how they think they have improved their reading of the sentences. Then have them read the sentences aloud on tape a second time, with improved pacing and tone.

INTERVENTION PRACTICE BOOK

page 119

Expressive Writing: Story Map

Build on prior knowledge. Tell students that "A Meteor Stopped Here" is nonfiction but that the information in it could provide ideas for a fiction story. Have them recall some fiction selections they have read. Remind students that the elements of a fiction story are the setting, characters, and a plot with a problem and solution.

Have students brainstorm ideas for a story about a main character who sees meteors or "shooting stars" in the sky. Display a story map like the one shown here.

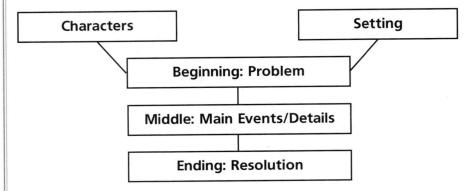

Characters

Setting

Beginning: Problem

Middle: Main Events/Details

Ending: Resolution

Construct the text. "Share the pen" with students in a collaborative group writing effort to complete the story map. As students dictate words and phrases, write them in the story map.

- To help students decide on characters and a setting, ask: **When and where does the story take place? Who is the main character? What other character or characters will be in the story?**

- To help students develop plot details, ask: **What is the main character's problem? What events take place in the middle of the story? How is the problem solved? How does the story end?**

Revisit the text. Have students read the information in the completed story map. Encourage them to add or change things to make the story better or more interesting. Ask: **Does the resolution of the story make sense? Is it believable?**

- Have students use the story map as a guide and tell oral versions of the story.

On Your Own

Think of a problem that a girl or boy your age might solve with help from others. Draw a story map and fill it in with ideas for your story. Then use the story map to tell your story to a partner.

Connect Spelling and Phonics

RETEACH digraphs /f/ *gh, ph.* Tell students that you will say six words in which the letters *ph* stand for the /f/ sound. Have volunteers write each word on the board. Then tell students you will say two words in which *gh* stands for the /f/ sound. Have volunteers write the words on the board. Work together to proofread spelling.

1. gopher	2. photographs*	3. phone	4. elephants*
5. dolphin	6. graph	7. rough	8. tough

*Word appears in "A Meteor Stopped Here."

Dictate the following sentences and have students write them: *This photograph shows an elephant talking on the phone to a dolphin. It must be tough to find a phone in the rough sea.*

Build and Read Longer Words

Remind students that they have learned that the letters *gh* and *ph* can stand for the /f/ sound. Now they will use what they have learned to help them read some longer words.

Write the word *graphics* on the board. Remind students that sometimes they can read a longer word by dividing it into syllables. Frame each syllable in *graphics* and help students read it. Point out that the *ph* stays together. Then help students blend the syllables to read the word. Follow a similar procedure with the word *toughen.* Use appropriate strategies to help students decode the words *roughly, pharmacy, phrases,* and *graphite.* Encourage students to build other long words in which the letters *gh* or *ph* stand for the /f/ sound. Suggest that they use a dictionary to look up words they are not sure about.

INTERVENTION ASSESSMENT BOOK

FLUENCY BUILDER Have students choose a passage from "A Meteor Stopped Here" to read aloud to a partner. You may have students choose a passage that they found particularly interesting, or have them choose one of the following options:

- Read page 239. (Total: 119 words)
- Read pages 240 and 241. (Total: 120 words)

Students read the selected passage aloud to their partners three times. Have students rate each of their own readings on a scale of 1 to 4. Encourage readers to note their improvement from one reading to the next by completing sentence frames such as *I know my reading improved because* _____. The partner who listens to the reading should also be encouraged to offer positive comments on the reader's improvement.

Review Vocabulary

To revisit Vocabulary Words with students prior to the weekly assessment, display or read aloud the following sentences. Have students tell whether each statement is true or false, and explain why.

1. A **particle** is too large to fit into a crater.
2. Something **fluorescent** will glow.
3. A **meteor** may be very small or very large.
4. If you **loop** around something, you are circling.
5. Gravity is a **force**.
6. **Solar wind** is part of a tornado.

Correct responses: 1. False, 2. True, 3. True, 4. True, 5. True, 6. False

You may want to display the Vocabulary Words and definitions on page 299 and have students copy them to use when they study for the vocabulary test.

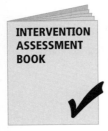

INTERVENTION PRACTICE BOOK

page 122

 Review Locate Information

To review the focus skill before the weekly assessment, distribute *Intervention Practice Book* page 122. Point out the title, Locate Information, and read the introductory material and directions aloud. You may choose to guide students through the activity, or have them complete it with a partner and then share and discuss their work with the group.

Review Test Prep

Ask students to turn to page 415 of the *Pupil Edition*. Call attention to the tips for answering the test questions. Tell students that paying attention to these tips can help them answer not only the test questions on this page but also other test questions like these.

ON YOUR MARK

page 415

Call attention to the index shown in the illustration. Ask a volunteer to read aloud the first test question, answer choices, and tip. Have students identify the correct page numbers and explain how they located the information. Then read aloud the second question, answer choices, and tip. Have students identify the correct choice and explain how they figured it out. Encourage students to tell how they might apply the tips on this page in other test situations.

INTERVENTION ASSESSMENT BOOK